Corporate Governance and Effectiveness

The book looks at the corporate management system and how it affects company performance. The main theme revolves around the notion that when a company values its workers and their satisfaction, that company can achieve success. The book is unique in its quantitative perspective and analysis, and it examines whether a corporate management system can be regarded as a source of a firm's competitive advantage by creating a sustainable competitive advantage and firm performance. The book examines how, in the context of Japanese multinational corporations (MNCs), corporate management can be part of an MNC's strategy in enhancing its capabilities, both at home and abroad, in Japan and in Thailand. Also, it analyses the reason for the demise of two major Indian companies, Dunlop and Hindustan Motors, in terms of their unsympathetic management systems.

Dipak R. Basu is Emeritus Professor at the Faculty of Economics, Nagasaki University, Japan.

Victoria Miroshnik is Professor of Management at Reitaku University, Japan.

T0384060

Routledge Studies in Corporate Governance

Corporate Governance and Effectiveness

Why Companies Win or Lose

Dipak R. Basu and
Victoria Miroshnik

Routledge
Taylor & Francis Group

LONDON AND NEW YORK

First published 2019
by Routledge
2 Park Square, Milton Park, Abingdon, Oxon OX14 4RN

and by Routledge
605 Third Avenue, New York, NY 10017

First issued in paperback 2020

Routledge is an imprint of the Taylor & Francis Group, an informa business

British Library Cataloguing-in-Publication Data
A catalogue record for this book is available from the British Library

Library of Congress Cataloging-in-Publication Data
A catalog record for this book has been requested

ISBN 13: 978-0-367-50416-8 (pbk)
ISBN 13: 978-1-138-32264-6 (hbk)
ISBN 13: 978-0-429-45190-4 (ebk)

Typeset in Galliard
by Apex CoVantage, LLC

To my friend
Alexis Lazaridis

Contents

Illustrations

Figures

Tables

Introduction

Japanese companies are at the top of the league of major successful companies in the world. They have already earned excellence in management (Bloom, Christos, Raffaella, and Van Reenen, 2012). To understand factors affecting corporate performance, a systematic analysis of the organizational culture is essential, which is missing in the economics-oriented literature on differences in performances of various companies of different national origins (Bloom and Van Reenen, 2010). Corporate organizational culture can affect corporate performance (Barney, 1991; Kotter and Heskett, 1992; Cameron and Quinn, 1999). In today's world of globalization, it is obvious that multinational corporations with its supposedly common organizational culture demonstrate different behaviors in different countries, which can influence their performances (Hofstede, 1980; Aoki, 1990; Axel, 1995; Triandis, 2006; Chen and Miller, 2010, 2011; Gupta, 2011; Bartlett and Yoshihara, 1988; Calori and Sarnin, 1991). National culture with its various manifestations can create unique organizational values for a country, which in conjunction with the human resources management practices may create some unique organizational culture for a corporation.

National culture may not always correspond to the geographical map of a country. However, in the case of Japan, Japanese national culture does not exist outside Japan, as Japan has no lasting colonies abroad; Japanese have not migrated *en masse* to other countries either. Minorities of Japan, indigenous Aino community and the Koran residents, are too tiny to have any impacts on Japanese culture. Thus, national culture in the case of Japan corresponds to the geographical map of Japan. The organizational culture described here corresponds to the large-scale manufacturing industries; other sectors normally try to emulate this organizational culture with various degrees of success. The purpose of this book is to provide a synthesis of various studies on Japanese management system to emphasize the core psychological values of Japanese culture that have created some unique Japanese management practices.

Kahneman and Tversky (1979) have analyzed the behavior of decision-making under risky situation and demonstrated some fallacy of the classical and neoclassical choice theory based on expected utility function. They have proved that economic rationality often is violated and that decision-making errors are widespread. They argued that people rely on a limited number of heuristic principles to judge probabilistic decisions, which may lead to errors. In most experiments they have conducted, frames are fixed by experimenters. However, in real life, frames are set by a manipulator or the decision maker (Laibson and Zeckhauser, 1998).

Questions can be raised how these frames are being evolved; how the manipulator change the frame; if there any endogenous frame selection process; and how that can affect future decision. The purpose of this book is to examine these issues by exploring the nature of decision making and their effects on business success or failure by going through the psychological process as it takes place in the real world rather than theorizing in a hypothetical world. In this book, first we try to analyze the decision-making process itself, which is different from what Kahnemann and Tversky thought it was. Then we focus on a series of experiments conducted in Japan, India, Thailand, and Britain for the employees in large multinational companies. The purpose is to examine whether the workplace alienation or alignments can affect business success of large organizations. In this book, we have analyzed a number of companies of India where workplace alienation was predominant and where they have failed. We also have analyzed a number of Japanese companies where workplace alignments are the norms.

Decision-making process is defined in terms of creation of a friendly culture in the organization where the values of the employees shaped by their societal values and culture can find a proper home. Organizational culture along with a leadership style, which is the product of organizational culture, national culture, and human resources management practices, creates a synergy, which shapes the fortune of the company's performances. Thus, national culture, organizational values (or purposes), organizational cultures, leadership styles, human resources practices, and corporate performances are interrelated and each depends on others (Chen and Miller, 2011; Triandis and Gelfand, 1998).

1 Personality and person–organization fit

Person–organization fit in the context of alienation of workers in modern environment was explained by Karl Marx more than 150 years ago (Aktouf, 1992, 1986; West, 1969). It was not taken up subsequently in the management literature except for some works on Japanese and Swedish organizational culture, which were developed during 1950s and 1960s under the environment of increasing militancy of the workers and their attractiveness toward the socialist system. Toyota in Japan and subsequently other Japanese companies adopted a system of molding the workers according to the value system of the organization so as to reduce or even eliminate militancy. Similar was the case in Sweden (Basu, Miroshnik, and Uchida, 2001).

In the traditional Western literature, person–organization fit correspond to the examination during recruitment whether a newly recruited employee would fit well with the organization. It does not take into account the systematic effort of the company to recognize the psychological characteristic of the employee with appropriate organizational set-up so as to achieve a perfect fit (O'Reilly, Chatman, and Caldwell, 1991; Cable and Judge, 1997a; Herold, Fedor, and Caldwell, 2007). That is however the ambition of the Japanese and Swedish companies. The Japanese system of management is not just a new production management technique, but it is a comprehensive system of management called Software of Mind to create an atmosphere where the employee will reorganize their psychological characteristic to the espoused goal of the organization. Japanese multinational companies even tried to implement the same system in their overseas subsidiaries. This study is an examination of the achievement of such a system.

Reformist managerial debates

Up until the end of the 1970s, a firm's success depended on meeting management production targets, with ever-greater speed and in large quantities. Combined with planned obsolescence, this philosophy inherited from Taylorism and Fordism (Aitken, 1960, 1985) would ensure lasting success to firms that first gained control of a product or range of products with which they could then flood the market. Managers and their theories were thus harnessed to the task of developing techniques and instruments that would help production move faster and faster at the plant. Creativity, initiative, and conceptualization were the sphere of specialists in noble R&D and planning departments. The rest of the firm was there to understand and execute orders as diligently and obediently as possible. The ideal employee was of course the "right person at the right place," executing plans developed by people hired and paid to be intelligent thinkers: management analysts and planners. In that context, the main problem of managers and their theorists was to find the means to mobilize and stimulate people to do work that specialization, technical division of work, and cost-cutting concerns had rendered more and more dull and meaningless.

With the economic success of the Japanese the Germans and Swedes, other concepts and factors of success began to surface. The objectives are no longer to make products faster and faster at the lowest cost but to produce them better, more "creatively," and more reliably. The era of quality has been extended to the business firm; now, *all employees must be active and intelligent participants.*

Management theorists cannot see that such dramatic shifts in the factors of success require an equally dramatic shift in management philosophy and in the conception of work and the worker (Scroggins, 2015). There can be no common measure between the employee who is expected to "do more faster and faster" in passive obedience and the employee from whom management expects constant initiative and creativity.

We may even wonder if the latter employee can be "managed" at all. Yet we have witnessed a proliferation of new "how to": how to construct a "good corporate culture," how to "manage symbols," how to generate and distribute "good values."

Who is this person that we want to actualize, liberate, and acculturate? To whom do we want to restore meaning in the workplace? With whom do we want to share? Is it the person we no longer want to treat like an instrument of short-term profits? This person is, in fact, constantly implied; he/she is considered a given. As Nord (1974) rightly pointed out, Maslow (1954, 1969) and Argyris (1957) are almost the only mainstream writers on management to show any real concern for a "non-industrial" definition of the "Man," but they are scarcely ever mentioned. It is as if we need only call on this person and tell him or her that we earnestly want him or her to embrace the right culture and symbols, to join the team, and become a champion. It is as if there were no need to have a clearer idea of the reasons, events, and circumstances that might bring about such a metamorphosis. Obviously, such clarity can be gained only if we are willing to take the point of view of the employee who is, after all, the "human element" that these theories want to promote. Thus, it is necessary to construct a vision of the person.

The solution is to open the way for managerial practices that will permit *development of the employee's* desire to belong and to use his or her intelligence to serve the firm, the employee as an active and willing accomplice. How can employees be expected to participate in shared values, to achieve personal success, and to express and liberate them if managers are often explicitly designated the quasi-unique artisans of liberation?

This notion does not deny the obviously determining role of managers, but it does underline the fact that this role must consist, essentially, in a radical change in everyone's concrete working conditions. A culture of synergy and collaboration – characterized by convergence, closeness, and sharing – must be injected into actual practice.

Radical-humanistic position

The first element is human beings as destined, that is, owing their unique status to their "self-consciousness," which forces them to search for what will liberate them, emancipate them (from all sorts of obstacles), restore them, and lead them to fulfill their vocations: They are endowed with consciousness, right judgment, and free will, and they aspire to their own elevation. Thus, people are "generic beings" who create their own milieu, their society, and, thus, themselves.

There are key role of social relations, class phenomena, fundamentally defined by community, society, and their relations with each others. The relations in and through which people live, help them to construct and grasp their sense of self (which make them the ground and condition of self-realization). "Man's" nature is undeniably social and community oriented.

Marx's thought can be found in the unrelenting search for the conditions dehumanizing man and for possible ways of restoring more human conditions (Engels and Marx, 1987). And the consideration is that people are most in danger of "ruin," of "losing themselves" (alienation), through the very act by which they can express their generic essence: the act of work.

The heart of the process of dehumanizing "man" is alienation through work. This idea explains the primordial importance of what takes place, concretely, in the work process. In this process, the workers alienate themselves by selling their capacity for work, while contributing to the development and the consolidation of forces (merchandise, profits, capital), which are exterior, foreign, and in the final analysis, hostile to them and, thus, even more "dehumanizing."

In sum, people are slipping into "self-estrangement" because of what they are led to do and experience as social and economic beings. An alienated person is caught up in production relations that are structurally, materially, and historically determined. Human beings are definitely not like mechanisms or organisms: They are ruled by *reasons, feelings,* and *choices.*

Mintzberg (1989) have used words calling for a *revolution;* management by *men who are still men;* suppression of *managerial rules* that degrade people; liberation of intelligence from the grip of the inhuman Taylorian machine; *disregard of now ossified top-down hierarchical authority;* renunciation of a *management that renders society's call* for recognition that managerial conceptions and practices foil any real possibility of giving "*man*" the status of subject, that of *an actor* personally and ontologically authorized to identify with and question the firm, to *reappropriate the acts* he or she is assigned to do, to experience them as an expression of his or her own desires.

The humanized firm

Almost all the authors of contemporary management best-sellers agree that facilitating the development of a new type of employee means the evolution of a new kind of firm. Whether it is called *excellent* or *third type* or *open*, it would still be a firm in which relations and the rules of the game will have changed radically. Workers must experience their relation to their work as a real, rather than a formal, appropriation. What they do in the firm must be experienced as a real extension of themselves, as an occasion for self-expression as well as for the pursuit and satisfaction of personal desires and interests that converge with those of the firm. Thus, the firm would become a place for partnership and dialogue, a workplace no longer run on the intensive use of workforce.

Surprisingly enough, this new trend seems to encompass one of Marx's most cherished principles: *abolition of wages*. Whether explicitly or not, many authors are advocating this principle, most often with reference to Japanese forms of remuneration (largely tied to corporate profits). This is the case for Weitzman (1984); for Peters (1987), who calls for profit sharing as part of remuneration; for Perrow (1979), who writes that control and coercion will be the only ways (more costly than profitable) to obtain maximum productivity as long as the salary system is the rule; for Etchegoyen (1990), who feels that salaries turn employees into mercenaries working in soulless enterprises (the "mercenary" element is seen here as an obstacle to individual commitment – a person no longer satisfied with doing what is asked, who has neither interest nor "soul").

At the present time, strong American and European trends are being shaped that will demand that an organization become a place where the employee can feel and act as a thinking, speaking, and questioning subject (Girin, 1990; Morgan, 1986, Sainsaulieu, 1983). This would be the place where the employee could find his or her essential availability, interest, and creativity. In other words, these are fee conditions for the advent of *vital work* (subjective and creative work, capable of constant adaptation and innovation), which Marx recognized as the main characteristic of humanity and which he deplored seeing replaced by dead, ossified work – that of machines, objective working conditions, maximum profits, and repetition.

The birth of industrial enterprise was marked by violence and suffering: It was a long struggle in which laws were won inch by inch and terrible clashes took place between workers and bosses to achieve slightly more just and human working conditions Marx based his terrifying descriptions of nineteenth-century working conditions on the reports of doctors and British government labor inspectors.

These descriptions point to the relevance of the element around which Marxism has always centered – the analysis of work relations, which is the original and still rampant contradiction between the interests of bosses and managers and those of the workers. For the bosses, it was and still is a matter of making the most profit possible, which is synonymous, among other things, with setting the lowest possible wages. For the workers, it has always been a question of fighting back to gain decent working conditions and wages.

Marxism sheds light on the powerful vogue of the management and organizational sciences. Thus, from management's viewpoint, the nineteenth century was the century of absolute surplus value, whereas the twentieth century is, at least in the West, mainly the century of relative surplus value. However, faced with competition from other countries such as Japan, it is becoming increasingly difficult to obtain a relative surplus value solely by organizing and disciplining labor and by making maximum profit from work time (Hassard, 1988). Japanese corporations stress the importance of human creativity over robotized automation in their manufacturing operations. This, however, does not imply that Japanese businesses are in general more humane, but that they make better use of the creative faculties of their employees. Even obtaining relative surplus value seems to depend more and more on a new attitude on the part of employees: The continued exploitation of labor (by relative surplus value) seems to imply, *paradoxically*, some kind of commitment from the employee and, thus, greater equity to him or her.

Real and concrete participation in management, in profits, in planning; workers' greater autonomy and polyvalence; and workers' adequate security; a finality of cooperative and shared production; and an organization that fosters commitment and interest through the *meaning* given to each person's daily work are now necessary to end the stagnation of productivity.

It will, for many companies, be the price to pay for survival. Because companies have reached the ultimate limits of Taylorism (Aitken, 1960, 1985), their only way of improving productivity seems to be making room in the firms for employees to adequately express their personal desires.

Recently, Pagès (1984) spoke about seeking to fuse the ideal of self with the ideal of the organization. To recognize this contradiction is to lay the groundwork for promoting labor to a position of active "co-management" with capital.

From corporate culture to management by symbols and from champions of the product to total quality, the aim is to change the behavior of employees, with no thought that the context must also be changed. In this case, employees are constantly being acculturated by self-cultured leaders, motivated by self-motivated leaders, and mobilized by self-mobilized managers.

However, although Marx's radical humanism may present an inescapable theoretical framework for constructing the know-how and bases of change suitable to today's managerial problems, it can be made by moving toward a form of organization where candor, symmetry, equity, and sharing would provide the grounds for humanizing the firm.

In sum, workers must no longer be considered as cost factors to be "compressed" or "rationalized," but as allies to be won – Although the pursuit of profit is a legitimate objective, it must not become the *only* factor to be considered and must stop being perceived as a short-term goal to be reached for the sole benefit of managers and shareholders. Instead, profit should be regarded as the result of collective efforts of all parties, and it should be administered accordingly. The rates and applications of profit should therefore be decided in common by all stakeholders, managers, shareholders, and workers alike.

Finally, we would argue that the Taylorist vision of the employee (Beissinger, 1988)as a cost factor and as a passive cog has now become a liability that must be discarded as quickly as possible to make room for a humanistic vision, whereby the employee is seen as an active and willing participant in the organization.

German system of workers participation in management

Germany has a well-established regulatory framework for worker participation. Rules were set out as early as the 1950s on how workers participate in management decisions – through board membership and works councils. It had a long history. It started in the eighteenth century to mitigate the sharp practices of capitalism that has seen in the United Kingdom the terrible scenes of exploitation.

Works councils provide representation for employees at the workplace, and they have substantial powers – extending to an effective right of veto on some issues. Employee representatives have a right to seats on the supervisory board of larger companies – one-third in companies with 500–2,000 employees, and half in companies with more than 2,000.

At national level, trade unions and employer associations participate in the decision-making process of the national legislator. Due to the act on co-determination, companies with over 2000 employees must allow workers representatives to participate in decision making. Workers representatives have 50 percent of the seats in the supervisory board. This is also known as parity codetermination because shareholders and workers are equally represented.

Japan followed the German system as far as possible. As Drucker pointed out:

> If there is one point on which all authorities on Japan are in agreement, it is that Japanese institutions, whether businesses or government agencies, make decisions by "consensus." The Japanese, we are told, debate a proposed decision throughout the organization until there is agreement on it. And only then do they make the decision.
>
> (Drucker, 1971)

One of the core mechanisms for labor–management relations within a large Japanese firm is joint labor–management committees (JLMCs). The majority of labor-side JLMC members are elected by employee vote. Thus, labor-side JLMC members usually legitimately represent the interests of the firm's workforce (Kato, 2003).

Corporate governance is characterized by the interplay between managers and owners of a firm. While the latter wish to maximize the value of the firm in the long run, executives maximize their own utility, for which compensation, prestige, power, etc. are relevant. Codetermination introduces a third interest group, employees, to the supervisory board and thus to the firm's decision-making process. Workplace representation in Germany takes place mainly through work councils rather than unions.

Person–organization fit and contributions of organizational culture and human resource management system

Organizational culture, which exists globally in a multinational company, is formed by major values introduced by of the founder/top management of that corporation, and it may or may not necessarily be influenced by the values of the country where that multinational corporation (MNC) is operating. That corporate global culture in turn forms company citizenship, a new organizational form in the era of globalization. Some successful multinational companies are transcending national cultural differences by developing a common pattern of drivers of business practices through the formation of the "company citizenship."

One of the central purposes of management is to facilitate communication across all of the organization's boundaries, so that the entire company works together to address given business challenges. With efficient dissemination of management system, the company's ability to make impacting decisions increases dramatically, because individuals throughout the firm gain access to important strategic ideas. This improves the organization's ability to make rapid decisions and execute them. To create a management system appropriate for transforming tacit knowledge into communal, explicit knowledge fear-based approaches to management must be abandoned in preference for a harmonious relationship-oriented management. The key is to create an environment of understanding, shared control, compassion, and learning.

Research has shown that human beings develop a sense of self that is a combination of beliefs, feelings, and knowledge, which is used to evaluate, organize, and regulate their intellectual, emotional, and behavioral reactions to the physical and social environment (Meyer, Irving, and Allen, 1998; Lok, Westwood, and Crawford, 2005). The "self" is constructed via experience, which is the primary means for humans to interpret and respond to external events.

Corporate culture encompasses basic assumptions and espoused values of the organization. It is a formal philosophy or mission of the organization, from which the behavior of the organization emerges. Corporate culture can be a strategy for the organization to achieve its goals. Values created over the years provide the foundation of ideas, expectations, ideals, boundaries of actions, and thought processes (Rokeach, 1973; Allaire and Firsirotu, 1984).

Thus, values are the basis of corporate culture. At the top level, there are patterns of behavior; at the secondary level, the values that influence behavior; and at the tertiary level, there are assumptions, beliefs, and perceptions that control behavior (Schein, 1968, 1984). According to Hofstede, corporate culture can be described as a combination of five values, which are *individualism/collectivism, power distance, uncertainty avoidance, masculinity/femininity,* and *long-/short-term orientation* (Hofstede and Bond, 1988), and the specific corporate culture of a company reflects the national culture of the country of establishment, which will have an overriding influence on the corporate culture of the company. In this book, we are to examine this in the context of several multinational companies.

Competitive advantages of firms can be created by a number of instruments; organizational culture is the most important one. Corporate culture in this book is perceived as the combination of three sub-systems from the perspective of its value components: (a) macro value system, (b) meso value system, and (c) micro value system. The first subsystem of culture, the *macro value subsystem* or "*national culture*," consists of the basic values (religious, moral, and habitual) that are common to a particular nation. The second subsystem of culture, the *meso value subsystem* or "*organizational culture*," embodies the myths, beliefs, and ideologies of the organization. Finally, the third subsystem of culture, the "*micro value sub-system*" or "*individual culture*," comprises the values that belong to individuals within the organization, who contribute their unique experiences, beliefs, goals, and personalities.

Motivation is the set of forces that cause people to choose certain behaviors from among the many alternatives open to them. Motivation is important because of its significance as a determinant of performance. Motivation contributes to the overall working culture in an organization. The heart of the motivation process is goal setting. All consciously motivated behavior is goal oriented, whether the goals are self-generated or assigned by others. Naturally occurring goals derive from the activation of basic human needs, personal values, personality traits, and self-efficacy perceptions shaped through experience and socialization. Individuals also set, or accept, goals in response to external incentives. The goals individuals choose can vary in difficulty and specificity, and these attributes, in combination with perceptions of self-efficacy, help determine the direction of behavior, the amount of effort exerted, the degree of persistence, and the likelihood that individuals will develop strategies to facilitate goal attainment. Corporate strategies may serve as the mechanisms by which goal choices and efficacy beliefs influence behavior (Locke and Latham, 1990, 2002). Humans are motivated by various needs, which exist in a hierarchical order. There are five general types of needs. These are, in ascending order, physiological needs, safety, belonging, social esteem, and self-actualization (Maslow, 1954).

"Work motivation is a set of energetic forces that originate both within as well as beyond an individual's being, to initiate work-related behavior, and to determine its form, direction, intensity, and duration" (Pinder, 1998). According to Locke (1997), the performance that results from these efforts affects the level of satisfaction experienced, which, along with motivation, can lead to other forms of action, a set of energizing forces that contributes to positive behavior. Motivation can be defined as the relative strength of an individual's identification with and involvement in a particular organization (Mowday, Porter, and Steers, 1979, 1982a, 1982b). Motivation is a psychological relationship between the employees and their organization, which would provoke employees' attachment to the organization so that they will not leave voluntarily (Meyer and Allen, 1984). Corporate culture is a major instrument in creating motivation. The question is how do we know when the level of motivation desired by the corporate culture has been achieved? In this book, we examine the proposition that if the value components of the prevailing corporate culture are similar to the values of the idealized vision of the corporate culture as perceived by the employees, we then would expect employees to be highly motivated and committed.

Organizational culture of a multinational company

Organizational culture, which exists globally in a multinational company, is formed by major values introduced by the founder/top management of that corporation, and may or may not necessarily be influenced by the values of the country where that MNC is operating. That corporate global culture in turn forms company citizenship, a new organizational form in the era of globalization. Some successful multinational companies are transcending national cultural differences by developing a common pattern of drivers of business practices through the formation of the "company citizenship."

One of the central purposes of management is to facilitate communication across all of the organization's boundaries, so that the entire company works together to address given business challenges. With efficient dissemination of management system, the company's ability to make impacting decisions increases dramatically, because individuals throughout the firm gain access to important strategic ideas. This improves the organization's ability to make rapid decisions and execute them. To create a management system appropriate for transforming tacit knowledge into communal, explicit knowledge fear-based approaches to management must be abandoned in preference for a harmonious relationship-oriented management. The key is to create an environment of understanding, shared control, compassion, and learning.

Values interact with aspects of culture to influence individual's attitude and response, which we can call commitments (Youssef and Luthans, 2007; Eisenberger, Fasolo, and Davis-LaMastro, 1990). The concept of person–organization fit, a psychological perspective in which both individual and the culture combine to affect an individual's response to the organization (O'Reilly, 1989; O'Reilly et al., 1991; Cable and Judge, 1997a; Herold et al., 2007), is defined as the compatibility between individuals and the organizations (Cable and Edwards, 2004; Aselage and Eisenberger, 2003; Schneider, 2001; Van Vianen, 2000; Kristof, 1996; Kristof-Brown, Zimmerman, and Johnson, 2005). The person–organization fit can be related to job satisfaction, organizational commitment, and turnover (Finegan, 2000). People are happier in settings that satisfy their individual needs or are suitable with their dispositions (Fredrickson, Cohen, Coffey, Pek, and Finkel, 2008; Cable, Aiman-Smith, Mulvey, and Edwards, 2000). Organizational culture is a very important factor in determining how well an individual fits an organizational context and thus, the analysis of "person–organization fit" is related to the analysis of the relationship between organizational culture and commitment (Caldwell, Herold, and Fedor, 2004; Barney, 2005; Van Vianen, 2000).

When a number of key or pivotal values concerning organizational-related behaviors and state of affairs are shared across units and levels by members of an organization, a central value system may emerge (Hayashi, 1989; Farh, Hackett, and Liang, 2007). To characterize an organization's culture in terms of its central values require first to identify these values and to measure the importance the members of the organization normally attach to these values. If the employees are attached to these central values of the organization, performance of the organization increases because of the increased commitment of the employees (Fedor, Caldwell, and Herold, 2006; Aselage and Eisenberger, 2003). It is essential to explore whether the employees have similar values as espoused by the organization, which create commitment of the employees.

Commitment and motivation help the firm to pursue strategic goals by discovering opportunities and utilizing existing opportunities. Entrepreneurship requires innovative activity, and strategic management requires stability (Hitt, Ireland, Sirmon, and Trahms, 2011). To achieve the balance between exploration and exploitation, specifications of organizational structure capable of supporting these twin needs are required. An effective organizational structure can combine existing resources and innovate future resources to create value for the organization and its stakeholders. The question is how formal and informal structures of the organization can create such a super structure for enhanced performance and entrepreneurial activities (Alvarez and Barney, 2010). The analysis presented in this chapter is an attempt to answer that question by elaborating the interrelationship between different components of the levels of cultures and the structure these support.

In quantifying the relationship between the organization and its members, researchers have taken two different roads (O'Reilly et al., 1991; Schneider, 2001; Cable and DeRue, 2002; Cable and Edwards, 2004; Carless, 2005; Kristof-Brown et al., 2005; Ostroff, Shin, and Kinicki, 2005). The first is the explorations of interrelationship between individual characteristics and occupational attributes. The second is to relate the skills of the individuals and job requirements. These have relationships with the congruence between individual's personality and the organizational culture, which has a close relationship with commitments of the individual.

Recent works in interactional psychology try to identify the characteristics of effective techniques to address the issue of person–organization–fit effects. O'Reilly et al. (1991) developed a profile-matching process to evaluate the person–organization fit. This is based on the idea that organizations have cultures that are more or less attractive to certain types of individuals. This begins with a set of values, which typically act as the definitions around which norms, symbols, rituals, and other cultural activities revolve (Kanter, 1968). It is based on the notion of a psychological process of identity formation in which individuals appear to seek a social identity that provides meaning and connectedness (Kilmann, 1981).

Values thus, provide the instruments to create a person–organization fit. Thus, it is essential whether there is a congruence between individuals' values (we call ideal organizational culture) and those of the organization (we call actual organizational culture) as a measure of the relationship between the organizational culture and commitment of the employees to stay in the organization. An employee may not leave the organization because he or she cannot get an alternative job, which pays just as much as he or she receives or in the same locality or of the same type. In those cases, he or she has limited psychological commitment for the organization. That may have effects on his or her ability to work in the most efficient way. A psychological attachment would be formed if the person is satisfied that he or she has obtained in his or her organization a similar organizational culture as he or she had imagined as the ideal organizational culture.

O'Reilly et al. (1991) focused more on the concept that certain types of organizations have cultures that are more or less attractive to certain types of individuals. In assessing person–organization fit, two components should be examined: First, preferences that individuals have for organizational cultures must be demonstrated, and second, the relationship between individual preferences and existing organizational culture should be evaluated (Del Campo, 2006).

Values interact with aspects of culture to influence individual's attitude and response, which we can call commitments (Youssef and Luthans, 2007; Eisenberger et al., 1990). The concept of person–organization fit, a psychological perspective in which both individual and the culture combine to affect an individual's response to the organization (O'Reilly, 1989; O'Reilly et al., 1991; Cable and Judge, 1997a; Herold et al., 2007), is defined as the compatibility between individuals and the organizations (Cable and Edwards, 2004; Aselage and Eisenberger, 2003; Schneider, 2001; Van Vianen, 2000; Kristof, 1996; Kristof-Brown et al., 2005). The person–organization fit can be related to job satisfaction, organizational commitment, and turnover (Finegan, 2000). People are happier in settings that satisfy their individual needs or are suitable with their dispositions (Fredrickson et al., 2008; Cable et al., 2000). Organizational culture is a very important factor in determining how well an individual fits an organizational context and thus, the analysis of person–organization fit related to the analysis of the relationship between organizational culture and commitment (Caldwell et al., 2004; Barney, 2005; Van Vianen, 2000).

When a number of key or pivotal values concerning organizational-related behaviors and state of affairs are shared across units and levels by members of an organization, a central value system may emerge (Hayashi, 1989, 2002; Farh et al., 2007). To characterize an organization's culture in terms of its central values, it is first necessary to identify these values and to measure the importance the members of the organization normally attach to these values. If the employees are attached to these central values of the organization, performance of the organization increases because of the increased commitment of the members of the employees (Fedor et al., 2006; Aselage and Eisenberger, 2003). It is essential to explore whether the employees have similar values as espoused by the organization, which create commitment of the employees.

Commitment and motivation help the firm to pursue strategic goals by discovering opportunities and utilizing existing opportunities. Entrepreneurship requires innovative activity, and strategic management requires stability (Hitt et al., 2011). To achieve the balance between exploration and exploitation specifications of organizational structure capable of supporting these twin needs are required. An effective organizational structure can combine existing resources and innovate future resources to create value for the organization and its stakeholders. The question is how formal and informal structures of the organization can create such a super structure for enhanced performance and entrepreneurial activities (Alvarez and Barney, 2010). The analysis presented in this chapter is an attempt to answer that question by elaborating the inter-relationship between different components of the levels of cultures and the structure these support.

In quantifying the relationship between the organization and its members, researchers have taken two different roads (O'Reilly et al., 1991; Schneider, 2001; Cable and DeRue, 2002; Cable and Edwards, 2004; Carless, 2005; Kristof-Brown et al., 2005; Ostroff et al., 2005). The first is the explorations of interrelationship between individual characteristics and occupational attributes. The second is to relate the skills of the individuals and job requirements. These have relationships with the congruence between individual's personality and the organizational culture, which has close relationship with commitments of the individual.

Recent works in interactional psychology try to identify the characteristics of effective techniques to address the issue of effects of the person–organization fit. O'Reilly et al. (1991) developed a profile-matching process to evaluate the person–organization fit. It is based on the idea that organizations have cultures that are more or less attractive to certain types of individuals. This begins with a set of values, which typically act as the definitions around which norms, symbols, rituals, and other cultural activities revolve (Kanter, 1968). It is based on the notion of a psychological process of identity formation in which individuals appear to seek a social identity that provides meaning and connectedness (Kilmann, 1981).

Values thus provide the instruments to create a person–organization fit. Thus, it is essential whether there is a congruence between individuals' values (we call ideal organizational culture) and those of the organization (we call actual organizational culture) as a measure of the relationship between the organizational culture and commitment of the employees to stay in the organization. An employee may not leave the organization because he or she cannot get an alternative job, which pays just as much as he or she receives or in the same locality or of the same type. In those cases, he or she has limited psychological commitment for the organization. That may have effects on his or her ability to work in the most efficient way. A psychological attachment would be formed if the person is satisfied that he or she has obtained in his or her organization a similar organizational culture as he or she had imagined as the ideal organizational culture.

O'Reilly et al. (1991) focused more on the concept that certain types of organizations have cultures that are more or less attractive to certain types of individuals. In assessing the person–organization fit, two components should be examined: First, preferences that individuals have for organizational cultures must be demonstrated, and second, the relationship between individual preferences and existing organizational culture should be evaluated (Del Campo, 2006).

A theory of corporate performance as a product of national and organizational culture

Culture is multidimensional, comprising of several layers of interrelated variables. As society and organizations are continuously evolving, there is no theory of culture valid at all times and locations. However, the core values of a society (macro values) can be analyzed by asking the following questions:

> What are the relationship between human and nature; (b) What are the characteristics of innate human nature; (c) What is the focus regarding time, whether past, future, or present or a combination of all these; (d) what are the modalities of human activity, whether spontaneous or introspective or result oriented or a combination of these; (e) what is the basic of relationship between one man to another in the society?

According to the classic model of culture proposed by Schein (1997), the artifacts or behavioral patterns form the top level of an organization's culture and are the most visible and tangible manifestations. They include the physical environment of an organization, its products, technology used or not used, as well as patterns of behavior, and the use of language and other symbolic forms. The second level is made up of values that influence behavior. A value system differentiates right feelings, thoughts, and behavior from wrong feelings, thoughts, and behavior. Values represent "what ought to be" or the ideals of the organization. They incorporate moral and ethical codes, ideologies, and philosophies of the organization. These form the espoused values of the organization (Basu, 1999, Ouchi, 1981). The final level forms the basis for fundamental cultural understanding; it comprises basic underlying assumptions: enshrined fundamental beliefs and perceptions that impact on individuals' thinking, behavior, and feelings (Kumazawa and Yamada, 1989).

Thus, values are considered to be the most important component of organizational culture. Values are defined as taken-for-granted presumptions about the self, physical, and social reality (Rokeach, 1973; Schwartz, 1994, 1996; Sagiv and Schwartz, 2000; Hofstede, 1980). Values are incontrovertible, personal truths that are unaffected by persuasion (Rokeach, 1973: 16) and can be changed only over a long time. Values have stronger affective and evaluative components than beliefs or knowledge (Kahle and Kennedy, 1988). Cultural values are transmitted across generations and maintain continuity through learning, technically termed enculturation. Thus, the values can be used as the major traits of the culture.

A subsystem of culture is a "macro-values system" or "national culture system" that combines basic values, religious, moral, and habitual, which are common for a particular nation. A second subsystem of culture is a "meso-values system" or "organizational values system" that embodies the myths, beliefs, and ideologies of the organization (Allaire and Firsirotu, 1984; Schein, 1997). Leaders attempt to influence the development of values and to define the organization's purpose, policies, and strategies to organize the work structure. Deal and Kennedy (1982) identified the "mythological" roles that leaders, as ceremonial heads of organizations, often play in the effort to clarify responsibilities, teach organizational values, and promote the organization's mission. A third component of culture is a "micro-values system" or "individual value system" (Cameron and Quinn, 1999). This subsystem is comprised of the collective individuals within the organization who contribute their unique experiences, beliefs, goals, and personalities.

One of the first models of culture based on value-components was proposed by Rokeach (1973). Rokeach differentiated people in terms of their race, sex, religion, occupation, political ideology, and a variety of other characteristics in the United States on the basis of their value orientations in his study on US companies. The Rokeach Value Survey (RVS) is a classification system of two sets of values, *terminal values* and other *instrumental values*. Terminal values refer to desirable end-states of existence. Instrumental values refer to preferable modes of behavior. The task for participants in the RVS survey is to arrange the 18 terminal values, followed by the 18 instrumental values, into an order of importance to the respondent (Rokeach, 1973:27). The purpose is to evaluate the characteristics of different national culture.

Another model of culture based on value-components was proposed by Hofstede (1980, 1993). Hofstede describes culture as combination of five values, which are *Individualism, Power Distance, Uncertainty Avoidance, Masculinity/ Femininity,* and *Long-Term Orientation*(Hofstede, 1993). *Individualism* would reflect the emotional independence of the person with respect to groups and organizations, while its absence would be similar to an emotional dependence.

An alternative model of culture based on value-components was proposed by Schwartz (1994). Schwartz develops an alternative theory of the structure of cultural values to that developed by Hofstede (1985). According to Schwartz (1994), cultures can be accounted for by seven basic cultural values (Schwartz, 1994): *Conservation*(values that emphasize the status quo and propriety, and traditional social order); *Hierarchy* (values which emphasize the legitimacy of the hierarchical ascription of roles); *Intellectual Autonomy* (values that situate the person as an autonomous entity); *Affective Autonomy* (values in promoting and protecting the attainment of positive affective experiences); *Competency* (values that give priority to self-affirmation); *Harmony* (values promoting harmonious fit with nature and the environment); *Egalitarian compromise*(values that share a concern for the well-being of others).

Schwartz's cultural model can be compared in relation to the dimensions of Hofstede's model. For example, Hofstede's *Individualism Index* is positively correlated with *Affective* and *Intellectual Autonomy* and with *Egalitarian Compromise*. On the other hand, it is negatively correlated with *Conservation* and with *Hierarchy*. These systems of values cannot be used to evaluate values at an individual level, but at the national level they can be used to categorize countries with different degrees of values. However, they are not useful in evaluating organizational culture.

Thus, the organizational culture can be characterized from the perspective of values because values are influencing behavior of people who are working in organizations. An organizational culture with a strong value structure (Cameron and Quinn, 1999) may create organizational effectiveness, and that may lead to competitive advantages of a company (Barney, 1986).

When this uniqueness provides increased profitability, the firm can outbid its rival companies using this uniqueness (Barney, 1986). Thus, a firm implementing a value creating strategy, which is not simultaneously being implemented by any current or potential competitors, can only create competitive advantages (Priem and Butler, 2001). Indeed, uniqueness of the organizational culture makes the organizational culture difficult to imitate. Values, symbols, and beliefs are difficult to describe and are not transferable (Barney, 1986, 2001) as there are unspoken, unperceived commonsense of the organization.

The culture of the major Japanese firms can have the combination of cooperative culture and passive culture (Ikeda, 1987; Imai, 1986). That kind of organizational culture promotes loyalty, harmony, hard work, self-sacrifice, and consensus decision making. These along with lifetime employment, seniority-based promotions, are considered the natural outcome of the Japanese national culture. A Japanese clan type of organizational culture can make an organization efficient (Ouchi, 1981). Unselfish and socially responsible behavior of the firms can improve their performances (Mintzburg, Simon, and Basu, 2002). Companies with progressive human resources practices can improve their performance (Peters and Watermann, 1982; Carroll, 1983). Organizational cultures emphasizing creativity, autonomy, and participatory management can improve productivity. The purpose of this chapter is to explore the basic ingredients and sources of this unique organizational culture of major Japanese companies and how these are interrelated form resources and effective corporate performances of Japanese companies.

Theory of structure of culture

In the structure of the national culture, there are certain *micro* or *individual values*, which include a sense of belonging, excitement, fun and enjoyment, warm relationship with others, self-fulfilment, being well-respected, and a sense of accomplishment, security, and self-respect (Kahle, Best, and Kennedy, 1988). Although Hofstede (1990, 1993) has the opinion that the perceived practices are the roots of the organizational culture rather than values, most researchers have accepted the importance of values in shaping cultures in organizations (O'Reilly et al., 1991; Triandis, 2006; Hayashi, 1989; Linclon and Kalleberg, 1990).

Combinations of micro and macro values can give rise to an organizational culture given certain *meso organizational values*, which are specific for a country. Meso-values are certain codes of behavior, which influences the future and the expected behavior of the members of the society if they want to belong to the mainstream. These vary from one society to another as the expectations of different societies, as products of historical experiences, religious, and moral values are different. Cultural values are shared ideas about what is good, desirable, and justified; these are expressed in a variety of ways. Social order, respect for traditions, security, and wisdom are important for the society that is like an extended family (Hayashi, 1989)

A combination of macro values, meso values, and micro values creates a specific organizational culture, which varies from country to country according to their differences in national culture. Hofstede (1980, 1985, 1990, 1993) showed the relationship between national culture and organizational culture. The Global Leadership and Organizational Behavior Effectiveness (GLOBE) research project has tried to identify the relationships between leadership, social culture, and organizational culture (House, 1999; House, Hanges, Javidan, Dorfman, and Gupta, 2004).

Cameron and Quinn (1999) have mentioned that the most important competitive advantage of a company is its organizational culture. If an organization has a "strong culture" with "well-integrated and effective" set of values, beliefs, and behaviors, it normally demonstrates a high level of corporate performances (Ouchi, 1981).

Denison and Mishra (1995) have attempted to relate organizational culture and performances based on different characteristics of the organizational culture. However, different types of organizational culture enhance different types of business (Kotter and Heskett, 1992). There is no single cultural formula for long-run effectiveness. As Siehl and Martin (1988) have observed, culture may serve as filter for factors that influence the performance of an organization. These factors are different for different organizations. Thus, a detail analysis regarding the relationship between culture and performances is essential.

Toward a theory of Japanese organizational culture and corporate performance

Japanese national culture (NC) has a specific influence on the organizational culture (OC) of the Japanese companies. To understand these aspects of culture that are affecting corporate performance, a systematic analysis of the NC and OC is essential. The purpose of this chapter is to provide a scheme to analyze this issue in a systematic way.

NC can affect corporate OC (Aoki, 1990; Axel, 1995; Hofstede, 1980) and corporate performance (CP) (Cameron and Quinn, 1999; Kotter and Heskett, 1992). MNCs with their supposedly common OC demonstrate different behaviors in different countries, which can affect their performances (Bartlett and Yoshihara, 1988; Calori and Sarnin, 1991). NC with its various manifestations can create unique organizational values for a country, which in conjunction with the human resources management (HRM) practice may create some unique OC for a corporation. OC along with a leadership style, which is the product of OC, NC, and HRM practices, creates a synergy that shapes the fortune of the company's performances. Thus, national culture, organizational values and organizational cultures, leadership styles, human resources practices, and corporate performances are interrelated and each depend on the other. If a company maintains this harmony, it can perform well, otherwise it declines.

Corporate performance and organizational culture

Culture is multidimensional, comprising of several layers of interrelated variables. As society and organizations are continuously evolving; there is no theory of culture valid at all times and locations. The core values of a society (macro values) can be analyzed by asking the following questions:

(a) What are the relationships between human and nature? (b) What are the characteristics of innate human nature? (c) What is the focus regarding time-whether past, future, or present, or a combination of all these? (d) What are the modalities of human activity, whether spontaneous or introspective or result-oriented or a combination of these? (e) What is the basis of relationship between one man and another in the society?

According to Schein (1997), organizational culture emerges from some common assumptions about the organization, which the members share as a result of their experiences in that organization. These are reflected in their pattern of behaviors, expressed values, and observed artifacts. OC provides accepted solutions to known problems, which the members learn and feel about and forms a set of shared philosophies, expectations, norms, and behavior patterns, which promotes a higher level of achievements (Kilman et al., 1985; Marcoulides and Heck, 1993; Schein, 1997).

Toward a theory of Japanese organizational culture

Organizational culture, for a large and geographically dispersed organization, may have many different cultures. According to Kotter and Heskett (1992), leaders create certain vision or philosophy and business strategy for the company. A corporate culture emerges that reflects the vision and strategy of the leaders and experiences they had, while implementing these strategies. However, the question is whether it is valid for every national culture.

Cameron and Quinn (1999) have mentioned that the most important competitive advantage of a company is its OC. If an organization has a "strong culture" with "well-integrated and an effective" set of values, beliefs, and behaviors, it normally demonstrates a high level of corporate performances (Ouchi, 1981).

Denison and Mishra (1995) have attempted to relate OC and performances based on different characteristics of the OC. However, different types of OC enhance different types of business (Kotter and Heskett, 1992). There is no single cultural formula for long-run effectiveness. As Siehl and Martin (1988) have observed, culture may serve as a filter for factors that influence the performance of an organization. These factors are different for different organizations. Thus, a thorough analysis regarding the relationship between culture and performances is essential.

Japanese firms are considered to be of a family unit with long-term orientations for human resources management and with close ties with other like-minded firms, banks, and the government. The organizational culture promotes loyalty, harmony, hard work, self-sacrifice, and consensus decision making. These, along with lifetime employment and seniority-based promotions, are considered to be the natural outcome of the Japanese national culture. (Ikeda, 1987; Imai, 1986; Ouchi, 1981). Japanese workers' psychological dependency on companies emerges from their intimate dependent relationships with the society and the nation.

Japanese national culture has certain micro values: demonstration of appropriate attitudes (*taido*); the way of thinking (*kangaekata*); and spirit (*ishiki*), which forms the basic value system for the Japanese (Kobayashi, 1980). Certain MEVs can be identified as the core of the cultural life for the Japanese, if they want to belong to the mainstream Japanese society (Basu, 1999; Fujino, 1998). These are (a) the *Senpai–Kohai* system; (b) *Conformity*; (c) *Hou-Ren-Sou*; and (d) *Kaizen* or *continuous improvements*.

The *Senpai–Kohai* or senior–junior relationships are formed from the level of primary schools where junior students have followed the orders of the senior students, who in turn, may help the juniors in learning. The process continues throughout the lifetime for the Japanese. In workplaces, *Senpais* will explain Kohais how to do their work, the basic code of conducts, and norms.

From this system emerges the second MEV, *Conformity*, which is better understood from the saying that "*nails that sticks out should be beaten down.*" The inner meaning is that unless someone conforms to the rules of the community or coworkers, he or she would be an outcast. There is no room for individualism in the Japanese society or in workplace.

The third item, *Hole-Rail-Sou*, is the basic feature of the Japanese organizations *Hou-Reel-Son*, and it is a combination of three different words in Japanese: *Houkoku*, or to report, *Renraku*, or to inform, and *Soudan*, or to consult or pre-consult.

Subordinates should always report to the superior. Superiors and subordinates share information. Consultations and pre-consultations are required; no one can make his or her decision by himself or herself even within the delegated authority. There is no space in which the delegation of authority may function. Combining these words, *Houkoku, Renraku*, and *Soudan*, "*Hou-Ren-Sou*" is the core value of the culture in Japan. Making suggestions, for improvements, without pre-consultations is considered to be an offensive behavior in Japanese culture. Everyone from the clerk to the president, from the entry day of the working life to the date of retirement, every Japanese must follow the "*Hou-Ren-Sou*" value system.

It is also called *Ringi* system. The *Ringi* system is a traditional way of managerial decision making in Japan. For example, when Japanese executives discuss the subject of decision making, they use the term *ringi seido*, that is, the ringi system. The system is based on decision making by group participation and consensus. The responsibilities for the decision making are highly diffused and cannot be associated with an individual person. The word *ringi* in reality consists of two parts. *Rin* means submitting a proposal to the superior or boss and receiving his or her approval (Yamashiro, 1967).

Kaizen, that is, continuous improvement, is another MEV that is one of the basic ingredients of the Japanese culture. Search for continuous improvement during the Meiji Government of the nineteenth century led the Japanese to search the world for knowledge. Japanese companies today are doing the same in terms of both acquisitions of knowledge by setting up R&D centers throughout the Western world and by having "*quality circles*" in workplaces to implement new knowledge to improve the product quality and to increase its efficiency (Kujawa, 1979; Kumagai, 1996; Miyajima, 1996).

Japanese organizational culture

To understand the Japanese organizational culture, it is essential to know the Japanese system of management, which gave rise to the unique Japanese style of OC. What follows is the result of several visits to the major Japanese corporations (e.g., Toyota, Mitsubishi, Honda, and Nissan) and interviews with several senior executives, including members of the board and vice-presidents of these companies.

Japanese system of management is a complete philosophy of organization, which can affect every part of the enterprise. There are three basic ingredients: lean production system, total quality management (TQM), and human resources management (Kobayashi, 1980). These three ingredients are interlinked in order to produce total effect on the management of the Japanese enterprises. Because Japanese overseas affiliates are part of the family of the parent company, their management systems are part of the management strategy of the parent company (Basu, 1999; Morishima, 1996; Morita, 1992; Shimada, 1993).

The basic idea of the lean production system and the fundamental organizational principles is the "*human-ware*" (Shimada, 1993), which is described in Figure 1.1. Human-ware is defined as the integration and interdependence of machinery and human relations and a concept to differentiate among different types of production systems. The purpose of the lean production philosophy, which was developed at the Toyota Motor Company, is to lower the costs. This is done through the elimination of waste, that is, everything that does not add value to the product. The constant strive for perfection (*Kaizen* in Japanese) is the overriding concept behind good management, in which the production system is being constantly improved; perfection is the only goal. Involving everyone in the work of improvement is often accomplished through quality circles. A lean production system uses "autonomous defect control" (*Pokavoke* in Japanese), which is an inexpensive means of conducting inspection for all units to ensure zero defects. Quality assurance is the responsibility of everyone. Manufacturing tasks are organized into teams. The principle of "*just in time*" (JIT) means each process should be provided with the right part, in the right quantity, and at exactly the right point of time. The ultimate goal is that every process should be provided with one part at a time, exactly when that part is needed.

The most important feature of the organizational set-up of the lean production system is the extensive use of multifunctional teams, which are groups of workers who are able to perform many different works. The teams are organized along a cell-based production flow system. The number of job-classifications also declines. Workers have received training to perform a number of different tasks, such as the statistical process control, quality instruments, computers, set-up performances, maintenance, etc. In the lean production system, responsibilities are decentralized. There is no supervisory level in the hierarchy. The multifunctional team is expected to perform supervisory tasks. This is done through the rotations of team leadership among workers. As a result, the number of hierarchical levels in the organization can be reduced. The number of functional areas that are the responsibility of the teams increases (Kumazawa and Yamada, 1989).

In a multifunctional set-up, it is vital to provide information in time and continuously in the production flow. The production system is changing and gradually adopting a more flexible system to adopt itself to changes in demand, which may reduce costs of production and increase efficiency. There are extensive usages of *Kaizen* activities and TQM and *Total Productive Maintenance* (TPM) to increase the effectiveness of CPs.

A nation-organization-leader-performance model

Organizational Culture is a product of a number of factors: National Culture, human resources practices, and leadership styles (LSs) have prominent influences on it. These in turn, along with the OC, affect corporate performances. The proposed model, as in Figure 1.1, is the synthesis of the ideas relating to this central theme. Figures 1.2 and 1.3 describe the proposed theoretical model relating organizational culture and corporate performances. Corporate performances are measured in terms of the following criteria: customers' satisfaction; employee's satisfaction; and commitment and contributions of the organization to the society and environment. Most companies in Japan use these criteria to signify corporate performances (Basu, 1999; Nakane, 1970).

There are several latent or hypothetical variables, which jointly can influence the outcome. National culture is affected by two constructs: micro values and macro values. MIVs are composed of several factors (Kahle et al., 1988). These are (a) the sense of belonging; (b) respect and recognition from others; (c) a sense of life accomplishments; and (d) self-respect.

Macro values, according to the opinions of the executives of the Japanese firms, are religious values, habitual values, and moral values. There may be other MAVs, which are important for other nations such as geography, racial origin, etc., but for the Japanese, these are not so important (Basu, 1999). Although moral and habitual values can be the results of religious values, it is better to separate out these three values as distinct. The moral and habitual values are different in Japan from other East Asian nations. Honor and "respect from others" are central to the Japanese psychology. Ritual suicides (*Harakiri*) are honorable acts for the Japanese, if they fail in some way to do their duty. Habitual values are extreme politeness on the surface, beautifications of everything, community spirit, and cleanness are unique in Japan, which are not followed in any other countries in Asia.

This is particularly true if we examine certain MEVs, which are neither MIV nor MAV values, but are derived from the national culture. It is possible to identify five different MEVs, which are important outcomes of the Japanese NC. These are discussed as follows:

1   Exclusivity or insider–outsider (*Uchi–Soto* in Japanese) psychology by which Japanese exclude anyone who is not ethnic Japanese from social discourse. (It is different from color or religious exclusivities. For example, the Chinese or Koreans, who are living in Japan for centuries, are excluded from the Japanese social circles).
2   Conformity or the *doctrine of "nail that sticks up should be beaten down"* (*Deru Kuiwa Utareru* in Japanese) – deviations from the mainstream norms are not tolerated.
3   Seniority system (*Senpai–Kohai* in Japanese) by which every junior must obey and show respects to the seniors
4   Collectivism in decision-making process (*Hou-Ren-Sou* system in Japanese)
5   Continuous improvements (*Keizen* in Japanese), which is the fundamental philosophy of the Japanese society

These MEVs are exclusively Japanese, a reflection of the unique Japanese culture (Basu, 1999; Nakane, 1970), and are fundamental to the Japanese organizations. National culture along with the MEVs affect both the organizational culture, Human resource management system, and the leadership style constructs. Japanese organizational culture construct is affected by the national culture, meso values, and the human resources management system. The similarities in organizational cultures in different companies are due to the similarities in national culture and meso values; the differences are due mainly to the differences in human resources management. In Japan, human resource practices vary from one company to another, and as a result, organizational cultures and corporate performances vary. In Toyota, it is very consistent and strong culture with great emphasis on discipline, *Keizen*, TQM and JIT production–inventory system. In many other companies in Japan, situations are not the same; as a result, organizational culture differs.

OC is affected by the NC, MEVs, and HRM. If the company's leader is also the founder, then only the leadership style can affect the human resources management and organizational culture. Otherwise, when the leaders are professional managers trained and grown up within the company (In Japan and in Japanese companies abroad, it is out of practice to accept an outsider for the executive positions. All executives enter the company after their graduation and stay until they retire), appropriate leadership styles are developed by the organizational culture and human resources management.

Due to the collective decision-making process (*Hou-Ren-Sou*) leadership, a meso value – in the model cannot affect an OC or the HRM system. It is very different from the Western (America, European, or Australian) companies where the leaders are hired from outside and are expected to be innovative regarding the OC and HRM system. This is quite alien to the Japanese culture. Leadership style in Japan is an outcome, not an independent, variable as in the Western companies. Leadership style is affected by the NC, MEVs, OC, and the HRM.

Organizational culture is affected by four factors, according to this proposed model. These factors are (a) stability, (b) flexibility, (c) internal focus, and (d) external focus (Cameron and Quinn, 1999). These factors are universal, not restricted to the Japanese companies. However, how an OC is being affected by national culture, meso values, and human resources management would vary from country to country.

Leadership style is a function of four factors. These factors are leader (a) as a facilitator, (b) as an innovator, (c) as a technical expert, and (d) as an effective competitor for rival firms (Cameron and Quinn, 1999). These four characteristics of a leader are universal, but the emphasis varies from country to country.

Finally, the corporate performance is affected by a number of influencing factors: (a) customers' satisfaction, (b) employees' satisfaction and commitments, and (c) the contribution of the organization to the society. If we consider the contribution of the organization to society that is already taken into account by the customers' satisfaction and employees' satisfaction, then CP has these two important contributory factors.

Theoretical relationship between the observed variables and the underlying constructs are specified in an exploratory model, represented in Figure 1.2. In Figure 1.3, a more elaborate model, including the unique human resources management system of the Japanese companies, is described. Figure 1.3 represents a Linear Structural Relations (LISREL) version (Joreskog and Sorbom, 1999) of the model, which can be estimated using the methods of structural equation modeling (Raykov and Marcoulides, 2000).

The proposed theory describes the relationship between national culture and corporate performances through organizational culture with the human resources management system affecting the nature of the culture and leadership. These interrelationships are important aspects of the Japanese corporate behaviors in a multinational setting, and this proposed theory is an attempt to understand the Japanese corporate culture.

Analysis of the Japanese culture and organizations by outsiders so far suffers from a number of defects (Ikeda, 1987; Watanabe, 1998). They neither try to understand the effects of the Japanese value system on their organizations nor do they give any importance to the relationship between performance and culture. So far, the success of the Japanese companies was analyzed only in terms of their unique production and operations management system. However, the interrelationship between the production and operations management system, which is a part of the organizational culture, and the specific human resources management system it requires for its proper implementation was not given sufficient attention. The typical example is the analysis of the failure of the implementations of Japanese operations management system in Britain by Oliver and Wilkinson (1992) or in China by Taylor (1999). They could not explain the reason for the failure, as they have not analyzed the Japanese OC and particularly the HRM system.

In a Japanese company, the leadership styles and the organizational culture are designed by the human resources management system: These are not coming from outside. An effective corporate performance is the result of these underlying determinants of organizational culture and leadership styles. Thus, in a Japanese organization, LS is rooted in the HRM system, which emerges from the meso values of the Japanese national culture.

Whether efficient corporate performances can be repeated in foreign locations depends on the transmission mechanism of the Japanese organizational culture, which in turn, depends on the adaptations of the Japanese style human resources management system. This can face obstacles due to the different meso values in a foreign society and as a result, organizational cultures in a foreign location may be different from the OC of the company in Japan. Adaptation of the operations management system alone will not create an effective performance of a Japanese company in a foreign location. Creation of an appropriate HRM system and appropriate OC are essential for an effective performance.

A relevant issue is how firms can create values and sustain competitive advantages. The issue is related to the concept of strategic entrepreneurship (Hitt et al., 2011), where there are four dimensions: (a) mindset, culture, and leadership; (b) management of internal resources; (c) creativity; (d) innovation. There are also environmental influences, which explain how resources can be utilized to create values over time.

This can be defined as strategic entrepreneurship, which means how and with what effects opportunities to create future achievements can be innovated and utilized. That requires creation of values, which is the central function of entrepreneurship. Value creation efforts are being enhanced by strategic entrepreneurship by creating competitive advantages. Japanese management system utilizing its layers of value system effectively tries to utilize strategic entrepreneurship inherent within its value system.

This can be done by combining environmental, organizational, and personal attributes into a dynamic process of creation of opportunities to enhance competitiveness. Corporate performance is affected by two variables, organizational culture and leadership style. As a result, CP is an outcome of practically all variables of the model. Two factors determine CP: (a) *Customers Satisfaction* and (b) *Employees Satisfaction and Commitment.*

Value system of different levels of culture supports the firm's ability to exploit opportunities. Culture of different levels and leadership, which in the Japanese system is being created endogenously, develop entrepreneurial activities to achieve growth of the firm. Leadership in that context is a dynamic entrepreneurship, which emphasizes exploitations of new opportunities. Thus, in this context, leadership and organizational culture are mutually inclusive. Social capital of the firm enhances its capability to identify and create opportunities. Human capital can be enhanced by adding social capital to create motivation to perform. Social capital can intensify its ability to perform by creating psychological factors needed to target setting, focused intensity, and aspirations of the leaders, which motivate the employees to be creative. This creates commitment resulting in the success of the firm.

These commitment and motivation help the firm to pursue strategic goals by discovering opportunities and utilizing existing opportunities. Entrepreneurship requires innovative activity, and strategic management requires stability (Hitt et al., 2011) to achieve the balance between exploration and exploitation. An effective organizational structure can combine existing resources and innovates future resources to create value for the organization and its stakeholders. The question is how formal and informal structures of the organization can create such a super structure for enhanced performance and entrepreneurial activities (Alvarez and Barney, 2010). The analysis presented here is an attempt to answer that question by elaborating the interrelationship between different components of the levels of culture and the structure these support.

The model can be translated into a path-analysis model. Theoretical relationship between the observed variables and the underlying constructs are specified in a path-analysis model, represented in Figure 1.1 and Figure 1.2. Figure 1.3 provides more elaborations, including the unique HRM system of Japanese companies.

Figure 1.1 Sub-model 1: culture-performance system

NC, National Culture; OC, Organizational Culture; LC, Leader Culture; CP, Corporate Performance.

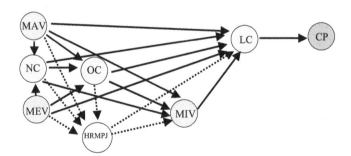

Figure 1.2 Culture-performance system

NC, National Culture; OC, Organizational Culture; LC, Leader Culture; MAV, Macro Values of Culture; MEV, Meso Values of Culture; MIV, Micro Values of Culture; HRMPJ, Human Resources Management Practices in Japan; CP, Corporate Performance.

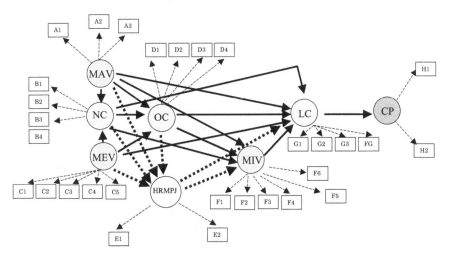

Figure 1.3 Values–culture–performance

NC, National Culture; OC, Organizational Culture; LC, Leader Culture; MAV, Macro Values of Culture; MEV, Meso Values of Culture; MIV, Micro Values of Culture; CP, Corporate Performance. A1, Religious Values; A2, Moral Values; and A3, Habitual Values are indicators for the MAV variable. B1, Power Distance; B2, Individualism/Collectivism; and B3 Masculinity/ Femininity are indicators for the NC variable; C1, Uchi–Soto Value; C2, Deru Kuiwa Utareru Value; C3, Senpai–Kohai Value; C4, Hou-Ren-Sou Value; and C5, Kaizen Value are indicators for the MEV variable. D1, Stability; D2, Flexibility; D3, External Focus; and D4, Internal Focus are indicators for the OC variable. E1, On-the-Job Training and E2, Emphasis on Personality of Recruits are indicators for the HRMPJ variable. F1, Sense of Belonging to a Group Value; F2, Respect and Recognition From Others Value; F3, Sense of Life Accomplishment Value; F4, Self-respect Value; F5, Kangaekata Value; and F6, Ishiki Value are indicators for the MIV variable. G1, Leader as Facilitator; G2, Leader as Innovator; G3 Leader as Technical Expert; and G4 Leader as Competitor are indicators for the LC variable. H1, Customers Satisfaction and H2, Employees Satisfaction and Commitment are indicators for the CP variable.

The initial stage for a value-based managerial intervention is the selected set of values, the current state of the organization. Through socialization, members learn OC and beliefs to participate as members of the organization. This process, through which established values are transforming into behavior and successful organizational commitments, is called management by values. Various value and mission statements are psychological contracts where the management promises the system that would be valid through enacting in employee behavior and create competitive advantages. Japanese corporations have strived to fulfill that goal to create a harmonious organizational climate not only for their main operation in Japan, but also in their overseas subsidiaries (Basu, 1999; Basu et al., 2001).

Harrison and Caroll (Harrison and Caroll, 1991, 1998, 2000, 2001) assumed that an individual's propensity to embrace the values and norms of a particular OC can be meaningfully represented by a single measure indicating the degree of fit with a cultural ideal. This measure of cultural fit is referred to as the *enculturation* (Selmer and De Leon, 1993). Although management groups differ in the types of factors they use to assess the level of enculturation, these often include knowledge, qualification, and willingness to embrace and comply with the culture, and they might reflect such factors as work experience and education.

As these set-of-value components are hard to imitate, they in turn create competitive resources for the company (Barney, 1986, 2001). Value creation can happen at the individual level and at the communal level (Felin and Hesterly, 2007; Nickerson and Zenger, 2008) and that demands individuals to cooperate with each other to create a collective value. Most individuals can be classified as self-regulators or reciprocator (Bridoux, Coeurderoy, and Durand, 2011). Self-regulators or individualists cooperate when they feel that such cooperation can enhance their own self-interest. Reciprocators or pro-socials cooperate because they feel that is the correct behavior. Collective value creation provides benefits to the organization and its individual members (Fehr and Gintis, 2007). OC created by different layers of culture in turn creates these prosocial activities (Dyer and Ouchi, 1993; Durand and Calori, 2006).

For a company, values of the original OC of the company can be transmitted to its subsidiaries as well by the HRM system (Shibata, 2008). Thus, OC can create competitive resources for a company in its subsidiaries as well. Japanese multinational companies with their proven competitive advantages in OC normally give priorities to the team spirit and involvement of the employees in quality enhancements. They have long and continuous training program to infuse the values of the parent units on the employees of the subsidiaries (Basu et al., 2001). Japanese firms given their competitive advantages in production and operations management, have greater employee involvement and team spirits (Liker and Morgan, 2006). They try to replicate these features in their overseas operations (Shimada, 1993).

A proposed theory of the relationship between national culture, organizational culture, human resources practices, and corporate performance for Japanese multinational companies, is narrated here. CP is a vast concept. According to the Balanced Score Card approach (Kaplan and Norton, 1996), it normally includes combination of both tangible and intangible concepts. Tangible factors of CP are sales, production, profit, return to assets, return to investments, market share, etc. Intangible factors of CP are job satisfaction, customer satisfaction, organizational commitment, product quality, etc. For a specific company, data on tangible factors, obtainable from the balance sheet of the company, are scalars, not variables in a given point of time (one year or one quarter, etc.). Data on intangible factors for that company depend on the opinion of the people concerned, workers, and customers, which vary according to the preferences of the individuals surveyed within a given point of time. As a result, these factors are variable with variance coming from the series of opinions expressed by the stakeholders of the company.

It is important to note that organizational culture is an intangible variable, and factors (value-components) that are composing culture are also intangible.

Therefore, there is a need to incorporate culture and performance in a model of quantitative relationship; the relevant factors composing the concept of the CP should be intangible too.

A number of studies have pointed out very close relationship between commitment of employees and the organizational performance (Mowday et al., 1979, 1982; O'Reilly et a 1991; Denison and Mishra, 1995). In fact, the relationship is so close that it is acceptable now to consider commitment as an index of performance (Meyer and Allen, 1991). Indeed, if employees are committed to work in an organization, corporate performance is considered to be very high in that organization. Thus, commitment is can be considered as one of the intangible measures of the CP.

The proposed theory describes the relationship between national culture and corporate performances through organizational culture with the human resources management system affecting the nature of the culture and the leadership. These interrelationships are important aspects of Japanese corporate behaviors in a multinational setting. This proposed theory is a synthesis to understand Japanese organizational and corporate culture.

Analysis of Japanese culture and organizations by outsiders so far suffers from a number of defects (Ikeda, 1987; Watanabe, 1998). They do not try to understand the effects of the Japanese value system on their organizations nor do they give any importance to the relationship between performance and culture. So far, success of Japanese companies was analyzed only in terms of their unique production and operations management system (Liker and Morgan, 2006). However, the interrelationship between the production and operations management system, which is a part of the organizational culture, and the specific human resources management system it requires for its proper implementation was not given sufficient attention.

The typical examples are the analysis of the failure of implementations of Japanese operations management system in Britain (Morris, Wilkinson, and Munday, 2000; Morris and Wilkinson, 1995) or in China (Taylor, 1999; Taylor, Levy, Boyacigiller, and Beechler, 2008). They could not explain the reason for the failure, as they have not analyzed the Japanese OC and particularly HRM system.

Adaptation of operations management system alone will not create effective performance of a Japanese company in a foreign location. Creation of an appropriate HRM system and appropriate OC are essential for effective performance.

Organizational commitment is thus one of the important intangible factors composing the concept of performance. Other intangible factors of CP (customers' satisfaction, job satisfaction, etc.) are not reflecting issues regarding OC so effectively as the organizational commitment does, as those are behavioral reactions toward the values already created by the OC, whereas organizational commitment itself is composed of values (Mowday et al., 1979).

However, there are controversies. Denison and Mishra (1995) provided a typography of OC and its relationship with organizational performance. On the other hand, Pavett and Morris (1995) in their quantitative study on the relationship between OC and performance concluded that there is no link between OC, and productivity or commitment. Clugston, Howell, and Dorfman (2000) in a quantitative study tried to apply Hofstede's thesis that certain national characteristics of OC can have relationship with commitment. Vandenberghe, Stinglhamber, Bentein, and Delhaise (2001) in their quantitative study of firms in several European countries observed that relationship between values of commitment and culture are culturally invariant and do not follow the pattern suggested by Hofstede (2002). Cultural differences are important, and these factors affect every component of the company behaviors and performances. The question was raised regarding factors, which are relatively more important than others, and whether it will be possible to manipulate these factors to increase performances of the multinational companies (Nag and Gioia, 2012; Puranam, Raveendran, and Knusden, 2012). The proposed theory may provide an answer to these issues.

There is a positive relationship between corporate ethical values and organizational commitment (Hunt, Wood, and Chonko, 1989). Clear personal values were more important in relation to attitudes about work and ethical practices than clarity about organizational values. These extra role activities carried out on behalf of the organization play a major influence in organizations' success and have a major role in enhancing CP (Smith, Organ, and Near, 1983, Smith and Elger, 2000). Research shows that commitment can create lower costs, less defects, higher productivity, and greater returns under influence of culture (Cutcher-Gershenfeld, 1991). Also commitment created by quality of work-life as manifestation of OC, quality circles, and labor–management teams can increase productivity (Katz, Kochan, and Gobeille, 1983). Moreover, commitment created by cooperative culture and innovative human resources practices has positive and significant effects on organization's productivity (Ichniowski, Shaw, and Prennushi, 1995). Palich, Horn, and Griffeth (1995) in their cross-sectional quantitative research across the United States, Canada, and Europe provides a major international study. The conclusion was that through job scope and extrinsic rewards, participatory management can promote commitment.

This chapter is based on conceptual aspects, as it does take into account the psychological value system inherent in the concepts of organizational culture and as a result of commitment as the source of corporate performance. Insignificant attention was paid in the literature on the value system inherent in OC and on the psychological aspects of CP, so this chapter has tried to fill up this important gap.

Value creation efforts are being enhanced by strategic entrepreneurship (Hitt et al, 2011) by creating competitive advantages. An effective management system utilizing its layers of value system effectively tries to utilize strategic entrepreneurship inherent within its value system. This can be done by combining environmental, organizational, and personal attributes into a dynamic process of creation of opportunities to enhance competitiveness (Ouchi, 1981; Jaeger, 1983).

The value system of different levels of culture supports a firm's ability to exploit opportunities. The culture of different levels develops entrepreneurial activities to achieve growth of the firm. Social capital of the firm enhances its capability to identify and create opportunities. Human capital can be enhanced by adding social capital with it, to create motivation to perform (Kirkman and Shapiro, 2001). Social capital can intensify its ability to perform by creating psychological factors needed to target setting, focused intensity, and aspirations of the leaders, which motivate the employees to be creative. This creates commitment resulting in the success of the firm. Such a commitment and motivation help the firm to pursue strategic goals by discovering opportunities and utilizing existing opportunities.

Entrepreneurship requires innovative activity and strategic management requires stability (Hitt et al., 2011). To achieve the balance between exploration and exploitation requires specifications of OC capable of supporting these twin needs. An effective OC can combine existing resources and innovate future resources to create value for the organization and its stakeholders. The question is how formal and informal structures of the organization can create such a culture for enhanced performance and entrepreneurial activities (Alvarez and Barney, 2010).

The initial stage for a value-based managerial interventions is the selected set of values, the current state of the organization. Through socialization, members learn OC and beliefs to participate as a member of the organization. This process, through which established values are transforming into behavior and successful organizational commitments, is called management by values (Shingo, 1985; Hayashi, 1989).

Various value and mission statements are psychological contracts where the management promises the system that would be valid through enacting in employee behavior and create competitive advantages. A successful corporation should strive to fulfill that goal to create a harmonious organizational climate through the corporate management system and operations management system not only for their main operation in the home operations, but also in its overseas subsidiaries (Basu et al., 2001; Selmer and DeLeon, 1996).

Although it is well-known that many multinational companies use OC as a control mechanism in their foreign subsidiaries, there are not any substantive studies of the phenomenon of the employees of the host country in foreign lands getting "acculturated" to the parent organizational system. This research is an answer to that. Since the parent organizational system reflects the parent companies' societal culture, employees in foreign subsidiaries could be subject to acculturation to a foreign culture of the parent company by learning novel values toward their work.

One of the central purposes of management is to facilitate communication across all of the organization's boundaries, so that the entire company works together to address given business challenges. With efficient dissemination of management system, the company's ability to make influential decisions increases dramatically, because individuals throughout the firm gain access to important strategic ideas. This improves the organization's ability to make rapid decisions and execute them. To create a management system appropriate for transforming tacit knowledge into communal, explicit knowledge fear-based approaches to management should be abandoned in preference for a harmonious-relationship-oriented management. The key is to create an environment of understanding, shared control, compassion, and learning. The leaders of the organization must take the reins in galvanizing and maintaining a persistent effort toward a management system of purposeful activity.

Successful multinational firms transcended national cultural differences to develop a common pattern of business performance by creating company citizenships. These included a primary focus on such values as organizational innovation, and a goal orientation. Corporate performances of the company, its espoused values, and vision of the leaders create values of its corporate management and operations management systems and for the organizational culture of the company as a whole. These values ultimately create commitment of the employees. Creation of commitment, an important index of a firm's successful corporate performance, in turn forms a company citizenship.

Organizational culture that "encouraged trust, participative-ness, and entrepreneurial behavior were effective across" the globe, both in the home country and in the host countries all over the world (Basu et al., 2001). In the context of a Japanese company, the role of culture should not be ignored, as culture implies resources of high economic significance.

With efficient dissemination of management system, the company's ability to make impacting decisions increases dramatically, because individuals throughout the firm gain access to important strategic ideas. This improves the organization's ability to make rapid decisions and execute them. To create a management system appropriate for transforming tacit knowledge into communal, explicit knowledge fear-based approaches to management must be abandoned in preference for a harmonious-relationship-oriented management. The key is to create an environment of understanding, shared control, compassion, and learning.

Thus, the organizational culture can be characterized from the perspective of values because values are the core components, which are in fact influencing the behavior of people working in the organizations. An OC with a strong value structure may create organizational effectiveness (Kotter and Heskett, 1992; Cameron and Quinn, 1999) and that may lead to competitive advantages of a company by creating unique resources (Barney, 1986; Barney and Clark, 2007).

The science and art of management can be understood as a sequential framework of purposeful activity designed to produce tangible management decisions resulting from a harmonious organizational system, toward the ultimate purpose of producing competitive advantages. Creation of such a corporate management and operations management system is a strategic process, which implies the goal of differentiation from competitors such that a sustainable competitive advantage is forged. For the end of competitive advantage to be achieved, all activities must be forged together to create a strong organizational system.

A firm's organizational culture can be a valuable resource to enhance corporate performance and create competitive advantages. The literature on culture and performance lacks emphasis on the individual's own experience of being committed. Current measures of culture and commitment may not accurately reflect the way people in organizations experience their own attachments to organizational life. There is a lack of examination of the nature of the OC and its value system (Kirkman and Shapiro, 2001). This research is designed to capture the individual's experience of the organizational culture based on his national and societal values and their relationship to the organization. Thus, this book provides deep insight in a methodical way to relate values of a society with the corporate performance.

2 Organizational strategy and design

Recently, all major multinational corporations (MNCs) utilize strategic planning by analyzing both the external and internal business environments (Drucker, 1959, Ackoff, 1970; Kaplan and Beinhocker, 2003). The success of this strategic planning largely depends on accurate forecasting of the external environment and a realistic appraisal of internal company strengths and weaknesses (Mintzberg, 1994; Rohrbeck and Schwarz, 2013). In recent years, MNCs have relied on their strategic plans to help refocus their efforts by abandoning old domestic markets and entering new global markets. This strategic global planning process has been critical in drive of modern MNCs to gain market share and to increase profitability (Hoskisson, Hitt, and Wan, 1999; Bereznoy, 2015).

Michael Porter in his book *The Competitive Advantage of Nations* (*1990*) asserts that competition itself is the key to success for multinational corporations. MNCs gain advantage against the world's best competitors because of pressure and challenge, and the best way to manage this global competitive challenge is through strategic planning (Mootee, 2016; Ruff, 2015).

Strategic planning process in multinational corporations

Strategic planning process in MNCs is the process of determining an organization's basic mission and long-term objectives of MNCs and then implementing a plan of action for attaining these goals. One of the primary reasons that MNCs need strategic planning is to keep track of their increasingly diversified operations (Grant, 2003). This need is particularly obvious when one considers the amount of direct foreign investment throughout the world. The second major reason for the increase in strategic planning is the need to coordinate and integrate diverse operations with a unified and agreed-upon focus. The third major reason for the increasing importance of strategic planning is the need to meet emerging international challenges (Vecchiato, 2015).

Many MNCs are convinced that strategic planning is critical to their success, and researchers are finding that these efforts are being conducted both at the home office and in the subsidiaries. Do these strategic planning efforts really pay off? Certainly, the fact that the strategic plan helps an MNC to coordinate and monitor its operations must be viewed as a benefit. Similarly, the fact that the plan helps an MNC deal with political risk problems, competition, and currency instability must be viewed as other benefits (Wiltbank, Dew, Read, and Sarasvathy, 2006).

Basic steps in strategic planning

In international management the basic steps in formulating strategic planning in MNCs can be summarized into the following:

1 Environmental scanning: scanning the external environment for opportunities and threats
2 Internal resource analysis: conducting an internal resource analysis of company strengths and weaknesses
3 Goal setting for strategy planning: formulating goals in light of the external scanning and internal analysis

Environmental scanning

Environmental scanning provides management with accurate forecasts of trends related to external changes in geographic areas where the firm is currently doing business and/or is considering setting up operations (Vecchiato, 2012). These changes relate to the economy, competition, political stability, technology, and demographic consumer data. Typically the MNC will begin by conducting a forecast of macroeconomic performance dealing with factors such as markets for specific products, per capita income of the population, and availability of labor and raw materials. A second common forecast will predict monetary exchange rates, exchange controls, balance of payments, and inflation rates. A third is the forecast of the company's potential market share in a particular geographic area as well as that of the competitors (Ruff, 2006).

Other considerations include political stability, government pressure, nationalism, and related areas of political risk. These assessments are extremely important in determining the profit potential of the region, which is always a major consideration in deciding where to set-up international operations (Vecchiato and Roveda, 2010).

Internal resource analysis

In formulating strategy, some MNCs wait until they have completed their environmental scanning before conducting an internal resource analysis. Others carry out the two steps simultaneously. An internal analysis identifies the key factors for success that will dictate how well the firm is likely to do (Miles, Saritas, and Sokolov, 2016). A key factor for success (KFS) is a factor necessary for a firm to compete effectively in a market niche.

For example, a KFS for a car is price. The car maker that discounts it price will gain market share vis-á-vis those that do not. A second KFS for the car is safety. A third

KFS is the quality. In the automobile industry, quality of products has emerged as the number one KFS in world markets. Japanese automobile MNCs have been able to successfully invade the US auto market because they have been able to prove that the quality of their cars is better than the average domestically built US car (Yoda, 2013). Toyota and Honda have had such a quality edge over the competition in recent years in the eyes of US car buyers. A fourth KFS for car is styling. The Mazda has been very successful in recent years because customers like its looks, and Mazda has gained market share both domestically as well as in Europe.

Internal resource analysis helps the MNC to evaluate its current managerial, technical, material, and financial strengths and weaknesses. This assessment is then used by the MNCs to determine its ability to take advantage of international market opportunities. The primary thrust of this analysis is to match external opportunities (gained through the environmental scan) with internal abilities (gained through the internal resource analysis).

Goal setting for strategic planning

In a sense, general goals concerning the philosophy of "going international" or growth actually precede the first two steps of environmental scanning and internal resource analysis. As used here, however, the more-specific goals for the strategic plan come out of the external scanning and internal analysis. Modern MNCs pursue a variety of such goals. Profitability and marketing goals almost always dominate the strategic plan of today's MNCs; because MNCs generally need higher profitability from their overseas operations than they do from their domestic operations. The reason is quite simple: setting up overseas operations involves greater risk and effort. In addition, an MNC has done well domestically with a product or service usually because the competition is minimal or ineffective. Firms with this advantage often find that there are additional lucrative opportunities outside their borders. Moreover, the more successful a firm is domestically, the more difficult it is to increase market share without strong competitive response. International markets, however, offer an ideal alternative to the desire for increased growth and profitability. Another reason that profitability and marketing are at the top of the list is that these tend to be more environmentally responsive, whereas production, finance, and personnel functions tend to be more internally controlled (Miles et al., 2016; Rohrbeck, Battistella, and Huizingh, 2015).

Once the strategic goals are set, the MNC will then develop specific operational goals and controls, usually a two-way process at the subsidiary or affiliate level. The head office management team will set certain parameters, and the overseas group will operate within these guidelines. Thus, for strategic planning in MNCs, profitability, and marketing goals are given higher importance and warrant closer attention (Bodwell and Chermack, 2010; Dibrell, Craig, and Neubaum, 2013).

Strategically plan implementation in multinational corporations

Strategy implementation provides goods and services in accord with a plan of action. International management must consider three general areas in strategy implementation: the MNC must decide where to locate operations; the MNC must carry out entry; and the MNC must implement functional strategies in areas such as human resources management (HRM), marketing, production, and finance. In choosing a location, today's MNC has two primary considerations: the country and the specific locale within the chosen country.

Traditionally, MNCs have invested in industrialized countries. For example, in the 1980s, the majority of all foreign investment by Japanese MNCs was in the United States, Canada, and Europe, and for US MNCs, it was in Europe and Canada. The small percentage that went into less developed countries was heavily concentrated in extractive (e.g., mining) rather than manufacturing activities. MNCs invest in industrialized countries primarily because these advanced nations offer the largest markets for goods and services. In addition, the established country or geographic locale may have legal restrictions related to imports, encouraging a local presence. Japanese MNCs, for example, in complying with their voluntary export quotes of cars to the United States as well as responding to dissatisfaction in Washington regarding the large trade imbalance with the United States, have established US-based assembly plants. In Europe, because of increasing EC 1992 regulations for outsiders, most Japanese and US MNCs have operations in at least one European country, thus ensuring themselves access to the European community at large. In fact, the Honda Motor operates in each of the original four EC countries, and huge US multinational corporation ITT now operates in each of the original 12 EC countries (Miles et al., 2016).

Second consideration in choosing a country is the amount of government control. MNCs tend to avoid entering or expanding operations in countries where there is political turmoil or spillover effects caused by retaliation from other nations, for example, in Arab countries in South Africa, etc. Also, traditionally, MNCs from around the world in the past refused to do business in Eastern European countries with central planning economies. However, the recent relaxing of the trade rules and the move toward free market economies in the former Soviet Union's republics and the other Eastern European nations has encouraged MNCs to rethink their positions; more and more are making moves into this largely untapped part of the global market. Recently the Japanese MNCs, as well as US MNCs, are investing in East Asian developing nations.

Third consideration in selecting a country is restrictions on foreign investment. Traditionally, countries such as China, Japan, and Mexico have required that control of the operation be in the hands of local partners. MNCs are reluctant to accept such conditions. In addition to the above considerations, MNCs will examine the specific benefits offered by host countries, including low tax rates, rent-free land and buildings, low-interest or no-interest loans, subsidized energy and transportation rates, and a well-developed infrastructure that provides many of the services found back home (good roads, communication systems, schools, entertainment, and housing).

However, these benefits will be weighed against any disincentives or performance requirements that must be met by the MNC such as job creation quotas; export minimums for generating foreign currency; limits on local market growth;

labor regulations; wage and price controls; restrictions on profit repatriation; and controls on the transfer of technology.

Once the MNC has decided the country in which to locate, the firm must choose the specific locale. A number of factors will influence this choice. Common considerations include access to markets, proximity to competitors, availability of transportation and electric power, and the desirability of the location for employees who will be coming in from the outside. In selecting US sites, a study found that both German and Japanese firms place more importance on accessibility and desirability and less importance on financial considerations. However, financial matters remain important: many countries attempt to lure MNCs to specific locales by offering special financial packages.

Very important common consideration is the nature of the workforce. MNCs like to locate near sources of available labor that can be readily trained to do the work. A complementary consideration that is often unspoken is the presence and strength of organized labor. Japanese MNCs, in particular, tend to avoid heavily unionize areas. Another common consideration is the cost of doing business. Japanese automobile companies often set-up operations in rural areas, because these are much less expensive.

Role of the functional strategies

Although marketing usually dominates strategy implementation, the production function also plays a role. If a company is going to export goods to a foreign market, the production process has traditionally been handled through domestic operations. In recent years, however, MNCs have found that whether they are exporting or producing the goods locally in the host country, consideration of worldwide production is important. For example, goods may be produced in foreign countries for export to other nations, including their home countries (Nash, 2013).

There are the following options in production: a plant will specialize in a particular product and export it to all of the MNCs' markets; a plant will produce goods only for a specific locale such as Western Europe or South America; and a plant will produce one or more components that are then shipped to a larger network of assembly plants. This latter option has been widely adopted by automakers such as Volkswagen and Honda or by pharmaceutical firms.

If the company operates production plants in different countries but makes no attempt to integrate overall operations, the company is known as a *multidomestic*. A recent trend has been away from this scattered approach and toward global coordination of operations. If the product is labor-intensive, as in the case of cars or microcomputers, then the trend is to farm the product out to low-cost sites such as Taiwan, Mexico, and Brazil, where the cost of labor is relatively low, and the infrastructure (electric power, communications systems, transportation systems) is sufficient to support the production. Sometimes multiple sources of individual components are used, and in other cases, one or two are sufficient. In any event, careful coordination of the production function is needed in implementing the strategy, and the result is a product that is truly global in nature (Bodwell and Chermack, 2010). MNCs can use three basic sources for filling the overseas positions: home country nationals (expatriates); host country nationals; and third country nationals. The most common reason for using the home country nationals in top management is to get the overseas operation under control of parent company. However, a host country national is more familiar with the culture and language and can often command a lower salary than the home country national. The primary reason for using a third-country national is that these people have the necessary expertise for doing the job.

The major criteria for selection the managers for overseas assignments include adaptability, independence, self-reliance, physical and emotional health, experience, education, knowledge of the local culture and language, motivation, family support to relocate, and leadership.

Usually in most MNCs, those managers who meet the selection criteria have to pass some form of screening. Some MNCs are using the psychological testing, but this approach have lost its popularity in recent years. More commonly, the candidates are given the various forms of interviews (Dibrell et al., 2013).

The implementation of marketing strategy must be determined on a country-by-country basis. However, in many cases, what works marketing wise in one locale may not necessarily succeed in another. In addition, the specific steps of the marketing approach are often dictated by the overall strategic plan, which in turn is based heavily on market analysis.

The Japanese provide an excellent example of how this process works. In many cases Japanese MNCs have followed a strategy of first building up their market share at home and driving out imported goods. Then the Japanese MNCs move into newly developing countries (e.g., China, Korea or Taiwan), honing their marketing skills as they go along. Finally, the Japanese MNCs move into fully developed countries, ready to compete with the best available. This pattern of implementing strategy has been used by Japanese MNCs in marketing automobiles, electronics, home appliances, petrochemicals, and steel.

However, for some products, such as computers, the Japanese MNCs have moved from their home market directly to fully developed countries and then on the newly developing nations. Finally, for products such as color TVs, videotape recorders, and sewing machines, the Japanese MNCs have gone directly to developed countries to market products because the market in Japan is small and stagnant. In general, once a MNC agrees on the goods it wants to sell in the international marketplace, the specific marketing strategy is implemented.

The implementation of marketing strategy in the international arena is built around the well-known four *P*s of marketing: product, price, promotion, and place. As noted in the example of the Japan, the local MNCs often develop and sell a product in local or peripheral markets before expanding to major overseas targets. However, if the product is designed specifically to meet an overseas demand, the process is more direct. Price is largely a function of market demand. The managers from the Japanese MNCs, for example, have found that the US microcomputer market is price sensitive; so, by introducing lower-priced clones, the Japanese have been able to make headway, especially in the portable lap computer market. The last two *P*s, promotion and place, are dictated by local conditions and are often left in the hands of those who are running the subsidiary or affiliate. Local management may implement customer sales incentives, for example, or make arrangements with dealers and salespeople who are helping move the product locally (Kaplan, 2012).

Financial function strategy is normally developed at the home office and carried out by the overseas affiliate or branch. In recent past, when a company become international, the overseas operation commonly relied on the local area for funds, but the rise of global financing has ended this practice. MNCs have learned that transferring funds from one place in the world to another or borrowing funds in the international money markets are often less expensive than relying on local sources.

One problem is representative of those faced by MNCs using a financial function to implement their strategies. Recently another biggest problem for MNCs in implementing the finance strategies has been the wide fluctuations of the exchange rates of the currencies. For example, when the dollar drops in terms of the Japanese Yen and Euro, the US overseas operations in Japan and Germany found their profits (in terms of dollars) rising sharply. However, the US operations holding pesos in Argentina or Mexico found their profits decreasing sharply because of the high inflation in their countries.

Theoretical review

Analyzing the strategic planning process in MNCs, we would like to give explanations of the reasons why MNCs exist; the description of the basic organizational structures of modern business; and organizational characteristics of the MNCs.

Therefore, we will now briefly describe "classic" theories such as Vernon's product life-cycle theory and Dunning's eclectic theory of direct investment. Thereafter, we will analyze the theories like Porter's theory of comparative and competitive advantage of nations, and Streek, Maurice–Sorge–Warner, and Lane's theory known as societal effect theory. All those theories attempt to explain why multinationals exist and to offer the systematic explanation of the multinationals in general (Hill, 2007; Verbeke, 2009).

Vernon: product life-cycle theory

Vernon's (1966) product life-cycle (PLC) theory takes its name from the similar PLC marketing theory. At the beginning, in the introductory phase, suppose a new product is introduced. It is innovative, it has not yet been standardized, and it is relatively expensive; because the product will evolve throughout this phase, the producer and the consumer must be in direct contact. Production and sales can only take place in the country where the product is developed, for example in the United States (Williamson, 2000; Appleyard, Field Jr., and Cobb, 2006).

In the next, expansion, phase the product becomes more standardized, and the price decreases slightly. Turnover increases sharply, and production costs begin to drop. To extend this phase, a company will attempt to export its product. As the price is still rather high, export will largely go to countries that have a similar income level, for example, Europe or Japan. At the end of the expansion phase and the beginning of the maturity phase, the company will start manufacturing the product in Europe. Turnover there will have increased to such an extent that it would pay to set-up foreign production, particularly in view of import tariffs and transport costs. By this time, however, the product has become standardized in such a way that European companies will be eager to produce by their own. In the end, the production process will be completely standardized, making economies of scale and mass production possible. The quality and level of skill of the workforce in the production process becomes less important than the costs. Production will, therefore, increasingly take place in labor-abundant countries like China. The PLC model made an important contribution to explaining the enormous scope of direct investment by American companies in the 1950s and 1960s (Kiritsis, Bufardi, and Xirouchakis, 2003)

However, the Vernon's model fails to answer two important questions. First, why does one company in a specific country become a multinational, while another does not? Second, why would a company choose to maintain control of the production process by setting up subsidiaries? It would be much simpler to license the know-how required to manufacture the product to a foreign company. Both of these questions can be answered by Dunning's eclectic theory, which also incorporates the location-specific advantages proposed in the classic theories of trade.

Dunning: eclectic theory

Dunning's eclectic theory (1985), known as the "transaction cost theory of international production," explains why corporations produce abroad, how they are able to compete successfully with domestic corporations, and where they are going to produce. The theory selectively combines elements of various other theories (hence the name "eclectic"). According to Dunning, a company that wishes to set-up production in a foreign country and wants to operate as a MNC must simultaneously meet three conditions: ownership advantages; location advantages; internalization advantages (Rugman and Verbeke, 2003, 2008).

Ownership advantages, also known as corporation-specific advantages, are advantages in the production of a good or service that are unique to a particular company. The range of advantages, both tangible and intangible, can be summarized as follows: proprietary technology due to research and development activities; managerial, marketing, or other skills specific to the organizational function of the corporation; product differentiation, trademarks, or brand names; large size, reflecting scale economies; large capital requirements for plants of the minimum efficient size (Bonaglia, Goldstein, and Mathews, 2007).

The presence of ownership advantages, however, in no way fully explains the existence of the multinational company. For example, if a company gains an ownership advantage over other companies for a certain foreign market, it could simply export its products to that market. For this reason, the second condition must also be met: location advantages.

Location advantages include all of the factors ranging from an abundance of fertile land and cheap labor to a liberal capital market and a sound infrastructure. To that we can also add the favorable investment conditions offered by some countries to attract foreign investors. These may be in the form of subsidies, tax exemptions, or cheap housing. At any rate, the benefits for the corporation must proceed from the combination of ownership advantages and location advantages. However, it will not necessarily lead to foreign direct investment and, therefore, to the establishment of a multinational concern. After all, the company can also sell its ownership advantages or license them out to another company in the foreign market. That is why finally the third condition must be met as well: the internalization advantages (Guillen and Garcia-Canal, 2009).

A company possesses internalization advantages if it is more profitable for this company to exploit its ownership advantages in another country itself than to sell or license them. In actual practice, there are countless arguments in favor of internalization. To a large, extent these arguments have their origin in Coase's (1937) and Williamson's (2000) transaction cost approach.

In the first place, if the ownership advantage is actually a combination of highly specific company factors, it might be difficult to sell or license it. And even if it were possible, the advantages and the contract for these advantages would be so complex that setting up and exploiting them would be highly expensive. This applies to a lesser degree if the advantage being sold is a specific, easily isolated invention. The problem in this situation, however, is that it would be difficult for the buyer/licensee to get a good idea, of what he is purchasing or acquiring a license for. After all, if the licensor releases too much information before concluding the contract, he will have very little left to sell or license. Finally, the company may be afraid that by licensing certain company-specific knowledge, this knowledge will either leak out, making further licenses difficult, or be used in such a way that it damages the name of the licensor. In each case, there may be some internalization advantages that the company will decide to carry out the relevant activity in the foreign country itself (Mathews, 2006).

Like rival theories, Dunning's approach is not seen as the best explanation for the existence of multinationals. However, it does succeed in elegant manner bringing together ideas from a number of relatively separate schools. We will, therefore, end the discussion of the explanations offered for the existence of multinationals with this theory.

The PLC theory has certainly made an important contribution to explaining the distribution of some high-tech products, but it raises almost as many questions as it answers. Why is it that one particular country is the leader in a new industry? Why are some industries seemingly immune to the loss of competitive advantage suggested by Vernon? And why is it that in many sectors of industry innovation is now seen as an ongoing process and not a one-off event, after which an invention quickly becomes standardized and production is taken over by low-wage countries? Finally, Dunning's eclectic theory provides very interesting and more or less comprehensive explanation of the existence of multinational enterprises. However, it does not explain why some countries gain particular ownership advantages, while others do not (Narula, 2006; Verbeke, 2009).

Thus, by now, we have discussed a number of reasons for MNCs existence and foreign direct investment. However, we have not yet concretely explain why a particular nation is able to achieve international success in a particular industry. The Porter's theory of comparative and competitive advantage of nations attempts to provide an explicit answer to this question.

Porter: theory of comparative and competitive advantage of nations

Now we will analyze Michael Porter's theory of comparative and competitive advantage of nations (1990), known as Porter's Analysis. According to Porter, the new theory of national comparative and competitive advantage of nations must meet the following criteria:

- as firms can and do choose strategies that differ, a new theory must explain why firms from particular nations choose better strategies than those from others for competing in particular industries;
- successful international competitors often compete with global strategies in which trade and foreign investments are integrated; most previous theories have set out to explain either trade or foreign investment – a new theory must explain instead why a nation is the home base for successful global competitors in a particular industry that engage in both;
- a new theory must move beyond the comparative advantage to the competitive advantage of a nation;
- a new theory must explain why a nation's firms gain competitive advantage in all its forms, not only the limited types of factor based advantage contemplated in the theory of comparative advantage;
- a new theory must start from the premise that competition is dynamic and evolving; much traditional thinking has embodied an essentially static view focusing on cost efficiency due to factor or scale advantages;
- a new theory must make improvement and innovation in methods and technology as central elements by explaining the role of the nation in the innovation process. Since innovation requires sustained investment in research, physical capital and human resources, it is necessary also explain why the rate of such investments is more vigorous in some nations and not in others;
- since MNCs play a central role in the process of creating competitive advantage, the behavior of MNCs must become integral to a theory of national advantage. From a manager's perspective much of trade theory is too general to be of much relevance. A new theory must give firms insight into how to set strategy to become more effective international competitors.

(Porter, 1990)

Porter naturally attempts to satisfy these conditions in his own analysis. After conducting a four-year study involving ten countries (Denmark, Germany, Italy, Japan, Korea, Singapore, Sweden, Switzerland, the United Kingdom, and the United States), he was convinced that national competitive advantage depends on four determinants such as factor conditions; demand conditions; related and supporting industries; firm's strategy, structure, and rivalry (Davies and Ellis, 2000).

Those four determinants were represented as a diamond. The complete model also includes the factors "government" and "chance," which make their influence felt through the four determinants. These four determinants are as follows.

Factor conditions

The first determinant, *factor conditions*, shows traces of the classic international trade theories proposed by Adam Smith as the author of the theory of absolute advantage of nations (Smith, 1776), David Ricardo – Richard Torrens as authors of famous law of comparative advantage of nations (Ricardo, 1821; Torrens, 1816) and Eli Heckscher (Heckscher, 2006) – Bertil Ohlin (1938) as a the authors of the Hecksher–Ohlin theorem postulating that each country has a comparative advantage in commodity that uses intensively the country's abundant factors such as asset, technology, tastes. However, whereas these theories concentrated mainly on the traditional production factors such as land, labor, and capital, Porter goes much further. He agrees with the factors such as labor (which he calls "human resources"), land ("physical resources"), and capital ("capital resources"), but in his view these categories are much broader than the classic theories suggest. For example, while Ricardo principally saw labor as a large, undefined mass of cheap workers, Porter emphasizes quality as well as quantity and divides human resources into "a myriad of categories, such as toolmakers, electrical engineers, engineers with PhDs, applications programmers, and so on." Physical resources also cover the location of a country with respect to its customers and suppliers, while capital resources can be divided into "unsecured debt, secured debt, 'junk' bonds, equity and venture capital." In addition to these "traditional" production factors, Porter also identifies knowledge resources and infrastructure as factors that can be decisive for the competitive advantage of a country. He considers knowledge resources as "the nation's stock of scientific, technical and market knowledge bearing on goods and services," while infrastructure includes transport and communications systems, the housing stock and cultural institutions with respect to education, training, skills, industrial relations, and motivation can all be seen as factor conditions that influence a country's competitive advantages (Kiritsis et al., 2003).

Demand conditions

The second determinant is *demand conditions*. Traditional trade theories tended to neglect the demand side. According to Porter, demand in the home market can be of great importance to a country's national competitive advantage. In addition to the size of the demand, which can lead to economies of scale, the quality of the demand is equally significant. If consumers in a company's own country, for example, are the most progressive and demanding in the world, this country will have to do its very best to deliver product quality, innovation, and service. In this way, the company and/or the country gains a competitive advantage on the world market.

Related and supporting industries

The third determinant, *related and supporting industries*, exercises a similar type of influence. The presence of related and supporting industries that can compete at an international level will force a company to meet the same high international standards.

Firms' strategy, structure, and rivalry

The fourth broad determinant of national competitive advantage is *firm's strategy, structure, and rivalry*. The goals and strategies of corporations can differ sharply from nation to nation. There are also huge differences in the way corporations in the same industry are organized in different countries. According to Porter, a good match between these choices and the sources of competitive advantage in a particular industry will result in national competitive advantage. If, for instance, the automobile industry demands flexible, non-bureaucratic organizational structures, and corporations in a particular country tend to favor this kind of organizational structure, they will – all other things being equal – have a good chance of succeeding in this industry (Rugman and Verbeke, 1993; Bellak and Weiss, 1993).

Thus, the important question related with the main topic such as strategic planning process in MNCs is, Why do corporations in particular countries favor particular strategies and structures? The answer is that there are many national characteristics that influence the ways in which corporations are organized and managed. According to Porter, some of the most important aspects are attitudes toward authority, norms of interpersonal interaction, labor–management relationships, social norms of individual or group behavior and professional standards. Porter places special emphasis on labor–management relationships because he believes they are central to the ability of corporations to improve and innovate. All these aspects in turn find their basis in a nation's educational system, its social and religious history, its family structures, and many other, often intangible but unique national characteristics (Clark, 1991; Jelinek, 1992).

Finally, domestic rivalry is a very important factor, in that companies force one another to lower their prices, improve quality, and introduce a constant stream of innovations, all of which also benefit the international competitive position of the country in which they operate (Rugman, 1992; Krugman, 1994; Waverman, 1995).

Japan as an example of Porter's analysis

We would like to examine Japan by using the Porter's analysis, because my research interest is mainly connected with Japan (Suzuki, 1994).

Thus, Japan's prominent position in automobiles, motorcycles, ships, consumer electronics, computers, and computing equipment, office machines, and sewing machines can in the first place be attributed to the country's rapid and continual upgrading of human resources, in which in-company training dominates. Porter's analysis focuses on applications and process optimization rather than basic technological innovation, resulting in high-quality products that are nevertheless competitively priced.

Second, demand conditions have also favored competitive advantage in these industries. In the 1950s and 1960s, while Japan's home market was growing rapidly in sectors such as sewing machines, ships, and motorcycles, and later automobile – these markets had begun to level off in other countries. As a result, Japanese corporations invested aggressively in large, efficient facilities with the latest technology. United States and European competitors, on the other hand, simply added on to existing, less efficient older plants. The result was higher productivity for Japanese corporations. The rapid growth of Japan's industrial economy also aided supporting industries such as robotics, copiers, and semiconductors. Even more important than the size of the home demand is the pressure from demanding and sophisticated buyers. Japanese consumers insist on quality and superior service and will readily switch brands if a quality difference is noticeable. It is important to note that this forces corporations continually to upgrade their products (Miroshnik, 2012; Suzuki, 1994).

As to the third determinant, Japan has a strong position in semiconductors, machine tools and robotics, which are essential supporting industries to many other sectors. Regarding the fourth determinant firm strategy, structure, and domestic rivalry – the strategy of Japanese corporations is geared largely toward standardization and mass production combined with high quality. This approach has made it the leader in industries such as consumer electronics and office machines. The commitment to their corporation of both workers and managers, and the corporation's investment in upgrading skills and norms of cooperation have led to an unusual rate of success in industries in which a cumulative learning effect is essential (consumer electronics, semiconductors, office machines).

Finally, in almost every industry in which Japan is internationally competitive, there are several and often a dozen or more competitors in automobile manufacturing, in semiconductors manufacturing and in shipbuilding.

Societal effect theory

Many of the factors identified by Porter, such as attitudes toward authority, norms of interpersonal interaction, labor–management relationships, social norms of individual or group behavior, professional standards, nation's educational system, nation's social and religious history, nation's family structures, and many other often intangible but unique national characteristics are considered as a part of a country's national science and can be seen in social science research as well.

Group of the authors such as Streeck, Maurice–Sorge–Warner, and Lane have pointed out national differences in the area of organizational structuring, differentiation and integration mechanisms, qualifications, and industrial relations (Streek, 1984; Maurice, Sorge, Warner, 1980; Lane, 1989). Such factors influence one another, and although this reciprocal effect can be found in every society, it is highly specific to the society in which it is taking place. This approach is known as the societal effect theory. For example, the strengths of German manufacturing enterprises are widely seen to emanate from two core institutional complexes – the system of vocational education and training and the system of industrial relations. The first not only creates high levels of technical skill throughout the industrial enterprise, but also engenders homogeneity of skills at all levels of the hierarchy, as well as fostering certain orientations to the work task and the work community. These characteristics, in turn, structure organizational relations, influence communication and cooperation along both horizontal and vertical lines and encourage labor deployment in accordance with the principle of responsible autonomy. The craft ethos permeates the whole of the organization and creates a common focus and identity for management and production workers, although not necessarily a community of interest. The cooperative works culture, fostered by the training system, is further reinforced by the system of industrial relations, particularly by the work council. The autonomy and responsibility encouraged by the organization of work is paralleled and enhanced by the participative industrial relations style, flowing from the system of codetermination (Kiritsis et al., 2003).

Organization structures and strategic planning

The organizational designs of many international operations are often similar to those used domestically. However, significant differences arise depending on the nature and scope of the overseas businesses and the home office's approach to controlling the operation. Ideally an overseas affiliate or subsidiary will be designed to respond to various concerns such as with production technology or the need for specialized personnel. However, the main concern is to meet the needs of both the local market and the home office. Importantly, an "if–then" contingency approach is used: if the strategy needed to respond to the local market changes, then there will be accompanying change in the organization structures. However, despite this contingency based approach, modern companies commonly use certain structural arrangements in international operations.

Initial division structure

Many firms make their initial entry into international markets by setting up a subsidiary by exporting locally produced goods. A subsidiary is a common organizational arrangement for handling finance-related businesses or other operations that require an onsite presence from the start. An export arrangement is a common first choice among manufacturing firms, especially those with technologically advanced products. Since there is little, if any, competition, the firm can charge a premium price and handle sales through an export manager. If the company has a narrow product line, this export manager usually reports directly to the head of marketing, and international operations are coordinated out of this department. If the firm has a broad product line and intends to export a number of different products into the international market, the export manager will head up a separate department and often will report directly to the president. These two arrangements work well as long as the company has little competition and is using international sales only to supplement domestic efforts.

If overseas sales continue to increase, local governments often make pressure in these growing markets for setting up on-site manufacturing operations. At the same time, many firms find themselves facing increased competition. The establishment of foreign manufacturing subsidiaries can help the MNCs to deal with both of these problems. The overseas plants show the government that the firm wants to be a good local citizen. At the same time these plants help the MNCs greatly reduce transportation costs, thus making the product more competitive. Each foreign subsidiary is responsible for operations within its own geographic area, and the head of the subsidiary reports either to senior executives coordinating international operations or directly to the home office.

International division structure

If the firm's international operations continue to grow, subsidiaries are commonly grouped into an international division structure, which handles all international operations out of a division created for this purpose. This structural arrangement is useful because it takes a great deal of the burden off the chief executive officer for monitoring the operations of a series of overseas subsidiaries as well as domestic operations. The head of the international division will coordinate and monitor overseas activities and reports directly to the chief executive on these matters. For example, PepsiCo recently reorganized its international soft drink division into such geographic business units covering 150 countries in which PepsiCo does business. These geographic units each have self-sufficient operations and broad local authority.

Companies that are still in the developmental stages of international business involvement are most likely to adopt the international division structures Other firms that use this structural arrangement include those with small international sales, limited geographic diversity, or few executives with international expertise.

A number of advantages are associated with the use of an international division structure: the grouping of international activities under one senior executive ensures that the international focus receives top management attention; the structural arrangement allows the company to develop an overall, unified approach to international operations; and the arrangement helps the firm develop a team of internationally experienced managers.

However, the use of this structure has a number of drawbacks: the structure separates the domestic and international managers and can result in two different camps with divergent objectives; as the international operation gets larger, the home office may find it difficult to think and act strategically and to allocate resources on a global basis; thus, the international division is penalized; most research and development efforts are domestically oriented, so ideas for new products or processes in the international market are often given low priority (Kiritsis et al., 2003).

Global structural arrangements

MNCs typically turn to global structural arrangements when they begin acquiring and allocating their resources on the basis of international opportunities and threats. This international perspective signifies a major change in management strategy and is supported by the requisite changes in organization structure. Global structures come in three common types: product, geographic, and functional.

Global product division structure

A global product division structure is a structural arrangement in which domestic divisions are given worldwide responsibility for product groups. The manager who is in charge of Product Division has authority for this product line on a global basis. This manager also has internal functional support related to the product line. For example, all the marketing, production, and finance activities associated with Product Division are under the control of this manager (Kiritsis et al., 2003).

The global product divisions operate as profit centers. The products are generally in the growth stage of the product life cycle, so they need to be carefully promoted and marketed. In doing so, global product division managers generally run the operation with considerable autonomy; they have the authority to make many important decisions. However, corporate headquarters will usually maintain control in terms of budgetary constraints, home office approval for certain decisions, and mainly "bottom line" (i.e., profit) results.

A global product structure provides a number of benefits: ability to respond to buyer needs (if the MNC is very diverse, for example, it produces automobiles, i.e., the products using a variety of technologies or has a wide variety of customers; the need to tailor the product to the specific demands of the buyer becomes important). A global product arrangement can help manage this diversity; ability to respond to local needs (if many geographic areas need to have the product modified to suit their particular desires, for example, cars, a global product division structure can be extremely important; ability to coordinate the marketing, production, and finance on a product-by-product global basis).

Also, MNCs also use a product division structure when a product has reached the maturity stage in the home country or similar markets but is in the growth stage in other markets such as third-world countries. An example might be automobiles, color television, computers, and mobile phones. These differing life-cycles require close technological and marketing coordination between the home market and the foreign market, best done by a product division approach (Rugman, 2005)

Some of the other advantages can be summarized as follows: it preserves product emphasis and promotes product planning on a global basis; it provides a direct line of communications from the customer to those in the organization who have product knowledge and expertise; it is enabling research and development to work on development of products that serve the needs of the world customer; it permits line and staff managers within the division to gain an expertise in the technical and marketing aspects of products assigned to them.

Unfortunately, the approach also has some drawbacks: the necessity of duplicating facilities and staff personnel within each division; division managers may pursue currently attractive geographic prospects for their products and neglect other areas with better long-range potential; many division managers spend too much time trying to tap the local market rather than the international market because it is more convenient, and they are more experienced in domestic operations.

Global area division structure

Instead of a global product division structure, some MNCs prefer to use a global area division structure. In this structure, global operations are organized on the basis of a geographic rather than a product basis. For example, the MNCs may divide international operations into two groups: domestic and foreign. This approach often signals a major change in company strategy, because now the international operations are put on the same level as domestic operations, that is, European or Asian operations are just as important to the Japanese MNCs as operations in Japan.

Under this arrangement, global division managers are responsible for all business operations in their designated geographic area. The chief executive officer and other members of top management are charged with formulating strategy, which ensures that the global divisions are all working in harmony. For example, excess resources in one region are transferred to others that need them.

A global area division structure is most often used by companies that are in mature businesses and have narrow product lines. These product lines are often differentiated based on geographic area. For example, the product has a strong demand in Europe but not in East Asia, or the type of product that is offered in Malaysia differs from the one sold in Thailand.

In addition, the MNCs usually seek high economies of scale for production, marketing, and resource-purchase integration in that area. Thus, by manufacturing in this region, rather than bringing the product in from somewhere else, the firm is able to reduce its cost per unit and bring the goods to market at a very competitive price. Firms that are producing autos, beverages, cosmetics, food, or pharmaceuticals often use such a global area arrangement.

The geographic structure allows the division manager to cater to the tastes of the local market and to make rapid decisions to accommodate environmental changes. A good example is provided by food products. In the United States, soft drinks have less sugar than in East Asia, so the manufacturing process must be slightly different in these two locations. In Turkey, Italy, Spain, and Portugal people like dark, bitter coffee; Americans prefer a milder, sweeter blend. In Europe, Canada, and the United States people, prefers less spicy food; in the East Asia they like more heavily spiced food. The global area structure allows for geographic unit in a foods company to accommodate such local preferences.

The primary disadvantage of the global area division structure is the difficulty encountered in reconciling a product emphasis with a geographic orientation. For example, if a product is sold worldwide, a number of different divisions are responsible for the sales. The lack of centralized management and control can result in increased costs and duplication of effort on a region-by-region basis. A second drawback is that new research and development efforts are often ignored by division groups because they are selling goods that have reached the maturity stage. Their focus is not on the latest technological superior goods that will win in the market in the local run, but on those that are proven winners and are now being conveniently marketed worldwide.

Global functional division structure

A global functional division structure organizes worldwide operations primarily on the basis of function and secondarily on the basis of product. The approach is not widely used other than by companies such as oil and mining companies. A number of important advantages are associated with the global functional division structure. These include an emphasis on functional expertise, tight centralized control, and a relatively lean managerial staff. Some of the important disadvantages include coordination of manufacturing and marketing is often difficult, managing multiple product line can be difficult because of the separation of production and marketing in different departments, and only the chief executive officer can be responsible for the profits.

As a result, the global functional process structure is typically favored only by those firms that need centralize coordination and control of integrated production processes, and those that are involved in transporting products and raw materials from one geographic area to another.

Multinational matrix structure or "mixed" organization structure

Some MNCs find that neither global product, global area, or functional arrangement is satisfactory. So, they combine all these structures in one called *multinational matrix structure* or mixed organization structure.

Thus, *mixed organization structur e* combines all three into a MNC that supplements its primary structure with a secondary one and, perhaps, a third one. For example, if a company uses a global area approach, committees of functional managers may provide assistance and support to the various geographic divisions. Conversely, if the firm uses a global functional approach, product committees may be responsible for coordinating transactions that cut across functional lines. In other cases, the organization will opt for a matrix structure that results in managers having two or more bosses. In this arrangement, the MNC coordinates geographic and product lines through the use of a matrix design (Roth, 1995).

Many advantages can be gained from the use of a mixed organization structure. In particular, it allows the organization to create the specific type of design that best meets its needs. The most important is that as the matrix design's complexity increases, coordinating the personnel and getting everyone to work toward common goals often becomes difficult. Too many groups are going their own way. Thus, many MNCs have not opted for a matrix structure; they are beginning to learn that simple, lean structures may be the best organization design. For example, well-known consultant Tom Peters claims that international firms that became wedded to the matrix concept of organization only kept the illusion of local control intact, but in reality engage "the New York-based, English-only-speaking, MBA-managers in charge of Thailand and Luxembourg and all stops in between" (Ghoshal, 2005).

The use of the subsidiary boards of directors as organization structure

Organizing the MNCs in recent years starts on the top with boards of directors. These boards are responsible for overseeing the corporation and ensuring that the senior managers are operating in accord with the overall policies and objectives established by the board. As firms increase their international focus, many are finding that subsidiary boards of directors are useful in helping shape and guide the activities of global operations. A subsidiary board of directors oversees and monitors the operations of a foreign subsidiary. In recent years this organizational arrangement has become increasingly popular. Some of the best known Japanese multinationals use this arrangement, including, the Nissan Motor Co., the Toyota Motor Co., the Honda Motor Co., the Matsushita Electric, as well as the Western multinationals such as Hewlett-Packard, Pilkington Bros., Ltd (Miroshnik, 2012; Grey and Antonacopoulou, 2003).

There are a number of reasons for the trend toward subsidiary boards. The main reason is that the external environment in which MNCs operate is becoming extremely complex, and rapid decision making is gaining in importance; subsidiaries must be given more authority for local operations. However, at the same time, the corporate board would like to ensure that the subsidiary does not become too autonomous. The solution to this dilemma is a local board that can play an important linking role between the two groups. The subsidiary board can also assist the unit in planning and controlling activities. Four major areas for which MNCs use subsidiary boards have been identified: to advise, approve, and appraise local management; to help the unit respond to local conditions; to assist in strategic planning; and to supervise the subsidiary's ethical conduct (Grey, 2004; Miroshnik, 2012).

Organizational characteristics of multinational corporations

Differences between domestic and multinational corporations

Now we will provide the further analysis of the strategic planning process of MNCs to determine the definition of the MNC by distinguishing the key differences between multinational and domestic corporations.

Multiculturalism and geographic dispersion

What are the fundamental difference s between domestic and MNCs? Adler (1982) tried to identify the major differences between domestic and MNCs by asking a selected group of experts in this field. Two factors were considered prime importance in differentiating between domestic and MNCs: multiculturalism and geographic dispersion.

Multiculturalism is defined as "the presence of people from two or more cultural backgrounds within an organization."

Geographic dispersion is defined as "the location of various subunits of the parent corporation in different countries."

In accordance to Adler, we think that the combination of both multiculturalism and geographic dispersion is of fundamental importance in definition of the MNC. However, so far, most international business studies have focused on the consequences of geographic dispersion and tended to give little attention to the consequences of multiculturalism. Most comparative management studies had the opposite preference. They tended to focus on cultural differences, while more or less neglecting the geographic dispersion aspect of MNC (Miroshnik, 2012; Grey and Willmott, 2005).

For a MNC, the main effect of multiculturalism and geographic dispersion must be considered with greater complexity. Actually, compare with domestic organizations, MNCs have to be more sensitive to government, labor, public opinion concepts, and business law regulations because home country business philosophies and practices are often inapplicable in foreign locations.

Multiculturalism and geographic dispersion can have advantages and disadvantages. Regarding multiculturalism, the number of authors made a distinction between current and future benefits. According to them, the most important future benefits of multiculturalism are

- increasing creativity and innovation (83.3 percent);
- demonstrating more sensitivity in dealing with foreign customers (75 percent);

- being able to get the best personnel from everywhere across the world (that is, not being stick with just local talent) (66.7 percent) and taking a global perspective (e.g., the MNC choosing the best opportunity globally) (62.5 percent);
- creating a "super-organizational structure," using the best of all cultures (based on needs for unifying, transcending culture) (62.4 percent);
- greater flexibility within the organization both to adapt to a wider range of environments (62.5 percent).

(Adler, 1982)

When the future benefits were compared with the benefits that were currently realized, the only major decrease in importance was that financial risks could be spread over a wider range of economies (−41.6 percent) and that more successful product-development and marketing strategies could be created in terms of both locally tailored and worldwide products (−25 percent). A general conclusion might, therefore, be that current benefits are related more to the functional areas of marketing and finance, whereas, potential future benefits are related more to HRM. It is very important to note that the HRM is one of fundamental factor in realizing an efficient and effective multinational organization.

MNCs have similar organizational structures. However, they do not all operate the same way. A variety of factors have been identified to help explain the differences such as overall strategy (Daniels, 1987), employee attitudes (Ronen and Shenkar, 1988), and local conditions (Brown and Schneck, 1979). Of particular significance to this discussion are the organizational characteristics of formalization, specialization, and centralization, which we will describe below.

Formalization

Formalization is the use of defined structures and systems in decision making, communicating, and controlling. Some countries make greater use of formalization than others, and this, in turn, affects the day-to-day organizational functioning. A good comparison is between Japan and United States. A study that investigated whether Japanese organizations are more formalized than US organizations found that although Japanese firms tend to use more labor-intensive approaches to areas such as bookkeeping and office-related work than do their US counterparts, no statistical data support the contention that Japanese firms are more formalized.

American and Japanese firms appear to have almost the same level of written goals or objectives for subordinates, written standards of performance appraisals, written schedules, programs, and work specifications, written duties, authority, and accountability. However, managers in Japanese firms perceive less formalization than do managers in American firms. Less reliance on formal rules and structure in Japanese firms is also revealed by the emphasis on face-to-face or behavioral mode of control indicated by the ratio of foreign expatriates to total employees in subsidiaries (Yeh, 1986).

The study also found that US MNCs tend to rely heavily on budgets, financial data, and other formalized tools in controlling their subsidiary operations (Basu, Miroshnik, and Uchida, 2001) This is in contrast to the Japanese, who make wider use of face-to-face, informal controls. These findings reveal that, although the outward structural design of overseas subsidiaries may appear similar, the internal functioning in characteristics such as formalization may be quite different.

Specialization

As an organizational characteristic, *specialization* is the assigning of individuals to specific, well-defined tasks. Specialization in an international context can be classified into horizontal and vertical specialization.

Horizontal specialization assigns jobs so that individuals are given a particular function to perform, and people tend to stay within the confines of this area. Examples include jobs in areas such as customer service, sales, and recruiting, training, purchasing, and marketing research. When there is a great deal of horizontal specialization, personnel will develop functional expertise in one particular area.

Vertical specialization assigns work to groups or departments where individuals are collectively responsible for performance. Vertical specialization is also characterized by distinct differences between levels in the hierarchy such that those higher up are accorded much more status than those further down, and the overall structure is usually quite tall.

The Lincoln–Hanada–McBride's comparative study of 55 American and 51 Japanese manufacturing plants, Japanese organizations had lower functional specialization of employees (Lincoln, Hanada, and McBride, 1986). Specifically, three-quarters of the functions listed are assigned to specialists in the US plants, but less than one-third are assigned in the Japanese plants. The later studies with regard to formalization echo this finding on specialization (Miroshnik, 2012). US subsidiaries have more specialists than do Japanese MNCs.

By contrast, both studies find that the Japanese rely more heavily on vertical specialization. They have taller organization structures in contrast to the flatter designs of their US counterparts. Japanese departments and units are also more differentiated than those in US organizations.

Vertical specialization can also be measured by the amount of group activity such as in quality circles. Japanese MNCs make much greater use of quality circles than do the US firms. Vertical specialization can also result in greater job reutilizations. Since everyone is collectively responsible for the work, strong emphasis is placed on everyone doing the job in a predetermined way, refraining from improvising, and structuring the work so that everyone can do the job after a short training period. Japanese organizations make much wider use of job reutilization than US organizations do.

Centralization

Centralization is a management system under which important decisions are made at the top. In an international context, the value of centralization will vary based on the local environment and the goals of the organization. Many US MNCs tend toward *decentralization*, pushing decision making down the line and getting the lower-level personnel involved. For example, the German multinationals centralize strategic headquarter-specific decisions independent of the host country and decentralize operative decisions in accordance with the local situation in the host country. The comparative study found that Japanese organizations delegate less formal authority than do their US counterparts, but the Japanese permit greater involvement in decisions by employees lower in the hierarchy (Besser, 1993). At the same time, however, the Japanese manage to maintain strong control over their lower-level personnel by limiting the amount of authority given to the latter and by carefully controlling and orchestrating worker involvement and participation in quality circles. Other studies have similar findings. In evaluating the presence of centralization by examining the amount of autonomy that Japanese give to their subordinates, it was concluded:

"... In terms of job autonomy, employees in American firms have greater freedom to make their decisions and their own rules than in Japanese multi-national corporations. Results show that managers in American multinational corporations perceive a higher degree of delegation than do managers in Japanese MNCs. Also, managers in American multinational corporations feel a much higher level of participation in the coordinating with other units and influencing the company's policy both in areas related to their work and in areas not related to their work". US managers in Taiwanese subsidiaries felt that they had greater influence than did their Japanese counterparts."

(Fujie and Shimada, 2017)

Perspective view of the organizational characteristics of multinational corporations

Research shows that MNCs tend to organize their international operations in a manner similar to that used at home. If the MNC tends to have high formalization, specialization, and centralization at its home-based headquarters, these organizational characteristics will probably occur in the firm, international subsidiaries. The Japanese and American MNCs in Taiwan are good examples. The researchers of the comparative study in Taiwan concluded:

"About 80 percent of Japanese firms and more than 80 percent of American in the sample have been operating in Taiwan for about ten years, but they maintain the traits of their distinct cultural origins even though they have been operating in the same (Taiwanese) environment for such a long time".

(Adler and Gunderson, 2007)

These findings also reveal that many enterprises view their international operations as extensions of their domestic operations, disproving the widely held belief that convergence occurs between overseas operations and local customs. In other words, there is far less of an "international management melting pot" than many people realize.

European countries are realizing that as they attempt to unify and do business with each other; differing cultures, languages, religions, and values are very difficult to overcome. One challenge for the years ahead will be bringing subsidiary organizational characteristics more into line with local customs and cultures.

Also, the Japanese MNCs operating in the United States provide another excellent example. Their failure sometimes to accept US social values has resulted in employment and promotion discrimination lawsuits and backlashes from workers who feel that they are being overworked and forced to abide by rules and regulations that are designed for use in Japan. Some years ago, Honda of America agreed to give 370 blacks and women a total of $6 million in back pay to resolve a federal discrimination complaint brought against them (Yoshikawa, 2018).

Strategic planning process in multinational corporations

Now we will describe the most important issues of the strategic managements of MNCs: the strategic planning process itself. Now we will develop the framework for strategic planning process in MNCs. This framework is integration of the organizational structure of a MNCs, external and internal environment, competitive strategy, and functional strategies. We will limit the analysis to four subjects: external analysis at global and industry level; internal analysis; competitive strategies; and functional strategies.

Strategic planning, in its broadest sense, seeks to match markets with products and other corporate resources to strengthen a MNC's competitive strategy. To be able to perform this matching process a MNC must execute both an external and internal analysis, which would result in a product/market combination (or in a number of those combinations), also called strategic business units (SBUs). For each SBU, a MNCs should define its market entry/participation strategy (the choice for export, licensing/franchising, or a wholly or partly owned subsidiary) and its competitive strategy. In implementing these strategies, the organizational structure, the functional strategies, the control and coordination strategies are of prime importance. A final important topic in this respect is the relationship with host and home country governments.

The process of strategic planning in MNCs is based on the environment–strategy–structure paradigm, which suggests that superior performance is the result of a good fit between strategy and environmental demands, and between organizational structure and strategy. For example, Harzing (2000) focuses explicitly on the internal factors of the corporation, which can facilitate, constrain, or form the basis of certain strategies by describing the organizational structuring and global strategic planning mechanisms. We believe that before addressing the different elements of the strategic planning process, two important remarks must be made; in reality, the process will not be as linear as it is shown here. There are numerous feedbacks and repetitions. Often strategy will be emergent (Mintzberg, 1994), incremental (Quinn, 1988), or take a muddling through approach (Lindblom, 1979). The very important intervening variable in strategic planning process is the manager himself or herself. Changes in the environment will not influence strategy unless they are enacted (Weick, 1979), and managers do have some choice of action (Child, 1972). An important influential factor in this process is the societal/cultural effect. Society/culture can on the one hand form a constraint on certain choices (for example, democratic leadership will not work in countries where people favor hierarchical decision processes) and on the other hand influence the values of managers so that certain environmental changes are not enacted, and certain choice options are not considered.

We believe that the society/culture can influence personnel and organization policies in different countries. MNCs will have to take these differences into account, but at the same time, they do bring the nationality of their home countries into the game. The MNCs from different countries have developed different strategies, structures, and policies in the past and probably will continue to do so in the future, despite common developments in the environment. Thus, in addition to national differences in management, there are also national differences in international management (Yoshikawa, 2018).

External analysis of the strategic planning process in multinational corporations

Strategic planning process should start with an analysis of the environment. The strategic planning process in MNCs must be considered much broader in internationalization process of business on global (world) and on an industry level.

When analyzing the environment on a global (worldwide) scale, one of the most important trends for MNCs is the increasing internationalization of the world economy. We will briefly describe the different eras that can be distinguished in the internationalization process (Bartlett and Ghosal, 1992).

The multi-domestic era (1920–1950)

The period between the wars was characterized by a rise in nationalistic feelings. Countries became increasingly protectionist and with high tariff barriers. There were large national differences in consumer preferences and communication, and logistical barriers remained high. These circumstances favored national companies. For MNCs, the strategy of centralized production in order to capture economies of scale, combined with exports to various countries, was made impossible by high tariff and logistical barriers. To be able to compete with national companies, MNCs had to set-up a larger number of foreign manufacturing subsidiaries. These subsidiaries were usually relatively small plants that produced for the national market only. Differences in consumer preferences and high communication barriers led to a decentralization of decision making, so that the foreign subsidiaries were relatively independent of their headquarters. European companies dominated foreign investment in this era.

The international and global era (1950–1980)

The postwar years were characterized by a worldwide boom in demand. Consumers were catching up for the years of scarcity and soberness. The United States was in a predominant economic position during this period and led the way. Most European companies were preoccupied with the reconstruction of their domestic operations, while American companies were almost untouched by the war. US companies developed more and more new technologies and products. They were almost forced into the international market by spontaneous export orders and opportunities for licensing. Later they started making their products in manufacturing facilities in Western Europe and in developing countries (Bartlett and Ghoshal, 1992).

In the 1960s and 1970s, the successive reductions in tariff barriers began to have their full impact. They were accompanied by declining international transport costs and communication barriers. Furthermore, new electronic technologies increased the minimum efficient scale in many industries. Finally, consumer preferences became more homogeneous because of increased international travel and communication. All these developments made centralized and relatively standardized production with exports to various countries profitable again. Japanese companies, which internationalized during this period, were very successful with their large-scale intensive production facilities they were able to produce low-cost, high-quality products under tight central control (Yoshikawa, 2018).

The transnational era (1980– till today)

By the late 1970s, there was a rising concern among host countries about the impact of MNCs on their balance of trade, national employment levels, and on the international competitiveness of their economies. As a consequence, they gradually started to exercise their sovereign powers. Trade barriers were raised again to limit exports and foreign direct investments were regulated by industrial policies. Other forces counteracted the previous globalization process as well. Flexible manufacturing, for instance, reduced the minimum efficient scale by employing robotics and CAD/CAM technologies. The use of software became very important in a growing number of industries (from telecommunications to computers and consumer electronics). This development facilitated conformity to consumers who were once again asking for products tailored to their local needs. The problem is, however, that we do not witness a complete reversal to the multi-domestic era again. The worldwide innovation of the international era and the global efficiency of the global era remain important competitive factors. Today, in more and more industries, companies struggle with three different and sometimes opposing demands: national responsiveness; global efficiency; and worldwide innovation or transfer of knowledge (Yoda, 2013).

Efficiency, quality, flexibility, and innovativeness

Thus, we have described different eras with a focus on either national responsiveness, transfer of knowledge, or global efficiency. The transnational era was characterized by the necessity to pay attention to all three of these market demands. I will discuss below a second study that distinguishes different phases in the business environment. Bolwijn and Kumpe (1990) distinguish four phases, each phase having different market demands and performance criteria and requiring a different ideal type of corporation.

The 1960s were characterized by growing internationalization, partly as a result of trade liberalization. A side-effect of this growth of international trade was fierce price competition, because products could be produced in low-wage countries. Price was the ruling market demand and efficiency the overruling performance criterion.

The 1970s brought a new competitive weapon: quality. Customers became more critical and demanded high-quality but affordable products. Thus, companies had to comply with the market demands of both price and quality. Japanese companies were and are especially good at higher quality with lower price.

In the 1980s, Japan once more took the lead in offering a large variety of products. Apart from price and quality, a wide range of choices and short delivery times were important market demands which forced companies to be flexible.

In the 1990s according to Bolwijn and Kumpe (1990), the market demand will be uniqueness. Companies will have to offer a product that is unique in one way or another. To be able to do this, companies have to be innovative. Flexibility is a prerequisite for this: innovation requires change and change requires flexibility. However, an innovative MNC also has to conform with the market demands of price and quality. The actual practice in MNCs companies lags behind, however. According to Bolwijn and Kumpe (1990), the industrial world as a whole is only in the phase of transition to flexibility, while some companies are still struggling with quality.

External analysis at industry level as a part of the strategic planning process in multinational corporations

External level of individual industries includes four familiar terms: multi-domestic, international, global, and transnational (Bartlett and Ghoshal, 1992).

Multi-domestic industries

In a multi-domestic industry, international strategy in fact consists of a series of domestic strategies. Competition in one country is essentially independent of competition in other countries. Typical industry characteristics are determined by cultural, social, and political differences between countries. A classic example of a multi-domestic industry is the branded packaged products industry, such as food and laundry detergents.

Global industries

In a global industry standardized consumer needs and scale efficiencies make centralization and integration profitable. In this kind of industry a corporation's competitive position in one country is significantly influenced by its position in other countries. The global industry is not merely a collection of domestic industries, but a series of linked domestic industries in which the rivals compete against each other on a truly worldwide basis. A classic example of a global industry is consumer electronics.

International industries

The adjective international refers to the international product life cycle, which describes the internationalization process in this type of industry. The critical success factor in these industries is the ability to transfer knowledge, particularly technology to units abroad. It is a process of sequential diffusion of innovations that were originally developed in the home market. A classic example of an international industry is telecommunications switching.

Transnational industries

Transnational industries are characterized by a complex set of environmental demands. Companies in these industries must respond simultaneously to the diverse and often conflicting strategic needs of global efficiency (as a characteristic of global industries), national responsiveness (as a characteristic of multidomestic industries), and transfer of knowledge (as a characteristic of international industries).

Thus, as shown above, the international environment has evolved toward the transnational era. However, the industry in which a company competes can be an important mediator in this respect. Some industries still have a distinctive multi-domestic, international, or global focus. And although more and more industries develop transnational characteristics, there will always be industries that continue to be more or less multi-domestic, international, or global. Now we will discuss internal analysis as a part of the strategic planning process in MNCs.

Internal analysis as a part of the strategic planning process in multinational corporations

Often the internal side of the analysis is forgotten or played down. Followers of the resource-based view of the corporation are refocusing their attention on internal resources that can be used to develop distinctive competitive advantages. According to them, corporation-specific resources and capabilities provide far stronger predictors of performance than industry characteristics. Due attention to the resources of the company, human resources being not the least important among these, implies a two-way or integrated relationship between business and FIRM strategy (Golden and Ramanujam, 1985; Yoda, 2013).

On the one hand, characteristics, quality, and limitations of the human resource pool influence, constrain, or form the basis for strategic options, and on the other hand, they are influenced by strategic options themselves.

In this section, we will discuss the approach advocated by Collis (1991). Collis identified three important elements of the resource-based view of the corporation: core competence, organizational capability, and administrative heritage.

Core competence as a part of the strategic planning process in multinational corporations

A corporation's core competence, a term that has become widely known through the writings of Hamel and Prahalad (1990), is the entire system of tangible and intangible resources in which a MNC has unique advantages. For example, the technological/marketing/production skills, a strong corporate culture, a well-trained workforce, a strong trade name, etc. It is important to note that a core competence should be "distinctive." A MNC should evaluate its resources in the light of the resources possessed by its competitors. Only if the corporation's own combination of resources has something unique or is superior to the combination of their competitors can the corporation be said to have an economically valuable core competence.

The external environmental demands and opportunities are the same for each MNC that is operating in a particular industry. However, the necessary resources every MNC must acquire to comply with these demands and exploit the opportunities of a certain product market will differ, because the combination of resources each MNC possesses (its core competence) is different. Therefore, MNC will choose product market positions that make the best use of their core competence, even if this leads them to choose product market combinations that are objectively seen to be second best. Furthermore, MNCs will in the first place acquire resources from their domestic factor markets. They will, therefore, preferably build their core competence around factors that are abundantly available in their country (Scroggins, 2015).

Organizational capability as a part of the strategic planning process in multinational corporations

Organizational capability consists of a very specific form of intangible resources. It comprises the managerial capability to improve and upgrade a MNC's efficiency, effectiveness, flexibility, and innovativeness in a continuous way. In fact, organizational capability can be a source of sustainable competitive advantage in its own right. According to Carr and Collis (2011), to achieve this organizational capability "the multinational corporation must create dynamic routines that facilitate innovation, foster collective learning, and transfer information and skills within the organization." This cannot be achieved by any specific organizational structure. Flexibility is, therefore, an extremely important element of organizational capability. The MNC needs to be able to perform the constant adaptations necessary to adjust to both changing external circumstances and the administrative heritage of the corporation. Thus, the organizational capability is very important when transforming to a transnational organization.

Administrative heritage as a part of the strategic planning process in multinational corporations

According to Bartlett and Ghoshal (1992), administrative heritage "can be, at the same time, one of the company's greatest assets – the underlying source of its key competencies – and also a significant liability, since it resists change and thereby prevents realignment or broadening of strategic capabilities". Both intangible (cultural) factors and tangible (physical) factors can form administrative heritage. Examples of the intangible factors are the charismatic and/or appropriate leadership of the company's leader or the culture of the organization. The physical factors can consist of plant locations, office facilities, and communication systems. New investments are clearly influenced by the physical assets already in place. Because these assets are generally very durable, most investments are essentially incremental decisions. For instance, once a decision in favor of a certain plant location is taken, it will continue to influence the location of new facilities, even if the original decision proved to be wrong. These two aspects of administrative heritage, cultural, and physical factors, can act as a constraint on strategy. Therefore, it is wrong to refer only to external product and factor markets to predict the behavior of a corporation. Furthermore, because most of these assets and resources are relatively difficult to change, MNCs will only periodically try to optimize their strategies and structures.

Thus, internal resources are certainly not to be overlooked in describing a MNC's strategic behavior. They can form both a constraint on and the basis for strategic choices. This is why both an external and internal analysis are necessary to justify choosing a number of product/market combinations, also called strategic business units (SBUs).

Analysis of the trends in the international competitive strategies as a part of the strategic planning process in multinational corporations

In the literature on competitive strategy, there are a few basic choice: a cost-efficiency or cost-leadership strategy; a differentiation strategy; a quality strategy (which can be considered as a form of differentiation); and an innovation strategy. In international management literature, the terms familiar from Bartlett and Ghoshal (1989, 1992) multi-domestic, global, international, and transnational are used to describe competitive strategy. Furthermore, we will show that the competitive strategies as distinguished by Bartlett and Ghoshal can be related to the transaction cost theory of international production.

Multi-domestic strategy

Companies following a multi-domestic strategy give prime importance to national responsiveness. Their products or services are differentiated to meet different local demands. Their policies are differentiated to conform to different governmental and market demands. The competitive advantage of multi-domestic corporations often lies in the downstream value chain activities such as sales and marketing or service. These activities are more closely related to the buyer and are usually tied to the buyer's location. This is the strategy traditionally followed by European multinationals.

Historically, branded packaged goods companies had to respond primarily to differing market needs. In Northern European countries "boil washing" had long been standard, whereas, hand washing in cold water represented an important demand segment in Mediterranean countries. Differences in water hardness, perfume preferences, fabric mix, and phosphate legislation made product differentiation from country to country a strategic necessity (Bartlett and Ghoshal, 1992).

Global strategy

Companies following a global strategy give prime importance to efficiency. They integrate and rationalize their production to produce standardized products in a very cost-efficient manner. The competitive advantage of global companies often lies in upstream value chain activities such as procurement, inbound logistics (warehousing, inventory control, material handling, etc.) and operations (machining, assembly, testing, etc.). These activities are optimized on a worldwide scale. This is the strategy traditionally followed by Japanese multinationals.

For example, the development of the transistor by the Bell Laboratories in 1947 signaled a new era in consumer electronics. The replacement of vacuum tubes by transistors greatly expanded the efficient scale for production of key components, and the subsequent development of printed circuit boards made mass production feasible by reducing both the amount and skill level of labor required to assemble radios, TVs, tape recorders, etc. The introduction of integrated circuits in the late 1960s further reduced the number and cost of components and increased optimum manufacturing scale. Through the 1970s, the clear dominant trend in the consumer electronics industry was a progressive increase in the benefits of the world-scale economies, driven primarily by technical changes and reinforced by the homogenization of customer tastes and a significant decline in trade barriers. In our rather constrained use of the term, this was a classic global industry – one whose basic characteristics were defined by the need for global scale, relatively unimpeded by national differences.

International strategy

Companies following an international strategy give prime importance to the development and diffusion of innovations worldwide. Their competitive advantage often lies in research and development. New technologies are developed in the home country and transferred and adapted to foreign countries, following the product life cycle. They do not strive for the efficiency of global companies or the complete national responsiveness of multi-domestic companies, but they do pay attention to both of these goals. This is the strategy traditionally followed by US multinationals.

For example, the telecommunications switching industry traditionally required a more multidimensional strategic capability than either consumer electronics or branded packaged goods. Monopoly purchasing in most countries by government-owned post, telegraph, and telephone authority (PTI) created a demand for responsiveness – a demand enhanced by the strategic importance almost all governments accorded to developing local manufacturers of telecom equipment. At the same time, global integration and coordination of activities were also required, because of significant scale economies in production and the need to arrange complex credit facilities for buyers through multinational lending agencies. However, the most critical task for switch manufacturers was the ability to develop and harness new technologies and to exploit them worldwide. This ability to learn and to appropriate the benefits of learning in multiple national markets differentiated the winners from the losers in this highly complex business.

Transnational strategy

Companies following a transnational strategy recognize that they should pay attention to global efficiency, national responsiveness, and worldwide learning at the same time. To do this, their strategy must be very flexible. To develop the transnational strategy, MNCs have to set such strategy where each strategic decision depends on specific developments. Thus, the transnational strategy would be a deliberately planned strategy to have an "adaptive" (Mintzberg, 1994), "incremental" (Quinn, 1988), "muddling through" (Lindblom, 1979), or "emergent" (Mintzberg, 1988) strategy.

Rugman–Verbeke's model of analyzing the competitive strategies

Rugman and Verbeke (1993) make an effort to link the transaction cost theory of international production to the configurations distinguished by Bartlett and Ghoshal. Their analysis is rather complex. However, it is probably the first analysis that managed to incorporate both the economic perspective on multinationals and the managerial perspective. Their analysis takes as a starting point that foreign direct investment has been chosen as a more efficient mode of entry than export, licensing or a joint venture. In terms of Dunning's eclectic theory, there are advantages to internalization.

Rugman and Verbeke then go on to distinguish two types of ownership-specific advantages, which they call firm-specific advantages (FSAs), namely *location-bound firm-specific advantages* and *non-location-bound firm-specific advantages*. The benefits of location-bound firm-specific advantages depend on their being used in one particular location (or a set of locations). They cannot easily be transferred and cannot be used in other locations without significant adaptation. An example would be a corporation's expertise in dealing with the idiosyncrasies of the Japanese distribution system. Transferring this specific expertise to other locations would be useless.

Non-location-bound firm-specific advantages do not depend on their being used in one particular location. They can be used on a global scale, because transferring them to other locations can be done at low-cost and without substantial adaptation. The best known example in this respect is proprietary technology resulting from research and development activities, but specific marketing skills and managerial capabilities can also form non-location-bound firm-specific advantages.

With regard to location advantages – or country-specific advantages (CSAs) as Rugman and Verbeke call them – they distinguish two sources: home and host country, and two ways of using them: *static and leveraged*. Home country-specific advantages, for example a highly skilled technical workforce, may be used in a *static* way, that is to support current firm-specific advantages. However, they can also be used in a *leveraged way*, that is to develop new firm-specific advantages, for instance a new type of technology. The same goes for host country-specific advantages.

Ragman and Verbeke distinguish the two types of firm-specific advantages discussed above, location-bound and non-location bound, and three different combinations of country-specific advantages: home country country-specific advantages, used in a leveraged way; host country country-specific advantages, used in a static way; a combination of home and host country country-specific advantages, used in either a static or a leveraged way. Also, the four types of companies are distinguished by Bartlett and Ghoshal (1989).

The type of company that is captured best by the original theory on MNCs (Dunning's eclectic theory) is the international company. The original framework assumes that firm-specific advantages are non-location-bound, that is that they can be used anywhere in the world. The actual choice for the optimum location for subsidiaries in this type of company is based on static host country country-specific advantages such as a cheap labor force. The product life-cycle model also describes the characteristics of this type of company.

In the case of multi-domestic companies, differences between countries with regard to customer preferences, market conditions and government regulation force companies to develop location-bound firm-specific advantages. These location-bound firm-specific advantages will often complement the country-specific advantages of the countries involved, such as the local marketing infrastructure or protected government markets.

Global companies would obviously have non-location-bound firm-specific advantages that can be exploited on a global scale. Home country country-specific advantages are more important than host country-specific advantages, because production operations are often concentrated in the home country.

The transnational company operates with a combination of location-bound and non-location-bound firm-specific advantages. Location-bound firm-specific advantages would be necessary in countries with a need for national responsiveness. Non-location-bound firm-specific advantages would permit global exploitation. With regard to country-specific advantages, the transnational company draws advantages from both home and host countries. And in contrast to the situation in international and multi-domestic companies, host country country-specific advantages can also be used in a leveraged way.

Analysis of the trends in the functional strategies in multinational corporations

Strategy formulation is the first step; succeeding in implementing this strategy is a second step, which is often a far more difficult one. Now we will describe the four major functional strategies: production, HRM, marketing, and finance.

Production

There are ethnocentric, polycentric, and geocentric solutions in production management (Rugman, 1987).

The *ethnocentric solution* would be *centralized sourcing*. Production takes place in one or a few plants that are tightly controlled centrally. The main function of the logistic manager would be to take care of exporting in the most cost- and time-efficient manner.

The *polycentric solution* would be *indigenous sourcing*. Production takes place in each country the multinational is serving and each manufacturing facility produces only for the local market. Therefore, international logistics is often de-emphasized.

The *geocentric solution*, finally, would be *distributed sourcing*. The same product could be manufactured in a number of countries, but some countries can also specialize in certain products, depending on their distinctive advantages (high technology, low wages).

Production can also be specialized into four different types of functions: low unit cost, seasonal, stockpile, and flexible plants (Rugman, 1987). The low unit cost plant (located in low-wage countries) should always produce at full capacity. If the demand for a product is seasonal, but the variations can be forecast accurately, a seasonal plant could be the solution. Ideally such a plant should be located in an area with a stable seasonal workforce (for instance tourist resorts in the winter). A stockpile plant would produce buffers and should be located in countries that offer inventory tax deductions or subsidies for warehousing. Flexible plants, finally, are destined to shift production flexibly into new or existing products. The geocentric solution requires a separate logistics department, which can coordinate all activities between the different input and output markets and manufacturing locations.

Human resource management

Perlmutter (1969) distinguished three states of mind or attitudes of international executives: ethnocentric (or home-country oriented); polycentric (or host-country oriented); geocentric (or world oriented). These attitudes should be regarded as ideal types. However, every MNC probably has the degree of ethnocentrism, polycentrism, and geo-centrism as a dominant state of mind.

The *ethnocentric attitude* implies that management style, knowledge, evaluation criteria, and managers from the home country are considered superior to those of the host country. A logical consequence is that only parent-country nationals are considered to be suitable for top management positions, both at headquarters and the subsidiaries.

The *polycentric attitude-takes* a completely different point of view. It explicitly recognizes differences between countries and believes that local nationals are in the best position to understand and deal with these country-specific factors. A local manager, however, will never be offered a position at headquarters, because parent-country nationals are considered more suitable for these positions.

A *geocentric attitude* is world oriented. A geocentric-oriented MNC draws from a worldwide pool of managers. Managers can be appointed at headquarters or subsidiaries regardless of their nationality. In later literature, Perlmutter's (1969) headquarters orientations became equated with strategies of international HRM, which is not surprising if one looks at the subjects he discusses. Three types of headquarters orientations have a rather high level of generality; so, they do not guide an HRM practitioner in making specific choices about task design, training programs, compensation packages, etc. Until now, there has only been a very limited amount of research done on the specific-HRM strategies MNCs should follow to achieve their strategic goals. The fact that HRM has only very recently been acknowledged as a strategic issue might be a reason for this lack of research.

Marketing

In a strategic sense, the choice in marketing management is often between standardization marketing, adaptation marketing, or combination of both. MNCs that choose *standardized marketing* see customers the world over as essentially having the same needs and tastes (that is, the same as the home country). This is rather ethnocentric view. However, for a fairly large number of products, this approach can work very well: for instance, Coca-Cola, Levi's Jeans, raw materials, or high-tech industrialized products.

MNCs that choose *adaptation marketing* see customers the world over as having different needs and tastes. They deliberately adapt their products to these differences. This is consistent with a polycentric view.

In a geocentric view, products would be rather standardized but adapted to foreign markets by means of slight product changes, distribution, and promotion. A corporation with a geocentric view would stress flexibility. Of course, a choice in favor of standardization or adaptation (or a combination of both) is largely dependent on the product, the country, and the customer group. All in all, however, the marketing function is often rather polycentric in attitude, since host country knowledge of consumer tastes is important.

Finance and accounting

International finance is often equated with the handling of foreign exchange rates, exchange controls, and tax optimization. These activities are usually centralized at the treasurer's office at headquarters (ethnocentric approach), because only at this level is there a complete overview of all factors involved. However, activities such as financial planning and control can have ethnocentric, polycentric, and geocentric solutions (Rugman, 1987).

The *ethnocentric solution* is to integrate all subsidiary operations completely into the planning and control system of the parent company. In the *polycentric solution* financial management is essentially portfolio management. The performance of each subsidiary would be evaluated individually against the performance of comparable domestic or foreign companies. Decision making on financial matters would be mostly decentralized. Only major new projects and financing subsidiaries would have to solicit permission from headquarters.

The *geocentric solution* promotes an "*it all depends*" attitude. Investment in developing countries is more likely to be centralized, because of the lack of local expertise and inadequately developed financial markets. In industrialized countries, the advantages of centralization are less evident, because the financial and economic systems of the various countries are already highly integrated. Furthermore, the quality of local management makes decentralization a more feasible option.

Closely associated with financial management are the numerous accounting problems. Accounting practices are culture-bound, in that every country has its own accounting rules. Local accountants have to meet local requirements, so a polycentric solution would be most logical. Consolidated accounts, however, will have to conform to home country standards.

Integration of strategic planning process in multinational corporations

Four configurations

The main conclusion is that corporations in a multi-domestic industry should preferably follow a multi-domestic strategy and have a multi-domestic organizational structure. The same goes for international, global, and transnational industries.

A MNC can choose to follow a strategy and choose a structure that would not provide an optimal fit with the industry, but is more in accordance with its core competence, organizational capability, and administrative heritage (Prahalad and

Doz, 1987). If these internal resources point to a very different choice than the industry the corporation is competing in, the corporation would have three basic options: to find a small niche in this industry that fits its internal characteristics; to try to modify the industry characteristics, which would often be very difficult, if not impossible; and to gradually move into other industries.

Integration of functional policies in the strategic planning process of multinational corporations

Broadly speaking, it is possible to say that ethnocentric policies would fit with global industries, strategies, and structures, polycentric policies with multi-domestic industries, strategies, and structures, and geocentric policies with trans-lational industries, strategies, and structures. However, there is another aspect such as motivation.

Perlmutter (1969), in describing his management attitudes, mentions many characteristics that can easily be recognized in the multi-domestic, global, and transnational organizational models. The ethnocentric orientation stands for a complex organization at headquarters and a simple one in subsidiaries, and for a high one-way flow of orders, commands, and advice from headquarters to subsidiaries, with the greatest authority at headquarters. This is consistent with the global concept of centralization of decision making at headquarters and the treatment of subsidiaries as simple delivery pipelines. A polycentric corporation is defined by Perlmutter (1969) as "a loosely connected group with quasi-independent subsidiaries as centers – more akin (close) to a confederation." There is little communication to and from headquarters and between subsidiaries with relatively low authority at headquarters. This is of course very consistent with the multi-domestic organizational model with its decentralized federation structure and its decentralized decision making.

In a geocentric corporation, according to Perlmutter (1969), "the firm's sub-sidiaries are neither satellites nor independent city-states, but parts of a whole whose focus is on worldwide objectives as well as local objectives, each part mak-ing its unique contribution with its unique competence." The organization is increasingly complex and interdependent. It is remarkable how well Perlmutter's (1969) headquarters orientations fit in with the organizational models sketched 20 years later by Bartlett and Ghoshal (1989).

Edström and Lorange (1984) found a fit between structure and HRM. Global companies tended to use more expatriates (ethnocentric HRM policy) than country-based (multi-domestic) companies. Then again, in one country-based company there were more expatriates as managing directors of subsid-iaries than host country nationals, and in another country-based company the difference was not that large. In management development and organization development all companies had a rather ethnocentric policy. HRM policies in multinationals still seem more likely to be ethnocentric than polycentric or geocentric, even if organizational strategy and structure would suggest otherwise.

International management research itself is also rather ethnocentric. International HRM is often equated with expatriate management. There is a large and growing number of studies on the problems encountered in recruitment and selection, training, compensation, career development and repatriation of expatriates. Research by Tung (1981, 1982, 1988) showed that Japanese corporations tend to use far more expatriates at all levels of the organization than American or European corporations, following an ethnocentric HRM policy. This is consistent with the fact that Japanese companies often have global strategies and structures that emphasize central control by headquarters. This can be most easily achieved by employing expatriates in subsidiaries, because they will propagate headquarters' attitudes (Florida and Kenney, 1991). Tung's research showed that European corporations do use fewer expatriates than Japanese corporations, which would be consistent with their dominant multi-domestic strategy focusing on local demands. Local employees will be more likely to be familiar with these. However, in Latin America and the Far East, the number of expatriates is very high (79 percent, 85 percent at senior management level). So, it seems that in countries at a greater cultural distance, ethnocentric HRM policies are still in use.

Strategic planning process in the major Japanese automobile multinational corporations

We decided to examine the Japanese automobile industry because the Japanese automobile MNCs are the major auto-producers and exporters in world-scale with global manufacturing bases. Analysis of the strategic planning process of Japanese automobile multinational companies includes the following: determination of the core competitive strategies common for all chosen Japanese automobile MNC; determination of the overall strategic planning philosophy for each chosen Japanese automobile MNC both in home and host countries; evaluations of the domestic strategies for each chosen MNC; evaluations of its transnational strategies in a global setting for each of the chosen Japanese automobile MNC; characteristics of the competitive and functional strategies as a part of the strategic plan implementing in each of the chosen Japanese automobile MNC.

Characteristics of the competitive strategies common in strategic planning process in major Japanese automobile multinational corporations

Japanese MNCs have made a significant contribution in overseas production bases (Wickens and Lopez, 1987). The successes of Japanese MNCs have raised interests on the system of production, organizational structure, and strategic planning process peculiar to the Japanese MNCs (Suzuki, 1994). Particularly in automobile industry, the Japanese strategic management techniques were adopted in a number of countries by non-Japanese MNCs to compete effectively against Japanese MNCs (Imai, 1986; Lillrank and Kano, 1989). Spread of this enthusiasm is basically due to the foreign production bases of the leading Japanese automobile companies.

There are three unique basic competitive strategies in Japanese strategic management system: the lean production system; the innovations in total quality management; unique HRM (Nohara, 1985). These three ingredients are interlinked in order to produce the total effect on the management of Japanese enterprises. As Japanese overseas affiliates in host countries are parts of the parent company, its strategic planning processes are the parts of the strategic planning process of the parent company as well (Shimada, 1993; Morita, 1992).

"Elimination of waste" strategy

The purpose of the lean production philosophy developed by the Toyota Motor Co. is to decrease the costs through the elimination of waste (i.e., everything that does not add value to the product). The "human-ware" is defined as the integration and interdependence of machinery and human relations and a concept to differentiate between different types of production systems. The fundamental idea is human-ware at all levels (Shimada, 1993).

According to the lean production system, the most important source of waste in the production process is inventory. Keeping parts and products in stock does not add value to them and should be eliminated. In a manufacturing company, the inventory as the form of work in progress is especially wasteful and should be reduced.

The effects of reducing work in progress go beyond that of reducing capital employed. So, the reasons for the existence of inventory must be removed. One way to reduce the inventory is by minimizing down time in machines. That can be accomplished through preventive maintenance.

Another way to reduce the inventories is through reducing the lot sizes. A reduction of the lot sizes also has other positive effects such as increasing flexibility since it is possible to switch between different parts more often. However, if the lot sizes were reduced, set-up times also have to be reduced; so, through the ingenious method – SUED – developed by Shingo (1981–1985), the set-up times in large punch presses have been reduced from several hours to less than ten minutes in the Toyota Motor Co., which has had dramatic consequences on the lot sizes.

The transportation of parts is another source of waste, because transporting parts from one location in the factory to another does not add any value to the product. It also adds to manufacturing lead time. If machines can be grouped together in a cell-based layout, the physical connection of the flow of products renders a faster truck useless.

Lack of quality is another source of waste, because manufacturing parts and products that are defective and therefore need to be reworked is wasteful. Even worse is the scrapping of parts. Therefore, eliminating scrap and rework is essential way to reduce waste.

Also producing the faults free manufacturing parts from the beginning of the production process have profound consequences for productivity (Flynn, Schroeder, Flynn, Sakakibara and Bates, 1997.

Continuous improvement of quality: "Kaizan" strategy

The constant battle for perfection or continuous improvement of quality, named "*Kaizan*" in Japanese, is the major concept in Japanese management, including the process of strategic planning. As perfection is the main goal, involving everyone in the work of improvement can be accomplished through quality circles, which is a common approach in Japanese automobile MNCs. These are activities where operators gather in groups to come up with suggestions on possible improvements. There are schemes for implementing the best suggestions, rewarding employees, and feeding back information on the status of the suggestions (Imai, 1986; Yoda, 2013).

"Zero defects" strategy

The major goal of Japanese automobile MNCs is to work with faults-free products to attain high productivity of its products worldwide. It means that all parts of products should be faults free from the very beginning of the producing process. That can be accomplished through the continuous improvements of the manufacturing system.

The idea is to prevent defects through discovering errors that can lead to those defects (Lillrank and Kano, 1989). Lean production system uses so-called autonomous defect control (in Japanese "*poka yoke*"), which is inexpensive way to conduct the inspection of all units to ensure "zero defects."

So, zero defects strategy denotes how a MNCs works in order to attain quality. In a lean production system, it is important to move toward a higher degree of process control. Each process is controlling by using the knowledge about each parameter of the process. Thus, instead of controlling the produced parts, the overall process of production itself is under control in Japanese automobile MNCs.

Quality assurance is the responsibility of every employee in Japanese MNCs. Identification of defective parts is the responsibility of every worker. Workers in Japanese automobile plant even allowed to stop the production line in case if defective parts were found. Every employee has responsibility for adjusting the defective parts workers. As a consequence, the number of personnel working in the quality control department can be reduced; therefore, the size of the adjustment and repair areas can be reduced too.

Manufacturing tasks are organized into teams. This makes the workers more aware of the need to manufacture only fault free parts. An important reason for the improved awareness was that the physical contact between manufacturing stages allowed for better communication. Working as a team, employees in Japanese automobile plants found beneficial to have the responsibility for correction of the part of the process where the error has been committed. Through the use of statistical process control, with tests after each process, the Japanese automobile MNCs can get better control over their production processes.

"Just-in-time" strategy

The principle of "just in time" means that each process should be provided with the right part, in the right quantity, and at exactly the right point of time. Accomplishing fault-free parts is a prerequisite to achieving just-in-time deliveries. The ultimate goal is that every process should be provided with one part at a time, exactly when that part is needed. It is possible to have different levels of just-in-time strategy application. First, there is the case when parts have been moved between different processes in lots. Second, the auto-parts have been differentiated according to product variants. Third, there is "sequential just-in-time" where the auto-parts have been arrived with reference to the individual products on the line. For example, the car seats may arrive at the assembly line in the exact order in which they are needed. In general, the higher the level of just-in-time strategy, the better Japanese MNCs can manage business. However, sequential just-in-time strategy is not always needed. It depends on the nature of the products, because if the products are standardized and relatively inexpensive, it may not be too important to achieve the highest level of the just-in-time strategy.

"Pull-instead-of-push" strategy

The word "pull" in given context means the demand of some certain parts for the operation process and supplying only the necessary parts after demand, and the word "push" means very common approach to supply the parts before the demand, and to store the parts as inventory.

Scheduling of materials is closely related to the principle of just-in-time strategy. It is useful to look at the relationship between forward scheduling and backward request. Before implementing the lean production strategy in the final assembly stage, the company has prepared the customer order. Actually, in the all other stages, the manufacturing process is conducted according to a forecast. Gradually the number of manufacturing stages producing according to customer order has to be extended. Thus, somewhere in the material flow is a point where "pull" meets "push." Behind this point, backward requests are used. Ahead of the point there is forward scheduling. This may create difficulties in stock-outs or too large stocks at this pull–push point, which can be due to the difficulties in making correct forecasts (Åhlström, 1998).

Multifunctional teams' strategy

The most important feature of the organizational set-up of the lean production system in Japanese automobile MNC is the extensive use of multifunctional teams. *Multifunctional teams* are the groups of workers who able to perform many different works. The multifunctional teams are organized along with a cell-based production flow system. Due to the rotation of the tasks in a team, the increased flexibility reduces the vulnerability of the production system. The number of job-classifications also declines. Workers have received trainings to perform a number of different tasks, such as statistical process control, quality instruments, computers, set-up performances, maintenance, etc. They also have to be trained in a number of functional areas such as materials management, purchasing, maintenance, and quality control. The company has to rotate the workers among tasks frequently, which possibly leads to decentralizing of responsibilities in due that the multifunctional team is expected to perform multiply supervisory tasks through the rotations of team leadership among workers. As a result, a number of successfully controlling functional areas have been increased. Workers who are not involving in process normally move to other areas because in Japan the company has no lay-off policy (Kumazawa and Yamada, 1989). However, recently some changes in that policy occurred in Japanese MNCs.

"Vertical information system" strategy

In a Japanese automobile MNCs, it is vital to provide information in time and continuously in the production flow. Operational information is more frequent than strategic information about market plans, production plans, process development plans, and financial performances.

Limits to lean

The Japanese "lean production system" strategy in automobile MNC is not the only alternative to the traditional production system. There are many different approaches that have been successfully implemented in different automobile MNCs, such as (a) German "style quality production" model based on a highly skilled work consensus; (b) "systemic rationality" model, which is common in the information technology firms; and (c) the Swedish model developed by Volvo Motor Co., so-called reflective production system, in which production teams have direct contact with the customers (Sandberg, 1995).

Recent changes in Japanese strategic planning process

Recently Japanese companies are no longer depending exclusively on the concept of lean production system. Due to changes in the external economic environments and collapse of the "bubble" economy of the late 1980s, the rising in the exchange value of Yen (which makes Japanese exports too expensive) and the rising costs of labor in Japan have provoked changes in the strategic management system in whole, including the strategic planning process in particular (Miyajima, 1996).

The main competitive pressure has been made to expand market shares, which in turn has resulted the reduced profits, thereby, inviting cost reductions and increased revenues. Cost reductions were associated with *Kaizen* (continuous improvements), which has stimulated further price competitions. Increased revenues needed the increased sales volumes, new products, and diversified products, which demanded new investments, more indirect labor, increasing break-even point, and reductions of profits during the period of the "bubble" economy.

Recently, the larger sales volumes are difficult to achieve due to stagnant consumptions. There are also reduced opportunities for Japanese companies to rely on exports as a means of compensating for lower domestic sales. Thus, the overall production system in Japanese automobile MNCs is changing and gradually adopting more flexible strategic planning system with relying on the following characteristics.

Production system must be more flexible to adopt itself to changes in demand, and therefore, to reduce the costs of production. Achievements of lower fixed costs using fewer frequent changes in products and fewer replacements of equipment must be implemented. Technological solutions must be implemented to have flexibility in a production system design on both down-stream and up-stream products.

Managers must develop the approach to reduce work-in-progress and set-up times by grouping of parts and products into similar classes/families; standardized modules of established and reliable design must be incorporated into new products which allow to mix the products; mix of productions must be organized to allow a variety of products to be manufactured without large inventories; extensive usage of *Kaizen* activities; total quality management and total productive maintenance must be used simultaneously.

We will provide below the detail analysis of strategic planning process of the three major Japanese automobile multinationals such as the Nissan Motor Co., the Toyota Motor Co., and the Honda Motor Co. to define and analyze the basic characteristics of their strategic planning process at home country Japan and host countries worldwide.

Strategic planning process in the Nissan Motor Co.

The Nissan Motor Co. (Japan) aims to build profitably the highest quality car sold in to achieve the maximum possible customer satisfaction and thus ensure the prosperity of the company and its staff. The all Nissan's plants in host countries across the world have strategic philosophy in accordance of one from Nissan of Japan.

Organization and production management system in the Nissan Motor Co.

Nissan's plants in Japan and in host countries across the world usually include a car and component manufacturing facility, an engine machining and assembly plant, a foundry, a plastics injection and molding plant, and a service parts operation all on one site. Environmental considerations are high in the list of priorities in the production system. Using the water-based paints helps to increase the volume of production and recycling activities. The strong operator–environment is one of the main elements of the production management system.

Nissan does not build a large buffer stock of doors, bonnets, and boot lids; so, Nissan is following the Toyota's just-in-time production system in its business operations in home country. Also, Nissan is implementing the just-in-time production system internationally in host countries where it is appropriate. For example, just-in-time system was successfully applied in Europe, particularly in Nissan's plant in Sunderland in Britain.

Quality management in the Nissan Motor Co.

Total quality is a philosophy that runs through every aspect of the business both in home and host countries. Quality control is not only the responsibility of quality control staff. It is the responsibility of every single person in the organization. Everyone is made fully aware that they have a valuable and significant role to fulfill. Quality standards and targets are settings in all areas and the plant's performance is monitored in accordance to them. Results are regularly being reviewed to get the feedback with workers and improve individual processes. Parts' quality is also constantly monitoring by using special test rigs backed by extensive chemical and metallurgy laboratory facilities. The plant's own quality cheek process is supplemented at random by Nissan's world auditors.

Human resource management system in the Nissan Motor Co.

The aim of the personnel management system in Nissan's plant both in home and host countries is "to create the mutual trust and cooperation between all people within the plant." It involves with the encouragement by top management the workers who are trying to make a significant contribution to business process, who are working together toward a common objective, and who are continuously seeking the ways to improve every aspect of the business. It aims for flexibility in the sense of expanding the role of all staff to the maximum extent possible and puts quality consciousness as the key responsibility above the all.

The production system builds in quality rather than to inspect and rectify. These strict targets are assisted by the fact that the company gives common terms and conditions of employment to all staff members. Every employee in a Japanese plant has the fixed salary compare with the Western system, where the employees have wage according to the quantity/number of the work/hours. In Japanese plants, every employee has the fixed sickness benefit scheme and private medical insurance, and company is paying approximately 33–44 percent of the medical care.

Also compared with Western plants, in Japanese plants, both in home and host countries, there are no time clocks and special discipline-controllers checking the exact time of worker's arrival on the working place. The performance appraisal system and cafeteria are the same for all staff, including the general manager at Nissan's plants both in home and host countries.

The main element of HRM in Nissan's plants, both in home and host countries, is training. The company believes that the "high caliber, well trained and motivated people are the key to success." Both on-the-job and off-the-job training are important parts of the Nissan's strategic planning process. Thus, the training expenditure in Nissan's represented 5.6 percent of total payroll costs with the training time as 4 percent of staff members' time. The emphasis on training has resulted in a sharp increase in productivity of the Nissan's plants in host countries. For example, the productivity level of the British workers at the beginning of the Nissan's operation in UK was very low compared to the productivity level of Nissan's operations in Japan; however, just after one year of extensive training of the British workers both in the United Kingdom and in Japan plants, the productivity level increased up to 78 percent.

Leadership style in the Nissan Motor Co.

To examine the characteristics of the supervisory style in Nissan, we have taken the survey by offering the questionnaire to the Nissan's shop-floor workers and managers of the middle and top levels both in home country and in host country (UK) to determine the features of the leadership style in the Nissan's plant and determine whether or not the leadership style differs in the home and host country of the same MNC.

Unfortunately, we got much less responses than we expected from home county employees compared with host country (UK) employees in Nissan. However, the given survey, the opinion of the employees, which was expressed by answering the questions from questionnaire: "Leadership style in The Nissan Motor Co.," and a number of interviews with top managers of Nissan Motor Co. in Japan and in the United Kingdom allowed us to summarize our conclusions as follows: the leadership style used in Nissan both in the home and host country is very Japanese in nature; the top managers are 100 percent Japanese in home plants and 99 percent Japanese expatriates in host countries to implement the home business culture at host country; the main aim of the leadership is to increase the motivation of the employees and therefore to increase the productivity by driving out class distinctions that exists in other industries in Western society, where the managerial staffs and ordinary workers live separate life, with separate facilities, and implementing "the equal opportunity for every employee" strategy.

Causes of the conflict in the Nissan. Motor Co.

Our survey shows that the "personal conflict" is not an important factor in the conflict. Analyzing the answers on our questionnaires, we came to conclusion that the causes of the conflict are objective rather than subjective such as the development of new markets and geographical diversifications along with the government regional policies.

Analyzing the survey, we also conclude that the causes for conflict with the suppliers are due to different management practices. We have noticed that in Nissan along with successful implementation of the internal just-in-time production–inventory management system, the external just-in-time production–inventory management system has not been successful so far because the network of suppliers and distributors are not ready to use the Japanese system due to economic, social, and psychological differences.

Partner selection in the Nissan Motor Co.

After analyzing the responses to questionnaire: "Objectives of Partner Selection in the Nissan Motor Co.," we came to the following conclusions that the objectives of partner selection in the Nissan Motor depend on similarities of technologies and management practice, and on the host country market conditions. The political connection is important because it helps to establish smooth relationships in supply chains and distributions.

Transnational strategic plan in the Nissan Motor Co.

The main goal of transnational strategic plan in the Nissan Motor Co. is to diversify the production bases. These have three main purposes: (a) to avoid the tariff and non-tariff restrictions on exports from its Japanese base; (b) to maintain cost by taking into account regional characteristics; and (c) to compete effectively with its Japanese rivals at home country and foreign car manufacturers by producing the higher quality cars abroad cheaper than its rivals.

Nissan's transnational strategic plan has been implemented in the tri-polar operating structure based on Japan and Asia, America (North America and Latin America), and Europe with research and development, production, sales, and finance capabilities in each region. To further localize overseas production and make them more self-sufficient, the company's transnational strategic planning process continues to strengthen sales of the local production in each region. At the same time, Nissan is increasing Japan-bound exports from overseas productions bases and pursuing natural supply of components and vehicles on a global level.

Other key initiatives of the Nissan's transnational strategic plan are the following: the improving cost competitiveness; constantly raising ability to compete on the basis of quality; and strengthening its presence in the growth markets of Asia.

However, while Nissan performed favorably in the US market, the Latin America's (Mexico) distressed economy and increasingly severe price competition in Europe made the operating environment in 1995–1996 outside Japan very difficult. Although in Japan Nissan's loss is declining. Nissan's loss is continuously because of Japan's recessions.

Thus, Nissan's goals in transnational strategic planning for the future must include expansions of global automobile and component manufacturing capabilities and increasing purchases from cost competitive overseas parts supplier. This effort will entail further progress in importing vehicles made by Nissan's plants overseas to Japan and these strategies will enhance the product line up, optimize efficiency, and help insulate Nissan against external factors such as currency fluctuations, etc. Current Nissan's transnational strategic plan, so-called Global Restructuring Policy, includes the expansion of local vehicle production and local production of major components; exports from its overseas production bases to Japan; and establishing strong overseas R&D functions and parts procurement systems. Also, Nissan is planning to increase its R&D base in Asia to have network of design centers connected to each other in Asia, Europe, and North America. This will strengthen the ability to design locally procured components, as well as tailor the vehicles to specific market needs.

Nissan is implementing the all above-mentioned strategies in its business. So, recently Nissan has created the in-house "Imports Production Committee," whose mission is to increase imports to Japan of both original equipment parts and after-market replacement parts from competitive suppliers. These efforts will continue in future.

Strategic plan in the Nissan Motor Co.'s plants in the United States and South-East Asia (ASEAN countries)

Nissan is building an engine and automatic transmission plant in Tennessee, the United States, and pursuing expansions in local production through joint ventures in China, Thailand, the Philippines, and Indonesia. Japanese production has declined, along with Mexican production, but in the United Kingdom, United States, Spain, and Asia, productions are increasing. Wagons and pickup trucks, designed for South-East Asia markets and manufactured in Thailand, Taiwan, the Philippines, and Malaysia are core models in Nissan's Asian line up. Nissan plans are ready to double the automobile production in ASEAN countries in cooperation with partners and joint ventures.

Strategic plan in the Nissan Motor Co.'s plants in East Asia

Nissan is expanding its operation in East Asia as well. For example, in Korea, Nissan established its office in Seoul as part of the comprehensive technical assistance agreement with Samsung Motors Inc. This agreement covers development of a new car model for Samsung and support for its other activities. Also, Nissan is collaborating with Nanjing Auto Works (now Yuejin Automobile Granp Corp.) in China. At the sometime, Nissan is to manufacture commercial vehicle in joint venture with Zhengzhou Light Track & Factory in China.

Strategic plan in the Nissan Motor Co.'s plants in Europe (UK)

Nissan Motor Manufacturing (UK) Ltd was established in 1984 as a part of the Nissan of Japan global strategic plan. The production started in 1986. Nissan announced that year its plans to accelerate the UK manufacturing program by increasing the local content to 60 percent by 1988 and 80 percent by 1991. The local content element was the obligation from the European Economic

Commission; otherwise the EEC can charge prohibitive tariffs. By 1987, Nissan has already internalized its sales in the United Kingdom, with the United Kingdom produced cars becoming the sole source of supply to the UK market. Plans for new investment were made. By 1988, the 60 percent of the content of the car was made in Europe, and the plant was modified to start production of engine and plastic infection molding facility. It has also invested heavily in research and development efforts within Europe. Britain was selected by Nissan as its European technology center, and a number of affiliated research and development organizations were planned. At the same time, coordination in research and development was enhanced by having design networks between development centers for Nissan in Japan, the United States, and Europe to coordinate developmental work. Exports to the European countries have started. Exports from Britain to the East European countries and to the Far East Asian countries have started. Productions of the cars were made as self-sufficient as possible, with engine produced in Britain being in use in all cars produced in Britain. In 1992, further automation of the plant was introduced by installing an automated pressing machine to build the body of the car. By 1994, Nissan from its UK production base has exported cars to 34 different world markets. So, Nissan has successfully used Britain as its export base. At the same time, it has created a network of suppliers throughout Europe. The number of suppliers varies from model to model and from country to country. Also, these networks of suppliers now satisfy most of the needs of production in the United Kingdom. However, the exit of the United Kingdom from the EEC raised the question about the sustainability of this strategy.

Thus, the Nissan Motor Co. is a transnational company with geocentric functional policies utilizing the appropriate transnational strategic planning process, which develops the progress through expanding its production capacity in home and host countries worldwide.

Overall strategic planning process of the Toyota Motor Co.

The Toyota Motor Co. (Japan) aim is to satisfy the customer by providing the highest quality at the lowest possible cost in shortest possible time by operating the competitive strategy such as just-in-time inventory–production management system.

Toyota was established in Japan in 1937 and became an MNC during 1950s. Its first overseas production began in 1959 in Brazil. Expansion continued throughout the 1950s, 1960s, and 1970s with the opening of the overseas plants in Africa, South America, South-East Asia, and Australia. In 1985, a joint venture company was established in the United States, and in 1988 its own vehicle plants were established in the United States and Canada.

In Europe, Toyota was established in 1989 in the United Kingdom. The production in the Toyota's UK plant started in 1992. All Toyota's plants located in host countries across the world have strategic management philosophy in accordance to the one from Toyota of Japan.

Characteristics of the functional strategies in the Toyota Motor Co.

We have to remember that so-called Japanese style production–inventory system including the following features such as just-in-time production, the *Kanban* system, total quality management, and cell-based layout designs were invented in Toyota plants in Japan during the early 1950s and later successfully implemented in its plants in home country as well as in its overseas plants at host countries.

The Toyota Motor Co. has a complete manufacturing operation including press and weld, paint, plastics, assembly, and engine plus a comprehensive environmental control facility. Quality is built in at every stage and confirmed throughout the process. In the press and welding section, coils of steel are out into "blanks" flat sheet shaped into the basic part in a pattern that minimizes waste steal. Operating to just-in-time production, Toyota has cut out all blanks in all operation lines. For example, when the press lines require parts to be sent forward, orders for details are entered on computers to ensure timely transferring by the automatic guidance vehicle (AGV) to the press machines. The presses give each part its third dimension using dies. Dies can be changed very quickly; thus, stocks are kept to a minimum according to Toyota's production system to save time, money, and space.

The completed body panels are welded together (90 percent done by robots) into larger main sub-assemblies. These sub-assemblies are then brought together by a robot to form a complete body shell. Throughout the process, team members and technology works together to build a high-quality vehicle. At each stage, team members check the quality of work before passing the vehicle on, while a number of automated intelligent systems interact to instruct and control the car-building system. The car then needed to go through painting, plastic moldings of instruments panels and engine assembly. Despite approximately 2500 parts having to be filled to each car, there are only two temporary parts storage areas where a maximum of eight-hour stock is held. A "manifest" (printed document or memo) is filled to the car, containing details of its specifications and providing visual control throughout the assembly process. The car then travels down the assembly line.

Throughout the process, each member is responsible for the quality of work they produce and pass on. The audio-cord is pulled once to call support from the team leader; in many cases the problem is addressed quickly, the cord is pulled again by the team leader, and the line continues never having stopped. If the problem is a bit more serious, the team leader will allow the line to stop until the concern is resolved. Although quality is built in at every stage, a complete functional and visual inspection is carried out before the line-off to ensure complete customer satisfaction.

Human resource management in the Toyota Motor Co.

We can see at every level that there are Japanese managers shadowing their local counterparts. However, recently, these local managers have been in command in Toyota's plants in the United States, while Japanese managers are very few compared with the Nissan Motor Co., which prefers to give managerial positions to Japanese expatriates. In the case of the "internal management" the style is very similar that of any Japanese MNCs, such as Nissan or Honda, with unified facilities and same job status for all staff members. In HRM, the major goal in host countries, for example, in the Toyota's UK plant, is to build an organization where all employees can develop to their full potential. Teamwork is an essential element of Toyota's HRM philosophy both in home and host countries, with the belief that a well-coordinated group can accomplish far more than the sum of individual effort. An average age of Toyota's workers is only 31. So, the young age of Toyota's workers is appropriate for continuous training.

The training process is a very important element of the HRM in Toyota both in home and host countries, like in any other Japanese automobile MNC, such as Nissan or Honda. The training facilities are available within the production system in Toyota's plants in home country, as well as in the most host countries. For example, Toyota's workers spend approximately 100,000 man/days on training prior to production startup. Training facilities are available in all locations throughout the world. For example, the British workers can go for training in Japan, United States, and Canada, and the workers from Toyota's foreign and Japanese establishments can come to Britain for training. Since the start of production, another further 20,000 man/days Toyota's workers have to spent on specific training courses off-the-job; the costs and time spent on continuous on-the-job training are almost immeasurable.

Characteristics of the transnational strategic plan in the Toyota Motor Co.

A transnational strategic plan in the Toyota Motor Co. was developed to design products to meet local needs of the host countries, to produce locally, and to involve the local talent of the host managers in business. In 1998, Toyota made agreement with French government to open the plant in France.

Implementing the strategic plan in the Toyota Motor Co.'s plants in North America and Latin America

For Toyota, the sales efforts are the instruments for globalization of production. Toyota had started exporting in the 1950s, initially to South-East Asia and Latin America and later to North America. Production was following the sales. In Latin America, Toyota opened the first plants in 1950s. These plants were small, producing a few thousand vehicles every year. However, plants located in Latin America helped Toyota to avoid paying a prohibiting tariff and obtain a foothold in the local market.

Thus, it was the protectionist policies of those countries that were responsible for local production of Toyota. Similarly, to obtain a presence in a highly protected market, plants were opened in the United Kingdom, the United States, and Canada. Design and development became international in 1970s, when design and technical facilities were set-up in North America. North American operations are localized in the sense that production and management should be self-sufficient.

Implementing the strategic plan in the Toyota Motor Co.'s plants in Europe (UK)

The operation in Europe is also increasingly localized. The capacity of the engine and vehicle plants in the United Kingdom will be expanded by added investment. These plants are exporting to other countries in Europe and throughout the world.

Currently Toyota (UK) exports most of its vehicle production to Europe, and the rest is for the UK market. Engines produced by its UK plants are exported to Turkey; similarly, cylinder blocks and crank staffs are exported to Toyota, Japan. Regarding the supply chain, there are 160 suppliers in ten countries in Europe for parts and components suppliers and 50 suppliers in various countries for raw materials. Eighty percent of the supply comes from the United Kingdom: there are 80 suppliers of parts and components and 30 suppliers of raw materials from the United Kingdom. The main objective of the supply chair network is to ensure quality and Toyota (UK) in developing long-term partnerships with suppliers based on mutual trust. There are internal just-in-time production and inventory system, but external *Kanban* system with the supplier is not yet developed in Toyota's plants in host countries. This is due to the fact that foreign suppliers abroad have not yet integrated their production and management system in that of Toyota in Japan.

Strategic plan in the Toyota in East Asia and South-East Asia (ASEAN countries)

East and South-East Asia will account for most of the growth in global demand for vehicles. Thus, Toyota has opened a second vehicle plant in Thailand in 1996. There is one more plant for Toyota in the Philippines as well. In Indonesia, the Toyota has started production in 1996. In China, there is now a joint venture company with Tianjin Automobile Industrial Group to manufacture engines that supplies engines to an affiliated company Daihatsu Motor Co. to produce vehicles. In 1996, Toyota Technical Center in Tianjin was opened to provide technical assistance to local parts manufactures. In Taiwan, an affiliate company Kuozui Motors began productions in 1995, and it is now expanding its association with Toyota affiliate Hino Motors of Japan.

Thus, the Toyota Motor Co. is a transnational corporation with geocentric functional policies utilizing the appropriate transnational strategic planning process that develops the progress through expanding its production capacity in home and host countries worldwide. So, given strategic plan allows to the Toyota Motor Co. to achieve the great progress by expanding production capacity outside Japan and serving its principal markets cost-effectively with using local workforce to make higher-quality products with competitive price and, therefore, to increase its global profits significantly.

Overall strategic planning process philosophy of the Honda Motor Co.

The Honda Motor Co.'s overall strategic planning philosophy is to achieve the main goal to satisfy the customer by providing the highest quality at lowest possible cost in shortest possible time by using the corporate policy that emphasizes originality, innovation, and efficiency in every step of its operations: from product developments and manufacturing to marketing.

Established 70 years ago in Japan, Honda Motor Co. Ltd. became one of the leading manufacturers of automobiles and the largest manufacturer of motorcycles in the world. The company is recognized internationally for its expertise and leadership in developing and manufacturing a wide variety of products ranging from general purpose engines to specially sports cars that incorporate Honda's highly efficient internal combustion engine technology. By following a corporate policy that emphasizes originality, innovation, and efficiency in every step of its operations from product developments and manufacturing to marketing Honda has striven to attain its goal to satisfy its customers. Through a worldwide commitment of advancing their goal, Honda and its many partners have succeeded in creating a global network with 89 production facilities in 33 countries that supply Honda products to most countries in the world.

Characteristics of the functional strategies in the Honda Motor Co.

Honda's plants in host countries have similar organizational structure as in Honda plants in home country. A significant part of Honda's income comes from motorcycles, which was the initial product. Establishing teamwork is the basic aim of Honda's HRM. The culture of teamwork exists throughout the company, breaking down many of the natural barriers between individuals and making apparently impossible tasks achievable. Honda's HR management works through NHC (New Honda Circles)/groups of Associates (i.e., workers and managers) taking responsibility for changing their own working environment to improve safety, build quality into the process, be more efficient in what they do, and improve their place of work. The teams' leaders sometime travel to the Honda plant in another country to analyze and solve problem in that plant and receive in the process understanding of how to use different techniques of different groups. By valuing the associates opinions, Honda, can make changes that improve working conditions, motivate, create a better understanding, and improve the overall quality of Honda products. In the survey of car quality, Honda has surpassed its competitions.

Transnational strategic plan in the Honda Motor Co.

The networks of Honda's manufacturing bases are throughout the world. North American sales are more important than the Japanese market. Recently the Asian and Latin American markets are also gaining importance. European sales are about one-tenth of sales of Honda automobile. European manufacturing activity is comparatively new considering Honda's manufacturing operation in Asia and North America. In Europe, total automobile demand was basically unchanged recently, but Honda's automobile sales in that region have represented consistent growth in unit terms. The Honda's plant in the United Kingdom produced automobiles accounted for approximately half of all Honda vehicle sales in this region. In Asia, Honda also has increased its investment. Honda is now manufacturing in a number of Asian countries: Thailand, Malaysia, Indonesia, the Philippines, Taiwan, Pakistan, India, and China.

While in Japan competition in the market intensified currency fluctuations and continued economic recessions have provoked Honda to shift its production overseas, its export from Japan declined. Honda has tried to improve its competitiveness to produce at the cheapest place using least expenditure materials and components from its worldwide suppliers and improving the quality by spending increasingly on R&D.

Honda's first overseas automobile production operations were in Taiwan in 1969. In 1982, Honda became the first Japanese automobile manufacturer to produce passenger cars in the United States. Then European production started in 1992. Honda's present global structure of automobile production is consistent with the company's corporate philosophy of manufacturing in those markets where demand exists. Honda currently makes automobiles in 15 facilities in 13 countries around the world.

The increased production level is for planned domestic sales rather than exports, which according to plan will be lowered due to shifts of production to the off-shore plants. After considering production costs as well as the viewpoint of producing vehicles in the local markets where demand is high, Honda suspended exports from Japan to the North American market in 1995 and increased the local production of this popular series. Over 75 percent were made locally and the rest came from Japan. Honda may resume exporting cars to North America if production capacity will exhaust. North America represented nearly half of Honda's overall exports from Japan. Honda has maintained a high utilization rate at Suzuki's compact car plant. This move does not necessarily mean a further acceleration of the shift to off-shore production. Honda plans to continue exporting some of the popular models to North America from Japan.

Strategic plan in the Honda in North America and Latin America

Production at Honda's Canadian manufacturing subsidiary Honda Canada Inc. (ACM) was started in 1995. In Canada, Honda built a second production line at its plant in Alliston, Ontario. This line will manufacture a new mini-van developed for the North American market. The new line will double Honda's automobile production capacity in Canada. Honda announced that it would accelerate its automobile strategy for America, expanding its US production of automobile engines and automatic transmissions, increasing R&D capabilities, and boosting local production in North America. In Latin America, in November 1995, Honda began production in Mexico, supported by its North American operations. Also, in December 1995, Honda invested in an automobile manufacturing facility in Brazil. The automobile produced at the plant will initially be sold only in Brazil with plans to export to other Latin American markets in future.

Implementing the strategic plan in the Honda Motor Co's plants in Europe

Honda's manufacturing plant in the United Kingdom (HUM) has started in 1985, and full-scale manufacturing began in 1992. Over 75 percent of the cars were exported, mainly to Europe, but also to Africa and Middle East. Honda's parts production facility at HUM (UK) began operations in May 1995, enabling Honda to consolidate production locally and enhance business among its local suppliers. Honda set its sights on the European market and announced plans to outsource European-made diesel engines for manufactured at HUM. HUM (UK) began to export models to the Middle East.

Implementing the strategic plan in the Honda Motor Co.'s plants in East Asia and South-East Asia (ASEAN countries)

Honda was very successful in advancing automobile production in the Asian markets as well, although Asia is Honda's most important market for motor-cycles. Honda has an agreement with Siel, a major Indian conglomerate for the production and sale of passenger cars in India. Under the agreement Honda Siel Cars India Ltd. was formed, which began production in 1997. In China, Honda is focusing on automobile parts production, which operations began at the joint venture Dongfeng Honda Auto Parts Co. Ltd in November 1995. Initially, all parts produced at this Guangdong plant are exported to the Honda Car manu-facturing (Thailand) Co Ltd (HCMT) and incorporated into models produced in Thailand. Thus, the Honda Motor Co. is a transnational corporation with very geocentric functional policies utilizing the appropriate transnational strate-gic planning process which develops further through expanding its production capacity in home and host countries worldwide.

Strategic planning process in multinational corporations

There is a growing need for strategic planning in MNCs. Some of the primary reasons of necessity of the strategic planning process in modern MNCs include the following: foreign direct investment is increasing; strategic planning is needed to coordinate and integrate increasingly diverse operations via an overall focus; and emerging international challenges require strategic planning.

A strategic plan in modern MNCs can take on economic focus, a political focus, administrative coordination, or some variation of the three. In addi-tion, the MNC is typically predisposed toward an ethnocentric, polycentric, region-centric, or geocentric orientation. MNCs may use a combination of these orientations in their strategic planning, but the geocentric is the one most commonly employed by global companies.

Strategy formulation consists of several steps. First, the MNC carries out external environmental scanning for the purpose of identifying opportunities and threats. Next, the firm conducts an internal resource analysis of company strengths and weaknesses. Strategic goals are then formulated in light of the results of the external and internal analyses.

Strategy implementation is the process of providing goods and services in accord with the predetermined plan of action. This implementation typically involves considerations such as (a) deciding where to locate operations; (b) carrying out an entry and ownership strategy; and (c) using functional strategies to implement the plan. The latter focuses on HRM, marketing, production, and finance. The organizational structure of MNCs and HRM should not be viewed in isolation. They depend on environment, industry and strategy, and in turn influence the feasible strategy.

Strategic planning process in MNCs includes different global and industrial characteristics, competitive and functional strategies, and organizational structures. Independent of environment and business strategies, however, some functional strategies will often be more centralized/integrated (e.g., finance) than others (e.g., marketing). Furthermore, internal resources also influence and constrain strategic choices.

Current environmental developments suggest that focusing on either efficiency/integration or differentiation/responsiveness will no longer be a very feasible choice. MNCs will have to comply with demands for efficiency and responsiveness simultaneously, while at the same time being internally flexible and innovative. Transnational companies will be best suited to comply with these demands. In spite of environmental demands and even in spite of their formal strategy, most multinationals are still rather ethno- centric oriented. Even international management researchers have a strong ethnocentric bias.

Organizational structures and the strategic planning process

A variety of factors helps explain the differences in the way international corporations operate. The classic theories of trade such as Vernon's product-life theory and Dunning's eclectic theory determined these factors such as land, labor, and capital. However, modern theories like competitiveness of nations or societal effect theory determined many more factors than simply labor, land, and capital. Those factors include nation's factor condition, demand condition, and related and supporting industry, MNC's organizational strategy, structure, and rivalry and national differences (Porter, 1990).

Many MNCs began by using the subsidiary to handle overseas business. As the operation grows or the company expands into more markets, the firm will often opt for an international division structure. Further growth may result in the adoption of a global structural arrangement such as a global production division, a global area division structure, a global functional division, or a mixture of these structures.

Some multinationals have subsidiary boards of directors that oversee and monitor the operations of a foreign subsidiary. As MNCs' operations increase worldwide, these boards are likely to gain in popularity. Three organizational characteristics of MNCs that are of particular importance are formalization, specialization, and centralization. These characteristics often vary from country to country so that Japanese MNCs will conduct operations differently than US-MNCs. When MNCs set-up international subsidiaries, they often use the same organizational techniques as they do at home without necessarily adjusting their approach to better match the local conditions.

Strategic planning process and overall strategic management

It is a very significant fact that Japanese MNCs being representatives of just one country from East Asia dramatically influenced the industrial and strategic management of the Western countries. There are three main elements of the strategic planning process of Japanese automobile MNCs, which have been introduced into Western industrial and strategic management: a commitment to *Kaizen* or continuous improvement; cooperative relationships between workers, managers, and suppliers; and emphasis on measuring all aspects of business, from serious faults to misplaced labels to identify precisely the needs of improvement. Before the establishments of Japanese manufacturing bases in the United States and Europe, American and European managers were reluctant to utilize these concepts because of their fear that it may lead to serious industrial disturbances due to social/cultural differences. However, with the entering of Japanese automobile MNCs like the Nissan Motor Co., the Toyota Motor Co., and the Honda Motor Co. in Western business world, it has become a compulsion to introduce Japanese style of management, including strategic planning techniques, in American and European management to increase the level of its productivity up to the Japanese level.

The Japanese effect in strategic management was introduced to the Western world through the Japanese automobile MNCs' way of dealing with its foreign suppliers of components. For example, in case of the Nissan Motor Co., the leading engineering firms in the United Kingdom such as GKN or small companies such as Frederick Woolley of Birmingham had to accept the standard of quality of these products and maintenance of supply line as necessary part of their business deal with the Nissan Motor Co. Immediately, the US competitors, like Ford Motor Company in the United Kingdom, were forced to change its own way of dealing with suppliers to increase the standards of quality and to be competitive to the Japanese car manufactures in car-manufacturing market in the United Kingdom.

Ford Motor Co. has introduced Japanese system of production–inventory system in collaboration with Mazda, another Japanese MNC, in its plants in Britain. The most significant change took place in Rover car plants (UK), which was in collaboration with the Honda Motor Co. of Japan. Honda has introduced both the Japanese management system and automated production system in Rover car plant.

However, what is true about the big rival European car manufactures is not true about the smaller suppliers of component. Europe and the United States have achieved significant improvements in productivity and quality standard by using the Japanese techniques, but the large manufactures are yet to accept fully the Japanese system.

The Japanese effect weakens with a distance from the source. For instance, Nissan has influenced small component suppliers such as Frederick Woolley who supplies to Lucas, who in turn supplies Nissan; Lucas has influenced its own suppliers. Recently, the Frederick Woolley had less than 100 faults per million parts; its own suppliers score 3500 or more. However, the smaller companies further down the supply chain have little direct contact with Japanese-inspired method, and their quality standards are low. So, to improve the quality of their products, the little companies in Europe and in the United States have to implement the Japanese techniques of the strategic planning process.

Also, some of the larger companies in Europe and in the United States are having difficulties to accept Japanese standards. For example, under Nissan's QCDDMI supplier evaluation system, suppliers are rated for quality, cost, delivery, development of new products, and management. Toyota and Honda have similar evaluation systems for supplier. Most European and American suppliers meet the first four elements of the evaluation system, but they dislike being rated in management.

Japanese MNCs' influence is not limited to the motor industry. Managers from all host countries are coming to Japanese automobile MNCs overseas plants to get training in management and to learn the strategic planning techniques. Governments of the host countries have sponsored the lot teams of experts to learn managerial techniques from Japanese MNCs.

Currently, when Yen has depreciated to levels below its recent peak, prospective economic trends in the United States and Europe are uncertain. The environments for exports from Japan remain severe. Japan is yet to recover from its recessions since 1991, although a gradual recovery is expected. However, large increases in domestic demand for all these producers we have discussed are hard to predict. Thus, competition for market share will intensify in future.

For the future, Japanese automobile companies are maintaining their efforts to enhance their competitiveness of their products by bolstering R&D, increasing the efficiency of their manufacturing system, strengthening their sales activities, and further localizing their overseas operations in accordance with its global strategic planning.

The significant effort of Japanese automobile MNC on Western strategic and industrial management is obvious and must be implemented by modern MNC in different countries to improve the quality of its products, to maintain the better relationship between the managers, supplier networks and workforce, and therefore, to compete worldwide successfully.

3 Leadership and decisions

Philosophical background

Leadership is as the process of influencing people to direct their efforts toward the achievement of some particular goal or goals. Leadership is widely recognized as being very important in the study of international management, but relatively little effort has gone to systematically study and compare leadership approaches throughout the world.

Leadership is often credited for the success or failure of international business operations. Recently, certain effective leadership styles such as the Western and Japanese have transcended the international boundaries. However, the effective leadership styles that have been very successful in one country would not necessarily succeed on other countries. Even within the same country, an effective leadership style tends to be very situation specific.

Most international research efforts on leadership have been directed toward a specific country or geographic area. In providing a leadership foundation for the international arena, two comparative areas can be examined: the philosophical grounding of how leaders view their subordinates, and leadership approaches as reflected through the use of autocratic-participative characteristics and behaviors of leaders.

Theories X and Y

The primary reason that leaders behave as they do is their philosophy regarding the most effective way to direct their subordinates. Managers who believe that their people are naturally lazy and work only for money will use a different leadership style than those who believe that their people are self-starters and enjoy challenge and increased responsibility. Douglas McGregor, the pioneering leadership theorist, labeled these two sets of philosophical assumptions with the terms Theory X and Theory Y.

A "Theory X" manager believes that people are basically lazy, and coercion and threats of punishment must be used to get them to work. The specific philosophical assumptions that Theory X leaders feel the following terms are most descriptive of their subordinates: People, by their very nature, do not like to work and will avoid it whenever possible. Workers have little ambition, try to avoid responsibility, and like to be directed. The primary need of employees is job security. To get people to attain organizational objectives, it is necessary to use coercion, control, and threats of punishments.

A "Theory Y" manager believes that under the right conditions people will not only work hard but will seek increased responsibility and challenge. In addition, a great deal of creative potential basically goes untapped, and if these abilities can be tapped, workers will provide much higher quantity and quality of output. Specific philosophical assumptions that Theory Y leaders feel are most descriptive of their subordinates are the expenditure of physical and mental effort at work is as natural to people as is resting or playing.

External control and the threats of punishment are not the only ways of getting people to work toward organizational objectives. If people are committed to the goals, they will exercise self-direction and self-control. Commitment to objectives is determined by the rewards associated with their achievement. Under proper conditions, the average human being learns not only to accept, but also to seek responsibility.

The capacity to exercise a relatively high degree of imagination, ingenuity, and creativity in the solution of organizational problems is widely distributed throughout the population. Under conditions of modern industrial life, the intellectual potential of the average human being is only partially tapped.

These philosophical assumptions help dictate the most appropriate leadership approach. through the managers' behaviors including the following: giving orders, getting and giving feedback, and creating an overall climate for business.

International division of leadership

The logical consequence of the theories discussed above is that a country must concentrate on the production of those goods and services in which it has a competitive advantage so, that it can export these goods and import goods and services to those industries where it is less productive. In this way, international competition helps to upgrade productivity over time. The process implies, however, that market positions in some segments and industries must necessarily be put aside if a national economy is to progress. This is certainly true in a macroeconomic sense, but on a micro-level, this means the loss of thousands of jobs in less productive industries, causing serious personal anxiety and social problems. This is the main reason why many governments have tried to maintain such industries by means of subsidies, protective tariffs, or other forms of intervention.

In these days of trade liberalization, globalization of the world economy and economic integration in many regions of the world is taking place. However, such policies are increasingly difficult to sustain. The world is moving toward a new international division of labor and leadership, a process in which multinational companies are playing a leading role.

Reich's new world order

In his book *The Work of Nations: Preparing Ourselves for 21st-Century Capitalism*, Reich (1991) prophesies a new world's order for leaders. The most important objectives for companies, including multinationals, are to satisfy the market demand and to make profits. If these companies can save money by moving production processes elsewhere, they will do it. This may not be so important to the companies themselves, but it does have an impact on the social structure and prosperity of the individual countries involved. The countries that have nothing to offer in international competition are doomed to lose out badly. First world countries that do not have a supply of cheap labor will have to concentrate on the production of other, more specialized products with a high knowledge and capital content. This will result in an increasing demand for highly educated and creative people, that is, leaders. A problematic social consequence is that Western nations will be confronted with a large surplus of unskilled production workers who cannot compete against low-cost labor in ex-second- and third-world countries. A proper education for all citizens (and not only the top 25 percent) is therefore an absolute prerequisite for future prosperity and the growth of the new generation of the leaders. The only problem is, who is going to supply the education for leaders? Governments very often do not have the necessary resources to do this. Businesses do, but they fail to see why they should apply their resources in this fashion. Furthermore, the global economy makes it possible to have special services performed anywhere in the world, so in-house training becomes unnecessary.

Reich's analysis of the professional categories in the new world order

Companies and their owners can look forward to a bright future, but can the same be said of their employees? Reich distinguishes three professional categories that in global terms cover three-quarters of the labor force (the remaining part mainly consists of employees working in agriculture and in the public sector).

Routine production services: The traditional example in this category is the employee who works on the assembly line performing short-cycle, repetitive tasks. However, according to Reich, this category also includes the "routine supervisory jobs performed by low- and mid-level managers, foremen, line managers, clerical supervisors and section chiefs – involving repetitive checks on subordinates' work and the enforcement of standard operating procedures." It has often been said that in the present and future information age, this type of work will become less and less important. Also, many information-processing jobs fit perfectly into this category. The raw material of the industrial era has simply been replaced by the raw data of the information age. Entering and processing such data is essentially just as routine and monotonous a task as working on an assembly line in an automobile plant. These routine production services are not associated with a particular country; they can be performed anywhere and everywhere. Wage costs are, therefore, the only criterion for deciding where to locate them.

In-person services. Like the previous category, this one also covers basically simple and repetitive tasks requiring relatively little training. Examples of jobs in this category are salespeople, hair stylists, waiters and waitresses, cleaning staff, and receptionists. The major difference between this category and routine production work is that in-person servers provide their services directly to the consumer and that their work must therefore be performed at the location where the consumer is present. Consequently, they have nothing to fear from lower wage costs in other countries (except, of course, from immigrants, whether legal or illegal, who may work for lower wages). They are, however, under greater threat from the increasing computerization of the many jobs they perform. Consider, for example, the cash dispensers that have become an indispensable part of life for so many people. And as many of these jobs require no special training, in-person servers are finding themselves competing more and more with unemployed routine production workers. Finally, this category of employee depends very heavily on the affluence of its customers. If a country is unable to attract enough economic activity, it will not have the financial resources to cover in-person services.

Symbolic-analytic services. The most important feature of the jobs in this category is that they require skills in problem solving and problem identification. Some examples are research scientists, engineers, consultants, and managers, but also architects, musicians, film producers, and journalists. These occupations are highly specialized; by definition, they entail a proper education. Most of the jobs in this group require at least a university degree or higher vocational training. This group of employees will benefit the most from prosperity, simply because they bring added value to the production process. Like the worker formed by a routine production worker, the activities of symbolic analysts are not bound to a particular location. By using the available communication and information technology, companies can avail themselves of their services anywhere in the world. And since the definitive criterion here is not wages but special skills, these activities are not automatically carried out in low-wage countries.

The number of people who can actually benefit from the new opportunities is, therefore, quite limited. The future seems particularly bleak for unskilled laborers in Western countries, simply because they will be unable to make a clear-cut contribution – either in the form of specific skills or in the form of low wages – to the global production process. They simply cannot compete against the wage levels of employees in poor countries who perform exactly the same type of work. Even dismantling the social security system – which in Europe is regarded as the main culprit behind the high cost of labor – offers no real alternative. After all, wages and terms and conditions of employment will never be cut so drastically that they can compete with low-wage countries. Because a large section of the population in the West remains under-qualified (there are by the way huge differences between different countries: the United Kingdom, for example, is much worse off in this respect than Germany), we will ultimately be dealing with increasingly greater differences in income and, possibly, the rise of a social underclass.

Reich's scenarios for leadership theory for the future

In this connection, Reich has described three scenarios for leadership theory for the future. He calls the first scenario *zero-sum nationalism*. The assumption is that there are only two outcomes possible in economic warfare: either we win or they win. Countries, therefore, close their eyes to globalization and try to protect and improve their own position. Government subsidies for deteriorating industries and a renewed interest in protectionism are the hallmarks of this scenario. Obviously, it will be the routine production workers and in-person service workers and their representatives (for example, trade unions) who will be particularly keen on this option and became the leader. This course of action will, however, be of very little benefit to companies and investors, meaning that in the long-term this scenario will simply not be sustainable.

The second scenario is *cosmopolitanism*, in which the ideal of free trade is championed. This is not a zero-sum game: the world as a whole can improve through free trade. By making products where they can be made most cheaply, we all benefit in the end. The major leaders of this scenario will often be symbolic analysts. After all, they have nothing to lose in such a world order; in fact, they will be the big winners. According to Reich, this is the attitude that will most likely determine the future.

Neither of the scenarios described above is ideal, but according to Reich, there is yet the third scenario: *positive economic nationalism*. The core of this idea is that "each nation's citizens take prime responsibility for enhancing the capacities of their countrymen for full and productive lives, but also work with other nationals to ensure that these improvements do not come at others expense." Nationalism as seen by the zero-sum nationalists and individualism as advocated by the cosmopolitans are traded in for globalization. This scenario combines a belief in the benefits of free trade with arguments for some form of government intervention. Governments should invest in education and infrastructure to form the new leaders, and they should even subsidize companies that offer high value-added production in their own country, regardless of the nationality of the company owners. To prevent a situation in which countries bid against each other to attract certain companies, they should instead negotiate with one another on the appropriate subsidy levels and targets. The result, according to Reich, would be a sort of GATT for foreign direct investment establishing guidelines for the way in which countries are allowed to grant such subsidies. Countries with a large unskilled labor force, for example, would be allowed to offer bigger subsidies than countries that already possess high-tech facilities and expertise. Ultimately, more people would be able to share the prosperity.

A second group of subsidies might go to basic research. This would involve projects of which the results could not be contained strictly within a country's borders. A good example is the exploration of space. Since the entire world benefits from such exploration, national governments will not be inclined to subsidize space research. Such subsidies should, therefore, be determined at supranational level. Decisions like these are already being made at regional level within the European Union (EU), although not always efficiently. The EU subsidizes countless studies carried out both at universities and in companies forming the new leaders. In any event, it is clear that this scenario calls for a new global/ supranational institutional order. It is less clear whether the scenario itself has a real future. According to Reich: "Those who are threatened by global competition feel that they have much to lose and little to gain from an approach that seeks to enhance world wealth, while those who are benefiting the most from the blurring of national borders sense that they have much to lose and little to gain from government intervention to spread such benefits."

Consequences for the leadership theory in the Western world

The cheap labor force of today will be the consumers of tomorrow. European and Japanese companies generally maintain a longer-term perspective than US companies; they invest more in personnel and leadership development and are less likely to relocate. In addition, because of protectionism, world markets are still less global than many people realize, while labor costs have become less significant in certain sectors of industry. Finally, it can sometimes be important for producers to stay close to their product market so that theme can register and process any changes in time. The final three comments were also made by the Japanese author Ohmae in his book *Triad Power: The Coming Shape of Global Competition* (*1985*). So, by switching to new high-tech growth sectors such as computers, semiconductors, and biotechnology, Western countries can escape having to compete with poorer countries on labor costs. As the examples given above show, however, cheaper labor is not the only issue. The West may specifically lack those leaders who have the right training and who can be found elsewhere, which is certainly a problem in many countries when it comes to technical qualifications. An additional factor is that, compared with the United States and certainly with Japan, Europe requires far more leaders to maintain the same level of production. To survive in the face of competition, the West must invest in continual education and training for the new generation of the leaders.

Leadership behaviors and styles

Leader behaviors can be translated into three commonly recognized styles of authoritarian, paternalistic, and participative.

Authoritarian leadership is the use of work-centered behavior designed to ensure task accomplishment. This leader behavior typically involves the use of one-way communication from superior to subordinate. The focus of attention is usually on work progress, work procedures, and roadblocks that are preventing goal attainment. Although this leadership style is often effective in handling crises, some leaders employ it as their primary style regardless of the situation. It is also widely used by Theory X managers who believe that a continued focus on the task is compatible with the kind of people they are dealing with.

Paternalistic leadership uses work-centered behavior coupled with a protective employee-centered concern. This leadership style can be best summed up by the statement, "work hard, and the company will take care of you." Paternalistic leaders expect everyone to work hard, and, in turn, the employees will be guaranteed employment and will be given security benefits such as medical and retirement programs. Paternalistic leaders are often referred to as "soft" Theory X leaders because of their strong emphasis on strictly controlling their employees coupled with their concern for their welfare. They often treat their employees as strict but caring parents would their children. Participative leadership is the use of both a work-centered and people-centered approach. Participative leaders typically encourage their people to play an active role in assuming control of their work, and authority is commonly highly decentralized as a typical Theory Y manager.

New approaches in leadership

Mention productivity in the manufacturing sector, and most people immediately think of the Japanese multinational corporations (MNCs). However, recently a revolution is taking place in manufacturing firms throughout the Western world, including Europe and North America. Objective evidence of this revival is in US manufacturing productivity. Many technological advances help account for the surge in US productivity, but leadership also seems to account for the success. Excellent example of such leadership is provided by major Japanese automobile MNCs and some Western MNCs.

Leadership in the international context

How do leaders in other countries attempt to direct or influence their subordinates? Are their approaches similar to those used in Japan and in the Western world? Research shows that there are both similarities and differences. Most international research on leadership has focused on Western world, including Europe and North America.

Indeed, recently the international management is becoming extremely important; thus, the demand for skilled managers as a new generation of leaders is increasing sharply. Currently, the new leaders can be considered as the students who now are pursuing master's degrees in Business Administration (MBA). In fact, many universities are now rethinking their MBA curriculum and adding new courses that are designed to give the student a global perspective.

MBAs of the 1990s, at least at leading US business schools, would take courses related to ethics, negotiation, communication, and technology. For better or worse, students would get more of what educators call experience learning, in which they act as consultants, intern in the United States and overseas, and join in activities such as mock negotiations and outward bound trips. Yet the biggest change may be that of a required foreign language.

However, recently US MBAs tend to be very parochial, believing that English will always be the international language of business. Although this may be true, MBAs in an increasing number of programs are going to get a semester or two of Japanese, Spanish, German, or a similarly important foreign language that will better prepare them for international business. Some schools are going even further and offering a course on formal entertaining, so that the students understand how to conduct themselves properly in social settings. Another major curriculum change will be a stronger focus on the behavioral area.

More emphasis will be given to people skills such as communication, motivation, and leadership in an international setting. The MBA has the functional emphasis that has traditionally been given to educating future business leaders in areas such as accounting, finance, production, personnel, and marketing may be replaced by a broader, more general education that better prepares one to manage in the global economy.

Will all business education move in this direction of forming the new generation of leaders? The answer will depend on the amount of support provided by both the faculty and the business community. Faculty members have been educated to focus on specialized functional areas applied to their own country. Now they will have to start thinking in more global terms. The business community likes the new business school products, and they are likely to provide financial support for these types of business programs. If they do not like what they see, the universities may end up going it alone. Academic administrators and faculty members that are now implementing these revised business education programs for future business leaders are guessing that their product will be accepted with open arms by the business community and that they will receive the necessary support to continue their efforts.

The role of level, size, and age on Western managers' attitudes toward leadership

In recent years, much research has been directed at leadership approaches in the Western world, including Europe and North America. Most effort has concentrated on related areas such as risk taking, strategic planning, and organization design. Some of studies examine the leadership practices in Europe. For example, British managers tend to use a highly participative leadership approach. This is true for two reasons: The political background of the country favors such an approach, and because most top British managers are not highly involved in the day-to-day affairs of the business, they prefer to delegate authority and let much of the decision making be handled by middle- and lower-level managers.

This preference sharply contrasts with the French and Germans who prefer a more work-centered, authoritarian approach. In fact, if labor unions did not have legally mandated seats on the board of directors, participative management in

Germany would likely be even less pervasive than it is. Scandinavian countries, however, make wide use of participative leadership approaches with worker representation on the boards of directors and high management–worker interaction regarding workplace design and changes.

As a general statement, most evidence indicates that European managers tend to use a participative approach. However, they do not entirely subscribe to Theory Y philosophical assumptions, since an element of Theory X thinking continues. This was made clear by the now-classic Haire, Ghiselli, and Porter (1966) study of 3641 managers from 14 countries.

The leadership-related portion of this study sought to determine whether these managers were basically traditional (Theory X or system 1/2) or democratic-participative (Theory Y or system 3/4) in their approach. Specifically, the researchers investigated four areas relevant to leadership.

Capacity for leadership and initiative

Does the leader believe that employees prefer to be directed and have little ambition (Theory X) or that characteristic such as initiative can be acquired by most people regardless of their inborn traits and abilities (Theory Y)?

Sharing information and objectives

Does the leader believe that detailed, complete instructions should be given to subordinates and that subordinates need only this information to do their jobs, or does the leader believe that general directions are sufficient and that subordinates can use their initiative in working out the details?

Participation

Does the leader support participative leadership practices?

Internal control

Does the leader believe that the most effective way to control employees is through the use of rewards and punishment or that employees respond best to internally generated control?

Responses by managers to the four areas covered in the Haire, Ghiselli, and Porter study (1966) are still the most comprehensive available and are relevant to the current discussion of leadership similarities and differences across cultures. The specifics by country may have changed somewhat over the years, but the leadership processes revealed should not be out of date. The results of the study indicate that none of the leaders from various parts of the world, on average, were very supportive of the belief that individuals have a capacity for leadership and initiative. The researchers put it this way, "In each country, in each group of countries, in all of the countries taken together, there is a relatively low opinion of the capabilities of the average person, coupled with a relatively positive belief in the necessity for democratic-type supervisory practice."

An analysis of standard scores compared each cluster of countries against the other and revealed that Anglo leaders tend to have more faith in the capacity of their people for leadership and initiative than do the other clusters, and they believe that sharing information and objectives is important. However, when it comes to participation and internal control, the Anglo group tends to give relatively more autocratic responses than all the other clusters except developing countries. Interestingly, Anglo leaders reported a much stronger belief in the value of external rewards (pay, promotion, etc.) than did any of the clusters except that of the developing countries.

Thus, these findings clearly illustrate that attitudes toward leadership practices tend to be quite different in various parts of the world. The research of Haire and his associates (1966) provided important additional details within each cluster of European countries. These findings indicate that in some countries, higher-level managers tended to express more democratic values than lower-level managers; however, in other countries, the opposite is true. For example, in England higher-level managers responded with more democratic attitudes on all four leadership dimensions, whereas in the United States, lower-level managers gave more democratically oriented responses on all four. In the Scandinavian countries, higher-level managers tended to respond more democratically; in Germany, lower-level managers tended to have more democratic attitudes.

Company size also tended to influence the degree of participative-autocratic attitudes. There was more support among managers in small firms than in large ones regarding the belief that individuals have a capacity for leadership and initiative. However, respondents from large firms were more supportive of sharing information and objectives, participation, and the use of internal control. Note that those from large US companies were most supportive of the first three attitudes. Those who were from small firms were more supportive of internal control.

There were findings that age also had some influence on participative attitudes. Younger managers were more likely to have democratic values when it came to capacity for leadership and initiative and sharing information on objectives; although on the other two dimensions of leadership practices, older, and younger managers differed little. In terms of specific countries, however, some important differences showed up. For example, younger managers in both the United States and Sweden espoused more democratic values than their older counterparts; in Belgium, just the opposite was true.

The Global Leadership and Organizational Behavior Effectiveness project and Hofstede on leadership based on national culture

Regarding national cultures and leadership, the recent study of the Global Leadership and Organizational Behavior Effectiveness (GLOBE) project is quite significant (House, Hanges, Javidan, Dorfman, and Gupta, 2004). GLOBE follows Hofstede (2002) and Peabody to a great extent (Peabody, 1985; Parboteeah,

Bronson, and Cullen, 2005). Hofstede (2002) has the following characteristic of international management, influenced by national culture:

1   **Power Distance**: it is an index of inequality of power and position within an organization and society.
2   **Individualism**: in individualistic countries, there is great importance on people's need for independence and their privacy; collectivist countries put more importance on harmony of the society and ignore the personal utility of the individuals.
3   **Femininity**: femininity, opposite to masculinity that represents competitiveness, achievements, heroism, assertiveness and material rewards for success, puts importance on cooperation and modesty.
4   **Uncertainty Avoidance**: high level of uncertainty avoidance means conservatism with strict rules of belief and behavior, intolerant for relaxed attitudes.
5   **Long-Term Orientation:** these are values associated with thrift and perseverance, respect for tradition.
6   **Indulgence:** it is an extension of uncertainty avoidance; indulgent societies allow free gratification of basic and natural human instincts related to enjoying life and having fun, restrained societies have a conviction that such gratification needs to be controlled.

The GLOBE study extended Hofstede (2002) study by adding new characteristics: assertiveness, human orientation, and performance orientation (Gunnell, 2016). The GLOBE study divided individualism versus collectivism into two groups: in-group collectivism and institutional collectivism. GLOBE defined assertiveness as the "beliefs as to whether people are or should be encouraged to be assertive, aggressive, and tough, or nonassertive, non-aggressive, and tender in social relationships" (House et al., 2004). Assertiveness is related to Hofstede's original characteristics of masculinity versus femininity. According to the GLOBE study, assertiveness is associated with a "community's adaptive capability to the external environment and the community's internal integration that allows daily functioning" (House et al., 2004). The GLOBE followed the work of Peabody (1985).

The GLOBE has six leadership characteristics: charismatic or value-based leadership, team-oriented leadership, participative leadership, autonomous leadership, human-oriented leadership, and self-protective leadership (Chhokar, Brodbeck, and House, 2008).

The nine GLOBE cultural characteristics of organizations are the following:

1   Performance orientation – rewards for improved performance
2   Assertiveness orientation – assertive, confrontational, and aggressive in social, individual and business relationships
3   Future orientation – planning and investing for future
4   Humane orientation – altruistic, caring, and kind to others
5   Collectivism I: Institutional collectivism – collective distribution of facilities

6   Collectivism II: In-group collectivism – loyalty and discipline to promote the organization
7   Gender Egalitarianism – minimizes gender role discrimination
8   Power distance – difference between the ordinary workers and the executives
9   Uncertainty avoidance – avoids the uncertainty of future risks

GLOBE made mistakes by putting countries with dissimilar religions and culture in one national grouping. For example, "Confucian Asia" grouping has Taiwan, Singapore, Hong Kong, South Korea, China, Japan, and Vietnam, who are not similar. Japan is quite different from China. Vietnam was anti-Chinese over many centuries. Korea is different from both Japan and China, Even Taiwan, Singapore, and to many extent Hong Kong are different from China. "South Asia" grouping has Pakistan, India, Bangladesh, Indonesia, Malaysia, Thailand, Iran, Philippines, and Turkey, which are very different characteristics with different religions and cultures (Javidan and Dastmalchian, 2009).

Regarding "in-group collectivism," Gupta, Hanges, and Dorfman (2002a) categorize South Asia, Confucian Asia, and Anglo cultures as, respectively, high, medium, and low on this dimension. This is different from "societal collectivism," where Confucian Asia is categorized as high, while Southern Asia and Anglo cultures are medium on this dimension. Anglo cultures are individualistic; Southern Asia cultures reflect loyalty to the in-group collectivism; while Confucian Asia is characterized by a societal collectivism.

Regarding "performance orientation," the United States and Singapore score high on this cultural practice, and businesses are likely to emphasize training and development. In countries that score low, like Russia and Greece, family and background count for more.

Assertiveness score is high in the United States, United Kingdom, Canada, and Australia in the Anglo Culture grouping, and they prefer competition in business. In less assertive countries such as Sweden, Japan, and New Zealand, harmony in relationships is preferred.

Regarding "future orientation" according to the GLOBE project, forms in countries with high degree of future orientation like Singapore and Switzerland tend to have longer-term horizons and have more systematic planning processes, but they tend to be averse to risk taking and opportunistic decision making. Firms in low future orientation countries like Russia and Argentina tend to be less systematic and more opportunistic in their actions.

According to GLOBE countries with high degree of "humane orientation," firms encourage and rewards individuals for being altruistic, generous, caring, and kind to others. According to GLOBE, it is very strange that countries like Egypt and Malaysia rank very high on this cultural practice and countries like France and Germany rank low. It is very difficult to accept this.

According to GLOBE, companies from countries with a high degree of "institutional collectivism" encourage and reward collective distribution of resources and collective action. Organizations in collectivistic countries like Singapore and Sweden tend to emphasize group performance and rewards, whereas those in the more individualistic countries like Greece and Brazil tend to emphasize individual in-group collectivism.

GLOBE has more controversial conclusions. According to it societies of Egypt and Russia, individuals express pride, loyalty, and cohesiveness in their organizations or families. "European countries generally had the highest scores on gender egalitarianism practices. Egypt and South Korea were among the most male dominated societies in GLOBE" (House et al., 2004).

According to GLOBE, "power distance" refers reflects unequal power distribution in a society. Countries that scored high on this cultural practice reflect leaders who expect, and receive, obedience like in Thailand, Brazil, and France. They tend to have hierarchical decision-making processes with limited one-way participation and communication.

According to GLOBE, "uncertainty avoidance" means the extent to which a leader relies on social norms, rules, and procedures to avoid unpredictability of future events and risks. Singapore and Switzerland are the examples. In contrast, firms in low "uncertainty avoidance" countries, like Russia and Greece, tend to prefer risks, opportunism, and simple processes.

GLOBE considered the following six dimensions of the leadership profiles:

1 Charismatic/value based

This kind of leaders inspire values, motivate others, and demand a high level of performance. "The highest reported score is in the Anglo cluster (6.05); the lowest score in the Middle East cluster (5.35 out of a 7-point scale)" (House et al., 2004).

2 Team oriented

This type of leaders creates effective teams with clear purpose and targets. "Highest score are in Latin American cluster (5.96); lowest score are in Middle East cluster (5.47) in 7-point scale" (House et al., 2004).

3 Participative

This type of leaders incorporate subordinates into the decision-making process and implementation of decisions. "Highest score are in Germanic Europe cluster (5.86); lowest score are in Middle East cluster (4.97)"(House et al., 2004).

4 Humane oriented

This type of leaders reflects compassion and generosity. According to GLOBE, however, they contribute only moderately in outstanding leadership. "Highest score are in Southern Asia cluster (5.38); lowest score are in Nordic Europe cluster (4.42)"(House et al., 2004). It is impossible to believe that most corrupt leaders of the Indian private sector, who systematically rob the banks and close down their factories leaving thousands of workers as destitute, can be also "humane."

5 Autonomous

This type of leaders is independent and individualistic. "Highest score are in Eastern Europe cluster (4.20); lowest score in Latin America cluster (3.51)" (House et al., 2004). Although we would have expected that Anglo-American leadership has this kind of characteristic, according to GLOBE, Anglo culture promotes democracy and fairness.

6 Self-protective

This type of leaders promotes the security of the individual, that is, themselves. It is self-centered and face-saving in its approach. Highest scores are in the Southern Asia cluster (3.83) and lowest in Nordic Europe (2.72). However, this is the typical characteristic of the Anglo culture.

Japanese Culture in the Globe project gives some idea about Japan that can be misleading.

According to the GLOBE project, in the management culture in Japan, performance orientation is medium, assertiveness is low, future orientation is medium, humane orientation is medium, institutional collectivism is high, in group collectivism is relatively high, gender egalitarianism is low, power distance is relatively high, and uncertainty avoidance is medium.

With regard to leadership, the GLOBE project results suggest, Japanese leadership is charismatic and team oriented, contribute slightly on participation and humane orientation, but has no impact on autonomous and self-protectiveness.

The interesting point is that both Japan and China scores are almost the same on both the account of culture and leadership, but in reality, these cultures are very different. It comes from the fact GLOBE does not differentiate between a Chinese and Japanese. According to GLOBE, they are both in the Confucius-cultural sphere, which is a debatable concept.

However, Chew and Putti (1995) and Yeh (1988) argue that the nature of collectivism is different between China and Japan. Chinese collectivism is family oriented, where people demonstrate loyalty to their family, relatives, party, and their close relationship with the government called "Guanxi." On the other hand, the Japanese demonstrate collectivism to workplaces and show loyalty to their firms. Yonaha (2011) discusses such differences stem from difference in political-economic systems of the two countries since the sixteenth century. He argues that "Japanese tend to identify themselves with both their community and workplace and consider their neighbours in such communities as their in-group, even if they do not share family relationships." For Chinese, family ties are necessary to accept one another in the collective unit.

GLOBE does not recognize that market institutions in Japan and China are also very different. Hall and Soskice (2001) argued that the Japanese institutional system involves long-term employment and consensual decision-making process inclusive of people throughout the firm. In China the labor market is fluid, job security is generally low, and decision-making power is concentrated in top management (Witt, 2011). The Japanese system tied them to firms, whereas the Chinese system makes stronger family ties as a source of security. Thus, GLOBE has a pro-Chinese and an anti-Japanese bias.

GLOBE study refuses to accept that Japan was not influenced by Confucian ideas, but by its own Bushido culture of the Samurai clans. But there are differences in the leadership style and employee expectation of leadership traits and behaviors between Japan and China (Shim and Steers, 2012; Yu and Meyer-Ohle, 2008).

Japanese respect very highly a leader who "creates a work climate that promotes cooperation among individuals," who "not only evaluates individual goal attainments but also their support to others," and who "makes decisions that prioritize the entire company's success" (Lee, Yoshikawa, Reade, and Arai, 2013; Shim and Steers, 2012). This cooperative and collective orientation was very highly rated by Japanese, but not by the Chinese. Japanese workers respect highly leaders who "not only appreciate results but also cares about process," and who "appreciates not only the member's achieved results but also their challenges in the process regardless of the results" (Lee et al., 2013). The Chinese workers do not have these considerations.

Chinese respondents clearly favor performance-based pay and promotion and are interested in fast promotion based on short-term goal achievement. Chinese employees prefer a transactional, particularistic leadership approach focused on individual, short-term goal attainment, while Japanese employees prefer a more paternalistic leadership approach focused on the collective good (Lee et al., 2013).

The Chinese labor market has experienced significant reform during the past two decades, and the stable, secure employment relationship has been dismantled. The employment relationship has taken the form of a fixed-period contract basis, and employees are prone to dismissal by employers (Witt, 2011). Once unemployed, individuals cannot receive social welfare such as healthcare. Thus, employees are exposed to considerable risks. It is likely that these external economic conditions create a "strong situation" (Mischel, 1977), "where employee behaviour is guided by the situation rather than by individual attributes such as personality, values and attitudes."

Young Chinese, born after the beginning of economic reform in 1978, are less collectivistic than elder generations (Sun and Wang, 2010). Ralston, Holt, Terpstra, and Kai-Cheng (2008) found that the introduction of capitalism results in individualistic work values. In China, state-owned firms and private/foreign firms form two distinct labor markets (Witt, 2011). State-owned firms tend to be associated with job security and work–life balance, whereas foreign firms are linked with international careers and challenging jobs. This suggests that employees in foreign firms may have a stronger interest in personal development and be more divergent from traditional culture. Chinese employees want leaders who will provide role clarity, and a clear link between pay and performance; this is fueled by institutional and economic uncertainty. Chinese employees prefer decisive leaders, and cultural values in China are likely to be more individualistic than in previous generations (Lee et al., 2013).

While Japanese respect their ideal leader as someone who drives collective goal attainment and creates a cooperative work environment, these characteristics did not figure highly in the Chinese image of their ideal leader. An ideal leader from the eyes of Chinese is the person who is "flexible and adaptable according to the changes in situations, as well as individual employees" (Shim and Steers, 2012). The interaction of traditional cultural values and modern economic development creates a unique set of work values (Ralston et al., 2008; Shenkar, 2012; Zaheer, Schomaker, and Nachum, 2012). The findings raise the question on the GLOBE findings on "Confucian Asian cluster."

Japanese leadership style

Japan is well-known for its paternalistic approach to leadership. Japanese culture promotes a high safety or security need, which is present both among home-country-based employees as well as MNC expatriates. The classic study (Haire et al., 1966) examined the cultural orientations of 522 employees of 28 Japanese-owned firms in the United States and found that the native Japanese employees were more likely to value paternalistic company behavior than their US counterparts. However, major differences appear in leadership approaches used by the Japanese and those in other location in Asia.

Haire, Ghiselli, and Porter study (1966) discussed earlier findings that Japanese managers have much greater belief in the capacity of subordinates for leadership and initiative than do most other countries. The Japanese also expressed attitudes toward the use of participation to a greater degree than others. In the other two leadership dimensions of sharing information and objectives and using internal control, the Japanese respondents were above average, but not distinctive. Overall, however, this classic research study found that the Japanese respondents scored highest on the four areas of leadership combined. In other words, they do provide evidence that the Japanese leaders have considerable confidence in the overall ability of their subordinates and use a style that allows subordinates to actively participate in decisions. Haire et al. (1966) study, although now quite dated, is more reliable than the biased study of the GLOBE project (House et al., 2004; Javidan and Dastmalchian, 2009) or of Hofstede (2002).

Japanese system of strategic management is a complete philosophy of organization, which can affect every part of the enterprise. There are three unique basic ingredients in the Japanese management system in whole: lean production system, total quality management, and human resources management (Nohara, 1985). These three ingredients are interlinked to produce total effect on the management of Japanese enterprises. As Japanese overseas affiliates are part of the parent company, their human resources management is part of the human resources management of the parent company (Shimada, 1993; Morita, 1992).

Now we will describe in detail some approaches of human resource management, including some characteristics of the Japanese leadership style, which have been observed by us in various plants of the major three Japanese automobile MNCs such as the Nissan Motor Co., the Toyota Motor Co., and the Honda Motor Co. during our research program supported by Nagasaki University, Japan. The study provides the most common characteristics of leadership style of the major Japanese automobile MNCs.

Leadership style of the Nissan Motor Co.

The Nissan Motor Co. (Japan) aims to build profitably the highest quality car sold in to achieve the maximum possible customer satisfaction and thus ensure the prosperity of the company and its staff. The all Nissan's plants located in host countries have same management philosophy in accordance of the one from the Nissan of Japan.

Human resource management system in the Nissan Motor Co.

The aim of the personnel management system in Nissan's plant both in home and host countries is "to create the mutual trust and cooperation between all people within the plant." It involves with encouraging by top management the workers who are trying to make a significant contribution to business process, who are working together toward a common objective, and who are continuously seeking the ways to improve every aspect of the business. It aims for flexibility in the sense of expanding the role of all staff to the maximum extent possible and puts quality consciousness as the key responsibility above the all.

The production system builds on quality rather than on inspection and rectifications. These strict targets are assisted by the fact that the company gives common terms and conditions of employment to all staff members. For example, every employee in a Japanese plant has the fixed salary compare with the Western system, where the employees have wage according with quantity of the work/hours. In Japanese, plants every employee has the fixed sickness benefit scheme and private medical insurance, and company is paying approximately 33–44 percent of the medical care. Also compared to Western plants in Japanese plants both in home and host country, there are no time clocks and special discipline-controllers checking the exact time of worker's arrival on the working place. The performance appraisal system and cafeteria are the same for all staff, including the general manager, at Nissan's plants both in home and host countries.

The main element of the human resource management in Nissan's plants both in home and host countries is training. The company believes that "high caliber, well trained and motivated people are the key to success." Thus, the training expenditure in Nissan's represented 5.6 percent of total payroll costs with the training time taking 4 percent of staff members' time. This emphasis on training has resulted into a sharp increase in the productivity of the Nissan's plants in host countries. For example, the productivity level of the British workers at the beginning of the Nissan's operation in the United Kingdom was very low compared to the productivity level of Nissan's operations in Japan; however, just after one year of extensive training of the British workers both in UK and in Japan plants, the productivity level increased up to 78 percent.

Leadership style in the Nissan Motor Co.

To examine the characteristics of the leadership style in Nissan, we have taken survey by offering the questionnaire to the Nissan's shop-flow workers and managers of the middle and top levels both in the home country and in host country (United Kingdom) to determine the features of the leadership style in the Nissan's plant and whether or not the leadership style differs in home and host country of the same MNC. Unfortunately, we have got much less response than we expected from home county employees compared with host country (United Kingdom) employees in Nissan. However, the given survey and the opinion of the employees, which was expressed by answering the questions from questionnaire "Leadership style in the Nissan Motor Co." allowed us to make the following conclusions: the leadership style used in Nissan both in home and host countries is rather paternalistic and very Japanese in nature; the top managers are 100 percent Japanese in home plants and 99 percent Japanese expatriates in host countries to implement the home business culture at host country; the main aim of the leadership is to increase the motivation of the employees and, therefore, to increase the productivity by driving out class distinctions that exists in other industries in Western society, where the managerial staffs and ordinary workers live separate life, with separate facilities, and implementing "the equal opportunity for every employee" strategy.

   Also, our survey shows also that the "personnel conflict" is not an important factor in the conflict. Analyzing the answers on our questionnaires, we came to conclusion that the causes of the conflict are rather objective than subjective, such as development of new markets and geographical diversifications along with the government regional policies.

Leadership style of the Toyota Motor Co.

The Toyota Motor Co. (Japan) aim is to satisfy the customer by providing the highest quality at the lowest possible cost in the shortest possible time by operating the unique strategic technique such as just-in-time inventory–production management system.

   Toyota was established in Japan in 1937 and became a MNC during 1950s. Its first overseas production began in 1959 in Brazil. Expansion continued throughout the 1950s, 1960s, and 1970s with the opening of the overseas plants in Africa, South America, South-East Asia, and Australia. In 1985, a joint venture company was established in the United States, and in 1988, its own vehicle plants were established in the United States and Canada. All Toyota's plants located abroad have the same management philosophy following the one from Toyota of Japan.

Human resource management and leadership style in the Toyota Motor Co.

If we look at the organization chart of the Toyota Motor Co. in Japan and compare it with its overseas plants, we can see at every level that there are Japanese managers shadowing their local counterparts. However, recently, these local managers are in command in Toyota's plants in the United States, while Japanese managers are very few unlike in the Nissan Motor Co., which prefers to give managerial positions to Japanese expatriates maintaining the participative leadership style. For example, Toyota, UK is striving to build an organization in which all employees can develop to their full potential and is maintaining the very participative leadership style.

However, in the case of "internal management," the leadership style is rather paternalistic, similar to Nissan. It is important, nevertheless, that the job status and facilities are same for all staff members in most of the Japanese automobile MNCs both in home and host countries.

Teamwork is an essential element of Toyota's human resources management philosophy with belief that the well-coordinated group can accomplish for more than the sum of individual efforts. An average age of the workers is only 31. So, the young age of Toyota's workers is appropriate for continuous training.

The training process is a very important element of the human resources management in Toyota just like it is in any other Japanese automobile MNCs such as in Nissan or in Honda. The training facilities are available within the production system in Toyota's plants in home country, as well as in the most host countries. About 100,000 man/days are spent on training prior to production startup. Training facilities are available in all locations throughout the world. For example, the British workers can go for training in Japan, United States, and Canada, and the workers from Toyota's foreign and Japanese establishments can come to Britain for training. Since the start of production, a further 20,000 man/days in Toyota usually are spent on specific "of-the-job" training courses; the costs and time which have been spent on continuous "on-the-job" training courses are almost immeasurable.

Leadership style of the Honda Motor Co.

The Honda Motor Co.' strategic planning philosophy is to achieve the main goal to satisfy the customer by providing the highest quality at the lowest possible cost in the shortest possible time by using the corporate policy that emphasizes originality, innovation, and efficiency in every step of its operations-from product developments and manufacturing to marketing.

Established 70 years ago in Japan, Honda Motor Co. Ltd. became one of the leading manufacturers of automobiles and the largest manufacturer of motorcycles in the world. The company is recognized internationally for its expertise and leadership in developing and manufacturing a wide variety of products ranging from general purpose engines to special sports cars that incorporate Honda's highly efficient internal combustion engine technology. By following a corporate policy that emphasizes originality, innovation, and efficiency in every step of its operations from product development and manufacturing to marketing, Honda has strived to attain its goal to satisfy its customers. Through a worldwide commitment of advancing their goal Honda and its many partners have succeeded in creating a global network with 89 production facilities in 33 countries that supply Honda products to most countries in the world.

Human resource management and leadership style in the Honda Motor Co.

The organizational structure in Honda's plants in host countries is more or less similar to Toyota's and Nissan's plants. However, in Honda's plants located in host countries, the Japanese managers are not shadowing their host countries' managers. Also, the leadership style on Honda's plants in host countries is very participative compared to the leadership style of other major Japanese MNCs.

After visiting the HONDA plants both in Japan and the United Kingdom, we have postulated the following conclusions: the philosophy and the basic aim of the human resources management and leadership of the Honda Motor Co. is to establish the teamwork; and the culture of teamwork exists throughout the company, breaking down many of the natural barriers between individuals and making apparently impossible tasks achievable. Honda has developed its own unique approach in human resource management to work through NHC (New Honda Circles)/groups of Associates (i.e., workers and managers) who are taking responsibility for changing their own working environment to improve safety, to build quality into the process, to be more efficient in business, and to improve their place of work; the teams sometime travel to the Honda plant in another country to analyze and solve problem in that plant and receive in the process understanding of how to use different techniques of different groups. By valuing the Associate's opinions, Honda can make changes that improve working conditions, motivate, create a better understanding, and improve the overall quality of Honda's products worldwide.

Comparative analysis of the Japanese and the Western leadership styles

The Japanese leadership style differs from the Western leadership style in a number of ways. The classic study of Haire et al. (1966) found that, except for internal control, large US firms tend to be more democratic than small ones, whereas in Japan, the profile is quite different.

A second difference is that younger Western managers appear to express more democratic attitudes than do their older counterparts on all four leadership dimensions, but younger Japanese fall into this category only in sharing information and objectives and in the use of internal control.

One of the most commonly cited reasons for different leadership styles between Japanese and Western managers is that each has a basically different philosophy of managing people. William Ouchi (1981) put forwards author the idea of Theory Z that combines Japanese and US assumptions and approaches. The Japanese leadership approach is group oriented, paternalistic, and concerned with the employee's work and personal life. The US leadership approach is almost the opposite.

Another difference between Japanese and the Western leadership styles is how senior-level managers process information and learn. Japanese executives are taught and tend to use *variety amplification*, which is the creation of uncertainty and the analysis of many alternatives regarding future action.

By contrast, Western executives are taught and tend to use *variety reduction*, which is the limiting of uncertainty and the focusing of action on a limited number of alternatives. When this study of processing information and learning examined the leadership styles used by Japanese and US senior managers, it found that the Japanese focused very heavily on problems, but the US managers focused on opportunities. The Japanese used specific guidelines; the Americans opted for general guidelines. The Japanese were more willing to allow poor performance to continue for a time so that those who were involved would learn from their mistakes, but the Americans worked to stop poor performance as quickly as possible. Finally, the Japanese sought creative approaches to managing projects and tried to avoid relying on experience, but the Americans sought to build on their experiences. Still another major reason accounting for differences in leadership styles is that the Japanese tend to be more ethnocentric than their US counterparts. The Japanese think of themselves as Japanese managers who are operating overseas; most do not view themselves as international managers. As a result, even if they do adapt their leadership approach on the surface to those of the country in which they are operating, they still believe deep down in the Japanese way of doing things and are reluctant to abandon it. For example, the study (Haire et al., 1966), shows that many Japanese managers are very ethno-centric oriented during their international assignments. The United States, with double digit billions in direct Japanese investment, is one of the major places where the Japanese managers end up. Unfortunately, for many, this US assignment often turns out to be more of a hardship tour than an enjoyable experience. The major reason is that the Japanese managers find themselves caught between two cultures. On the one hand, they must adapt to US values; on the other hand, they do not want to lose their Japanese ways. In addition, most Japanese want to send their children to universities back home, where they have to pass very difficult, but important, entrance examinations. Getting them prepared for these exams while living in the United States is no easy task. Yet the problems run deeper than just their children's education.

As Japanese business-people begin to become part of the local community, their lifestyle starts to change. Unlike social customs in Japan, in the United

States, they find themselves and their spouses socializing a great deal more. They also find that their children soon become fluent in English and speak Japanese only at home. Worse yet, the Japanese find that their way of doing business is strange to Americans. The Japanese solicit everyone's opinion and methodically make calm decisions. American managers get the facts that they feel are important and make rapid-fire decisions. In the process, they may do some yelling and screaming. Japanese often find this approach not only strange, but absolutely inappropriate for business and sometimes even frightening.

Perhaps the biggest challenge facing Japanese expatriates is to adopt the Western methods without becoming too reliant on them. Japanese managers do not want to return home and be labeled as "Americanized." For example, a repatriated Japanese manager has to deliberately be patient and methodical when making decisions. Any sign of discontent with the typical consensus style used by the Japanese is likely to be regarded by the repatriated Japanese manager's peers as an example of becoming Americanized – something that needs to be stamped out. In fact, repatriated managers who are identified as having become too Americanized are likely to be assigned to a small office in a remote locale in Japan until they change their ways.

Of course, not everyone on an international assignment returns to Japan. A few Japanese managers like living in their overseas location and simply change jobs and work for a local firm. However, more than 95 percent do return, and for them, the challenge is one of fitting back in as quickly and smoothly as possible.

International context

Leadership is a complex and controversial process that can be defined as influencing people to direct their efforts toward the achievement of some particular goal or goals. In providing a foundation for the study of leadership in an international setting, two areas warrant attention: philosophical assumptions about people in general and leadership styles. The philosophical foundation is grounded in Douglas McGregor's Theories X and Y. Leadership styles relate to how managers treat their subordinates and incorporate authoritarian, paternalistic, and participative approaches. These styles can be summarized in terms of Likert's management system (Hall, 1972) or styles data from the classical Haire, Chiselli, and Porter study (1966), although as mentioned is now quite dated, do show, nevertheless, the differences in the attitudes toward leadership practices between European managers. In most cases, these leaders tend to reflect more participative and democratic attitudes, but not in every country. In addition, organizational level, company size, and age seem to greatly influence attitudes toward leadership. Since many of the young people in this study are now middle-aged, European managers, in general, are highly likely to be more participative than their older counterparts of the 1960s and 1970s. However, no empirical evidence proves that each generation of European managers are becoming more participative than the previous one. Also, just because they express favorable attitudes toward participative leadership does not mean they actually practice this approach. More research that actually observes today's European managers' style in their day-to-day jobs is needed before any definitive conclusions can be drawn.

The attitudes of Western managers toward dimensions of leadership practice such as the capacity for leadership and initiative, sharing information and objectives, participation, and internal control were examined in a classic study by Haire et al. (1966). They found that the Europeans, as a composite, had a relatively low opinion of the capabilities of the average person, coupled with a relatively positive belief in the necessity for participative leadership styles.

The study also found that these European managers' attitudes were affected by the hierarchical level, company size, and age. However, overall European managers espouse very participative leadership style. It is a very significant fact that Japanese MNCs being representatives of just one country from East Asia can dramatically influence the Western countries. The Japanese managers in the Haire et al. (1996) study had a much greater belief in the capacity of subordinates for leadership and initiative than did most other countries. The Japanese managers also expressed a more favorable attitude toward a participative leadership style than managers in most other countries. In terms of sharing information and objectives and using "internal control" the Japanese responded above average but were not distinctive. In a number of ways Japanese leadership styles differed from Americans. The company size and age of the managers are two factors that seem to affect these differences. Other reasons include the basic philosophy of managing people, how information is processed, and the high degree of ethnocentrism by the Japanese. However, some often overlooked similarities are important, such as how effective Japanese leaders manage high-achieving and low-achieving subordinates.

The main conclusion about the leadership style of the major Japanese automobile MNCs such as the Nissan Motor Co., the Toyota Motor Co., and the Honda Motor Co. have been obtained during our research and can be summarized as follows:

1   There are two main elements influencing the human resource management of Japanese MNCs, which have been introduced into Western human resource management in the past ten years from 1986 to 1996: a commitment to *Kaizen* or continuous improvement; cooperative relationships between workers, managers, and suppliers; and strong inclination to change the paternalistic leadership style to participative one in plants located in home country.
2   Before the establishments of Japanese manufacturing bases in the United States and Europe, American and European managers were reluctant to utilize these concepts because of their fear that they may lead to serious industrial disturbances because of social/cultural differences. However, with the entering of Japanese automobile MNCs in the Western business world, it has become a compulsion to introduce the Japanese style of management, including the Japanese leadership style to American and European management in order to increase the level of productivity of the workforce up to the Japanese level.

3   Japanese MNCs' influence is not limited to the motor industry. Top managers and humen resources managers from all host countries are coming to Japanese automobile MNCs overseas plants to get training in management and to learn the Japanese leadership techniques. Some, of the larger companies in Europe and the United States are having difficulties to accept Japanese standards because of the social/cultural differences between Japan and the Western world. However, despite of these facts, the governments of the host countries have sponsored the lot teams of experts to learn human resources management techniques from Japanese automobile MNCs.

Thus, Japanese leadership style of the leading Japanese automobile MNCs such as the Nissan Motor Co., the Toyota Motor Co. and the Honda Motor Co. has a significant influenceon Western human resources management on one side, and on the other side, it is absorbing the best features of the Western leadership style of the host countries to achieve the best relationship between the managers, as a leaders and workforce, and therefore, to significantly improve the quality and to increase the productivity worldwide.

Leadership is a complex and controversial process that can be defined as influencing people to direct their efforts toward the achievement of some particular goal or goals. In providing a foundation for the study of leadership in an international setting, two areas warrant attention: philosophical assumptions about people in general and leadership styles. The philosophical foundation is grounded in Douglas McGregor's (1960) "Theories X and Y Leadership styles," which relate to how managers treat their subordinates and incorporate authoritarian, paternalistic, and participative approaches. Data from the study by Haire et al. (1966) examined the differences in the attitudes toward leadership practices among European managers. In most cases, these leaders tend to reflect more participative and democratic attitudes, but not in every country. In addition, the organizational level, company size, and age seem to influence the attitudes toward leadership in many ways. Since many of the young people in this study are now middle-aged, European managers, in general, are highly likely to be more participative than their older counterparts of the 1960s and 1970s. However, no empirical evidence proves that each generation of European managers are becoming more participative than the previous one. Also, just because they express favorable attitudes toward participative leadership does not mean they actually practice this approach. More research that actually observes today's European managers' style in their day-to-day operations is needed before any definitive conclusions can be drawn.

The attitudes of Western managers toward dimensions of leadership practice such as the capacity for leadership and initiative, sharing information and objectives, participation, and internal control were examined in the study by Haire et al. (1966) They found that the Europeans, as a composite, had a relatively low opinion of the capabilities of the average person coupled with a relatively positive belief in the necessity for participative leadership styles. The study also found that these European managers' attitudes were affected by the hierarchical level, company size, and age. However, overall European managers espouse a very participative leadership style.

It is very significant fact that Japanese MNCs being representatives of just one country from East Asia can dramatically influence the Western countries. The Japanese managers had a much greater belief in the capacity of subordinates for leadership and initiative than did most other countries. The Japanese managers also expressed a more favorable attitude toward a participative leadership style than managers in most other countries. In terms of sharing information and objectives and using "internal control," the Japanese are above average, but not distinctive. In a number of ways, Japanese leadership styles differed from the Western style. The company size and age of the managers are two factors that seem to affect these differences. Other reasons include the basic philosophy of managing people, how information is processed, and the high degree of ethnocentrism by the Japanese. However, some often overlooked similarities are important, such as how effective Japanese leaders manage high-achieving and low-achieving subordinates.

The main conclusions about the leadership style of the major Japanese automobile MNCs such as the Nissan Motor Co. and the Toyota Motor Co. have been obtained during our research and can be summarized as follows.

There are two main elements influencing the human resource management of Japanese MNCs that were introduced into the Western human resource management from 1986 to 1996: a commitment to *Kaizen* or continuous improvement; cooperative relationships between workers, managers, and suppliers; and a strong tendency to change the paternalistic leadership style to a participative one in plants located in home country.

Before the establishment of Japanese manufacturing bases in the United States and Europe, American and European managers were reluctant to utilize these concepts because of their fear that they would lead to serious industrial disturbances because of several social and cultural differences. However, with the entry of Japanese automobile MNC in the Western business world, it has become a compulsion to introduce Japanese style of management, including Japanese leadership style in American and European management to increase the level of productivity of the workforce up to the Japanese level.

Japanese MNCs' influence is not limited to the motor industry. Top managers and HR managers from all host countries are coming to Japanese automobile MNCs overseas plants to get training in management and to learn the Japanese leadership techniques. Some of the larger companies in Europe and the United States are having difficulties to accept Japanese standards due to social and cultural differences between Japan and Western world. However, despite of this fact, the governments of host countries have sponsored teams of experts to learn human resources management techniques from Japanese automobile MNCs.

Thus, the leadership style of the leading Japanese automobile MNCs, such as the Nissan Motor Co. and the Toyota Motor Co., has a significant influence on the Western human resources management system. At the same time, Japanese managers are absorbing the best features of the Western leadership style from the host countries to achieve the optimum relationship between the managers and the workforce. The Japanese system is undergoing serious transitions mainly due to the acquisitions of management controls of some of the major Japanese multinational companies by Western companies. Nissan is now controlled by Renault, and as a result, it is going through structural changes including downsizing, which is certainly affecting the leadership style, organizational culture, and human resource management system Although Toyota is so far unaffected by any of these, it is not immune to the influences of managerial transformations that are taking place in Japan. Thus, the future directions of the organizational cultures and leadership styles in Japan are uncertain.

Appendix 1

Leadership style in the Nissan Motor Co.: Britain and Japan –questionnaire

Would your superior show disapproval of a member who regularly arrived late for work by a certain amount of time?

Answer (a): It does not happen; Mean = 4.79; S. D = .18
Answer (b): It does not happen; Mean =- 4.93, S. D = .26

How many hours per week is your superior usually at work, compared to other members of the group?

Answer (a): 39 hours or like others; Mean = 4.99; S. D = .01
Answer (b): 40 hours or like others, Mean = 4.98 S. D = .04

How many hours per week is your superior usually at work compared to official work hours?

Answer (a): For all the official hours; Mean = 4.98; S. D = .07
Answer (b): For all the official hours; Mean = 4.96; S. D = .16

How does your superior dress at work, compared to others in the group?

Answer (a): Same as others; Mean = 3.79; S. D = .15
Answer (b): Same as others; Mean = 4.82; S. D = .34

Where does your superior usually eat lunch?

Answer (a): In the same canteen with others; Mean = 3.51; S. D = .27
Answer (b): In the same canteen with others; Mean = 4.21; S. D = .38

How often does your superior eat lunch with other members of the group?

Answer (a): Always; Mean = 4.67; S. D = .27
Answer (b): Always; Mean = 3.58; S. D = .45

When members experience personal difficulties, do they tell their superior about them?

Answer (a): Yes; Mean = 2.21; S. D = .78
Answer (b): Yes; Mean = 4.79; S. D = .89

When your superior learns that a member is experiencing personal difficulties, does your superior discuss the matter sympathetically with the person concerned?

Answer (a): Yes; Mean = 2.85; S. D = .56
Answer (b): Yes; Mean = 3.89; S. D = .18

When your superior learns that a member is experiencing personal difficulties, does your superior discuss the matter in the person's absence with other members?

Answer (a): Sometime; Mean = 2.97; S. D = .85
Answer (b): Sometime; Mean = 3.57; S. D = .35

When your superior learns that a member is experiencing personal difficulties, does your superior arrange for other members to help with the person's workloads?

Answer (a): Yes; Mean = 3.51; S. D = .32
Answer (b): Yes; Mean = 3.76; S. D = .26

On average, how often does your superior check with members concerning the quality of their work?

Answer (a): Continuously; Mean = 4.87; S. D = .13
Answer (b): Continuously; Mean = 4.98; S. D = .07

On average, how often does your superior talk about progress in relation to a work schedule?

Answer (a): Regularly in weekly meeting: Sometime more often than that.
Mean = 4.37; S. D =.32
Answer (b): Regularly in weekly meeting: Sometime more often than that.
Mean = 4.93; S. D = .38

On average, how often does your superior demonstrate or us any of the equipment used by the group?

Answer (a): Training is part of the work so when ever needed; Mean = 4.76; S. D = .24
Answer (b): Training is part of the work so when ever needed; Mean = 4.97; S. D =.21

On average, how often does your superior instruct you on how to increase your job skills?

Answer (a): Whenever needed; Mean = 4.86; S. D = .32
Answer (b): Whenever needed; Mean = 4.98; S. D = .11

On average, how often does your superior send you written notes or memos instead of speaking to you in person?

Answer (a): That is not the practice to use written notes;
Mean = 4.92; S. D =.16
Answer (b): That is not the practice to use written notes,
Mean =-4.04; S. D =.37

On average, how often does your superior explain to you how to carry out a new task?

Answer (a): Always; Mean = 4.78; S. D = .31
Answer (b): Always; Mean = 4.98; S. D = .26

About how many suggestions for work improvements would your superior hope that you would make each month?

Answer (a): As many as possible; Mean = 3.85; S. D = .27
Answer (b): As many as possible; Mean = 4.05; S. D = .36

When group members make suggestions for improvements, what does your superior usually do?

Answer (a): Members can discuss in group meeting; Mean = 4.71; S. D = .31
Answer (b): Members can discuss in group meeting; Mean = 4.89; S. D = .21

For what proportion of the day are you within sight of your superior?

Answer (a): Most of the time or sometime less, it depends on the type of work;
Mean = 4.67; S. D = .32
Answer (b): Most of the time; Mean = 4.65; S. D = .15

(20) How often do you spend time with your superior socially?

Answer (a): There are social clubs, sports club we all join; Mean = 4.75; S. D =.31
Answer (b): There are social clubs, sports club we all join; Mean = 4.95;
S. D = .07

How often do you spend time with your superior discussing your career plans?

Answer (a): Whenever needed; Mean = 3.06; S. D = .38
Answer (b): Whenever needed; Mean = 3.67; S. D = .45

How often do you spend time with your superior talking about immediate work problems?

Answer (a): Whenever needed; Mean = 4.32; S. D = .35
Answer (b): Whenever needed; Mean = 4.89; S. D = .09

Does your superior's evaluation depend more on your own work or on that of the group as a whole?

Answer (a): We work as a group; Mean = 4–87; S. D = .37
Answer (b): We work as a group; Mean = 4.91; S. D = .32

How much of your entitlement to paid holidays did you take in the twelve months?

Answer (a): All; Mean = 4.5 S. D = .34
Answer (b): Most but not All; Mean = 4.2; S. D = .28

How often do you work more – hours than those for which you are paid?

Answer (a): We don't do; Mean – =4.45; S. D = .37
Answer (b): We don't do; Mean = 3.42 S. D = .48

On average, how often does your superior meet the group for social or recreational purpose outside working hours?

Answer (a): Quite often; Mean = 4.2; S. D = .35
Answer (b): Quite often; Mean = 4.67; S. D = .17

What does your superior do when he or she believes that there is a substantial problem in the group's work procedures?

Answer (a): Discuss in the group meeting, invite suggestions; Mean = 4.31; S. D = .39
Answer (b): Discuss in the group meeting, invite suggestions; Mean 4.98; S. D = .13

Who is consulted when substantially new work procedures are being discussed?

Answer (a): Training department, all associates; Mean = 4.96; S. D = .17
Answer (b): Training department, all associates; Mean = 4.99; S. D = .01

How do you address your superior?

Answer (a): By name, which are written on our uniform; Mean -= 4.-56; S. D = .34
Answer (b): By name, which are written on our uniform; Mean = 3.45; S. D = .32

How much of the information available to your superior concerning the organization's plans and performance is shared with the group?

Answer (a): We share every detail; Mean = 3.05; S. D = .26
Answer (b): We share every detail; Mean = 3.56; S. D = .38

How often does this group as a whole have meetings with your superior?

Answer (a): At least once a week; Mean = 4.86; S. D = .14
Answer (b): At least once a week; Mean = 4.98; S. D = .01

How many hours do you usually spend discussing work problems with three or more People from your own workgroup at the same time?

Answer (a): It varies from group to group; Mean = 4.56; S. D = .32
Answer (b): It varies from group to group; Mean = 4.88; S. D = .06

How frequently do you communicate with members of other workgroup in the organization on the same level as yourself?

Answer (a): Quite often; Mean = 4.21; S. D = .39
Answer (b): Quite often; Mean = 4.02; S. D = .18

(34) How does your superior react when you communicate with members of other workgroups?

Answer (a): With encouragement and sympathy; Mean = 3.52; S. D = .38
Answer (b): With encouragement and sympathy; Mean = 3.89; S. D = .27

(35) How does your superior react when you help co – workers with their work problems?

Answer (a): With encouragement and sympathy; Mean = 4.06; S. D = .38
Answer (b): With encouragement and sympathy; Mean = 4.85; S. D = .04

(36) How does your superior react when you undertake work additional to the hours for which you are paid?

Answer (a): That is not the practice; Mean = 4.576; S. D = .31
Answer (b): That is not the practice; Mean = 3.21; S. D = .35

Notes: Answer (a) is for the British plant, answer (b) is for the Japanese plant; the mean and standard deviation are calculated using a Likert scale (Likert, 1932) from 1 (disagree) to 5 (strongly agree).

Appendix 2

Leadership styles in the Toyota Motor Co.; British and Japanese: questionnaire

(1) Would your superior show disapproval of a member who regularly arrived late for work by a certain amount of time?

Answer (a): Yes, the team is closely controlled by the team leader;
Mean = 4.57; S. D -= .11
Answer (b): Yes, the team is closely controlled by the team leader;
Mean = 4.99; S. D = .02

How many hours per week is your superior usually at work, compared to other members of the group?

Answer (a): Same as others; Mean = 4.53; S. D = .32
Answer (b): Same as others; Mean = 4.24; S. D = .27

How many hours per week is your superior usually at work compared to official work hours?

Answer (a): Same; Mean = 4.57; S. D = .36
Answer (b): Same; Mean = 3.57; S. D = .31

How does your superior dress at work compared to others in compared to others in the group?

Answer (a): Same dress as others; Mean = 4.03; S. D = .37
Answer (b): Same dress as others; Mean = 4.97; S. D = .02

Where does your superior usually eat lunch?

Answer (a): Same canteen; Mean = 3.58; S. D = .25
Answer (b): Same canteen; Mean = 4.96; S. D = 28

How often does your superior cat lunch with other members of the group?

Answer (a): Regularly, but there are lunch time meetings sometimes for the team leaders only; Mean 4.53; S. D = .21

Answer (b): Regularly, but there are lunch time meetings sometimes for the team leaders only; Mean = 4.98; S. D = .03

When members experience personal difficulties, do they tell their superior about them?

Answer (a): Yes; Mean = 3.21; S. D = .32
Answer (b): sometime; Mean = 4.76; S. D = .16

When your superior learns that a member is experiencing personal difficulties, does your superior discuss the matter sympathetically, with the person concerned?

Answer (a): Yes; Mean = 3.5; S. D = .37
Answer (b): Yes; Mean = 3.02; S. D = .28

When your superior learns that a member is experiencing personal difficulties, does your superior discuss the matter in the person's absence with other members?

Answer (a): Yes; Mean = 2.58; S. D = .69
Answer (b): It is not normal; Mean = 3.98; S. D = .31

When your superior learns that a member is experiencing personal difficulties, does your superior arrange for other members to help with the person's work-loads

Answer (a): Yes; Mean = 3.53; S. D = .58
Answer (b) Sometime; Mean = 4.32; S. D = .39

(11) On average, how often does your superior cheek with members concerning the quality of their work?

Answer (a): Regularly, daily; Mean -= 4.86; S. D = .14
Answer (b): Regularly, daily; Mean = 4.99; S. D = .01

(12) On average, how often does your superior talk about progress in relation to a work schedule?

Answer (a): Regularly; Mean -= 4.04; S. D = .21
Answer (b): Regularly; Mean = 4.67; S. D = .08

On average, how often does your superior demonstrate or use any of the equipment used by the group?

Answer (a): Regularly; Mean = 4.09; S. D = .35
Answer (b): Regularly; Mean = 4.89; S. D = .21

On average, how often does your superior instruct you on how to increase your job skills?

Answer (a): Regularly; Mean = 3.78; S. D = .38
Answer (b): Regularly; Mean = 4.88; S. D = .17

On average, how often does your superior send you written notes or memos instead of speaking to you in person?

Answer (a): Regularly; Mean = 4.01; S. D = .45
Answer (b): Almost never; Mean = 4.35; S. D = .27

On average, how often does your superior explain to you how to carry out a net task?

Answer (a): Regularly, no fixed number; Mean = 4.67; S. D = .38
Answer (b): Regularly, no fixed number; Mean = 4.82; S. D = .14

(17) About how many suggestions for work improvements would your superior hope that you would make each month?

Answer (a): As many as possible; Mean = 4.57; S. D = .25
Answer (b): As many as possible; Mean = 4. 82; S. D = .42

When group members make suggestions for improvements, what does your superior usually do?

Answer (a): Examine and sometime accept; Mean = 4.42; S. D = .31
Answer (b): Examine and sometime accept; Mean = 4.27; S. D = .25

For what proportion of the day are you within sight of your superior?

Answer (a): Always; Mean = 4.51; S. D = .32
Answer (b): Most of the time; Mean = 4.38; S. D = .27

(20) How often do you spend time with your superior socially?

Answer (a): Often; Mean = 3.52; S. D = .36
Answer (b): Often; Mean = 4.06; S. D = .52

(21) How often do you spend time with your superior discussing your career plans?

Answer (a): 3 times per year at least; Mean = 3.01; S. D = .37
Answer (b): Not very often; Mean = 3.89; S. D = .35

(22) How often do you spend time with your superior talking about immediate work problems?

Answer (a): Always; Mean = 4.56; S. D = .38
Answer (b): Always; Mean = 4.89; S. D = .07

(23) Does your superior's evaluation depend more on your own work or on that of the group as a whole?

Answer (a): Individual performances; Mean = 3.7; S. D = .45
Answer (b): Performances of the group as a whole; Mean = 4.02; S. D = .37

How much of your entitlement to paid holidays did you take in the past twelve months?

Answer (a): Almost all, 25 days per year; Mean -=- 4.89; S. D -=.25
Answer (b): Not very much; Mean = 3.67; S. D = .48

How often do you work more hours than those for which you are paid?

Answer (a): Never; Mean = 4.30; S. D = .38
Answer (b): Never; Mean = 3.05; S. D .23

On average, how often does your superior meet the group for social or recreational purpose outside working hours?

Answer (a): Depends on group, every 2–3 months; Mean = 4.09; S. D = .22
Answer (b): Normally every day; Mean 4.2; S. D = .38

(27) What does your superior do when he or she believes that there is a substantial problem in the group's work procedures?

Answer (a): Discuss with the group; Mean = 4.30; S. D = .47
Answer (b): Discuss with the group; Mean = 4.24; S. D = .39

(28) Who is consulted when substantially new work procedures are being discussed?

Answer (a): Team leaders and workers; Mean = 3.58; S. D = .38
Answer (b): Team leaders and workers; Mean = 4.52; S. D = .31

(29) How do you address your superior?

Answer (a): First name always.; Mean = 3.02; S. D = .36
Answer (b): First name always.; Mean = 3.67; S. D = .24

How much of the information available to your superior concerning the organization's plans and performance is shared with the group?

Answer (a): All. Mean 3.03; S. D = .43
Answer (b): All. Mean = 3.67; S. D .32

How often does this group as a whole have meetings with your superior?

Answer (a): Several times a day. Mean = 4.01; S. D =- .34
Answer (b): Several times a day. Mean = 4.52; S. D = .32

How many hours do you usually spend discussing work problems with three or more people from your own workgroup at the same time?

Answer (a): Regular meeting.; Mean = 4.89; S. D = .26
Answer (b): Regular meeting; Mean = 4.98; S. D = .06

How frequently do you communicate with members of other workgroups in the organization on the same level as yourself?

Answer (a): Frequently. Mean = 3.56; S. D = .39
Answer (b): Frequently. Mean = 4.35; S. D = .36

(34) How does your superior react when you communicate with members of other workgroups?

Answer (a): Encourages; Mean = 3.76; S. D = .32
Answer (b): Encourages; Mean = 3.51; S. D = .25

(35) How does your superior react when you help co-workers with their work problems?

Answer (a): Gladly accept, appreciate; Mean = 3.05; S. D = 31
Answer (b): Gladly accept, appreciate; Mean = 4.34; S. D = .16

(36) How does your superior react when you undertake work additional to the hours for which you are paid?

Answer (a) – it does not happen here; Mean = 4.39; S. D = .35
Answer (b) – it does not happen here; Mean = 3.05; S. D = .28

Notes: Answer (a)is for the British plant, answer (b)is for the Japanese plant; the mean and standard deviation are calculated using a Likert scale (Likert, 1932) from 1 (disagree) to 5 (strongly agree).

4 Person–organization fit in Japan

In this chapter, we compare the ideal organizational culture as perceived by the employees and the organizational culture they observe in reality in both the parent operation of a Japanese multinational company (MNC) and in its subsidiary operation in Thailand. If the ideal and the observed organizational culture are similar, then a "person–organization fit" exists in that organization. As a result of this harmony, the committed employees are expected to give their best to maximize the potentiality of the organization. For a multinational company, it is not enough, as foreign subsidiaries provide important intermediate products along with the market for final products, manufactured either in the parent company or in the subsidiaries. Thus, a person–organization fit should be ideally achieved both in the parent operation and in the subsidiaries.

Value characteristics in Japanese companies

In a Japanese company, the leadership styles and the organizational culture are designed by the human resources management (HRM) system; these are not coming from outside as the leaders are recruited from inside the organization. Effective corporate performance is the result of these underlying determinants of organizational culture and leadership style. Thus, in a Japanese organization, the leadership style is rooted in the HRM system, which emerges from the values of the organizational culture (Sekiguchi, 2006).

An organization with informal cultural control relies on an implicit organization-wide culture within the organization for the control of the members of that organization. In a classical bureaucratic model of organization, control relies on the use of explicit formal rules and regulations. Japanese organizations follow the first type of control through culture (Baliga and Jaeger, 1985). Japanese corporations have strived to fulfill that goal to create a harmonious organizational climate through the corporate management system and operations management system not only for their main operation in Japan, but also in their overseas subsidiaries (Basu, Miroshnik, and Uchida, 2001; Miroshnik, 2012, 2009). Japanese management system utilizing its layers of value system effectively tries to utilize strategic entrepreneurship inherent within its value system. This can be done by combining environmental, organizational, and personal attributes into a dynamic process of creation of opportunities to enhance competitiveness (Pascale and Athos, 1982; Hayashi, 1989, 2003).

In a Japanese company, control is based on a broad organizational culture (Ouchi, 1981). This type of company, "Type J," is different from the American style of organization (Type A) and the emerging Western global ideal style (Type Z). A Type Z company has values, which are shared by the members of the organization, as well as model code of conducts for the members. Type A has explicit formalized control. Type J has implicit informal control. Type Z has implicit informal control with explicit formalized measures. In Type J, responsibility is collective. In both Type A and Type Z, responsibility is upon the individuals. In a Type A, subsidiary would have a reasonable flexibility to adapt to the local laws and customs. Type J and Type Z may not allow these flexibilities.

An individualistic culture fits with American style organizations and a collectivist culture fits with Japanese style organizations (Kranias, 2000). The Japanese organizational culture of Type J was evolved in response to the changing industrial climates, and the national culture was manipulated to create an organizational culture suitable for efficient industrial performances. Scandinavian multinational companies appear to have some features similar to the above-mentioned Japanese-style organizations (Henson, 2012; Hedlund, 1994). Thus, the question is whether the Japanese-style organizational culture can be transmitted to a subsidiary in a country where the national culture is dissimilar to that of Japan.

Quantitative analysis of the organizational culture: procedure

To measure organizational culture and its impacts, this research has created a set of questionnaires. The method is to describe the central values that may be important to a worker's self-concept or identity as well as relevant to the organization's central value system.

The instrument to measure organizational culture included a set of value statements that could be used to assess both the extent to which certain values characterize a target organization and an individual's preference for that particular configuration of values. To develop a profile of an organization's culture, respondents familiar with the organization were to evaluate these value statements according to a Likert's scale. There are eight dimensions of the organizational culture (O'Reilly, Chatman, and Caldwell, 1991): (1) Innovation; (2) Entrepreneurship; (3) Decisiveness; (4) Emphasis on Security; (5) Supportiveness; (6) Emphasis on Performance; (7) Team orientation & Spirit; (8) Attention to detail or Preciseness. This research has adopted 25 items, which are related to the above value statements. Out of these 25 items, it is possible to identify eight factors that are similar to the eight dimensions as mentioned by O'Reilly et al. (1991). The reason for the adaptation of the methodology of O'Reiley is that it was used widely by nearly 200 other researchers (according to a Google Scholar search), and it has established psychometric properties and also satisfies the reliability criteria.

The full sets of questionnaires (in English, Japanese, and Thai) were distributed in various plants and offices of a Toyota automobile company in Japan. Altogether, 500 forms were distributed, and out of that, 300 employees have responded. After eliminating forms that were incomplete or wrongly filled, 150 answers were selected. Responses sought according to a 7-point Likert scale (Likert, 1932). The instrument contains a set of value statements that can be used to assess both the extent to which certain values characterize a target organization and an individual's preference for that particular configuration of values. In the questionnaire of this research, in order to measure organizational culture, there are 26 items, which can be distributed within these eight dimensions of the organizational culture mentioned above. The numbers of items were reduced following the approach of Cable and Judge (1997b).

In the Japanese sample (in Table 4.1), employees have long tenure. That would mean the employees in Japan have longer time to absorb the organizational culture. There are very few foreigners, if any at all. The employees are almost all men; there are few females. Most of the Japanese employees have not received training in cultural adaptations or foreign language because most of them would not work abroad.

Table 4.1 The characteristics of the sample in Japan

Items	Employees in Japan
Number of respondents	150
Gender	Male = 142, Female 8
Tenure	
Length of service (mean)	17.25 years
Age	
Under 35	27.5%
35–45	64.5%
Above 45	8%
Educational level	
Senior High School	12.0%
University Graduate	79.5%
Post-graduate	8.5%
Nationality	
Japanese	98%
Thai	0%
Other Asian	2%
Formal cultural training	
Posted abroad	4.5%
Received cultural training	15.6%
Received language training	13.6%

Statistical analysis for organizational culture in the parent operation of Toyota

In the questionnaire (in the Appendix to this chapter), there were 25 items described, which were divided into eight values as described below. These values were Innovation, Entrepreneurship, Decisiveness, Emphasis on Stability & Security, Supportiveness, Performance Orientations, Team Spirit, and Preciseness.

Definitions of values of organizational culture

OCJV1, Innovation; OCJV2, Entrepreneurship; OCJV3, Decisiveness; OCJV4, Stability & Security; OCJV5, Supportiveness; OCJV6, Emphasis on Performance; OCJV7, Team Spirit; OCJV8, Preciseness

All the values were measured using Likert's scale (Likert, 1932) from 1 to 7:

7, Strongly agree; 6, Agree; 5, Moderately agree; 4, Slightly agree or slightly disagree; 3, Moderately disagree; 2, Disagree; 1, Strongly disagree

Detailed characteristics of each scale are provided below.

Innovation scale (OCJV1) characteristics

The Mean Score for OCJV1 (Innovation) = 5.44 Standard Deviation= .84

This scale reflects the activity of the organization to encourage and implement new ideas, products, and mechanisms to improve the performance of the company.

Entrepreneurship scale (OCJV2) characteristics

The Mean Score for Entrepreneurship (OCJV2) = 5.30 Standard Deviation= .70

This scale is also composed of items reflecting the risk-taking activity of the company to improve the quality of the product and the efficiency of the management.

Decisiveness scale (OCJV3) characteristics

The Mean Score for Decisiveness (OCJV3) = 5.57 Standard Deviation= .82

This scale reflects that the managerial system is caring for the employees to do their task without being constrained by inhuman rules, while at the same time, the managers use rules rather than discretions to deal with their subordinates so as to create a stable atmosphere not dominated by fear but by tradition. This is the basic Japanese system of management that may prevail in most organizations in Japan.

Emphasis on stability scale (OCJV4) characteristics

This scale represents the basic elements of Japanese organizational culture to provide complete security and stability to the employees to remove any tension due to uncertainty regarding their tenure or future prospect in the company. As far as the Japanese organizational culture is concerned, this is the cornerstone of industrial relations in Japan.

The Mean Score for Stability (OCJV4) = 5.39 Standard Deviation= .82

Supportiveness scale (OCJV5) characteristics

This scale is measured by items, reflecting the fellow-feelings that are being promoted by the company to create a harmonious relationship between the employees.

The Mean Score for Supportiveness (OCJV5) = 4.24 Standard Deviation= .82

Orientations scale (OCJV6) characteristics

This scale is measured by items reflecting the evaluation system within the company, which is based on performance and action with high rewards for merits. The performance evaluation system in Japan has changed rapidly from a seniority-based system to a performance-based system with due regards for experience in order to maintain the stability and harmony among employees.

The Mean Score for Performance Orientations (OCJV6) = 5.15 Standard Deviation= .82

Team spirit scale (OCJV7) characteristics

Team orientation is one of the fundamental values of every Japanese organization, and thus in the Samurai MNC, it is being promoted very seriously throughout in its operations management system. Most of the operations management methods commonly in use in Japanese organizations will be inoperative without this characteristic.

The Mean Score for Team Spirit (OCJV7) = 5.65 Standard Deviation= .82

Preciseness scale (OCJV8) characteristics

This scale has items reflecting the analytical approach the company has implemented in its operations so as to implement basic rules of the Japanese operations management system. Japanese operation requires preciseness so as to have "zero" defects in the product rather than tolerating an acceptable level. It requires also the exact detail regarding requirements and supply routes for each and every department so as to maintain an analytically precise production and inventory system, which are fundamental for the operations management system in Japanese manufacturing. The system was devised in Samurai to start with and as a result, and it has considerable experience to train the employees in the precise nature of the operation.

The Mean Score for Preciseness (OCJV8) = 5.47 Standard Deviation = .82

The Cronbach Alpha provides us the reliability regarding internal consistency of the perceptions of the employees. In the "Structural Equation Modelling" analysis, given later, we can see that these eight values can effectively compose organizational culture.

Reliability

Alpha = .9435   Standardized item alpha = .9364

In Table 4.2, we present basic statistics for the organizational culture as observed in this company in Japan. In Table 4.3, we present the organization culture as perceived or idealized by the employees of this company. In both tables, the value components of organizational culture show high scores, indicating high acceptance and approval of these features of organizational culture of the Samurai MNC in its parent operation. All standard deviations demonstrate that means are significantly different from zero at the 5 percent level of confidence. Thus, the calculated means from the small sample of 150 employees are not spurious but can represent the population of the total number of employees. Skewness is a measure of symmetry, or more precisely, the lack of symmetry. Kurtosis is a measure of whether the data are peaked or flat relative to a normal distribution. Considering the above descriptions, the assumptions of normal distributions of the variables can be maintained. As a result, most of the testing procedures in the factor analysis and regression analysis will be valid. The mean responses are more or less close to 5.5 on average in the Likert's scale of 7.

The covariance matrix (Table 4.4) of the observed organizational culture shows variances are similar between OCJV1 and OCJV3, 6, 7, and 8. As a result, the values such as Innovation, Decisiveness, Emphasis on Performance, Team Spirit, and Preciseness are highly correlated according to the correlation matrix given later. The values such as Entrepreneurship and Supportiveness are not correlated with other values but are quite independent. It is possible that Entrepreneurship is related to the psychology of the top executives; ordinary employees are unrelated to it. High emphasis on performance demands preciseness, and continuous innovation (*Kaizen* in Japanese). Team spirit supports these values in the work–place. Supportiveness is related more on interpersonal relationship than on operational culture. It is possible that Japanese employees are working as a highly glued team in their operational activities, but their social relationships are not so close. This is a characteristic of the psychology of the Japanese people, who normally work very meticulously in their workplace but can be distant in

Table 4.2 Basic statistics for observed organizational culture, Japan

	OCJV1	OCJV2	OCJV3	OCJV4	OCJV5	OCJV6	OCJV7	OCJV8
Mean	5.5938	5.2923	5.6108	5.5923	5.2985	5.5862	5.6077	5.6015
Std. error of mean	3.459E-02	2.841E-02	3.424E-02	3.453E-02	2.806E-02	3.490E-02	3.439E-02	3.442E-02
Median	6.0000	5.0000	6.0000	6.0000	5.0000	6.0000	6.0000	6.0000
Mode	5.00	5.00	5.00	5.00	5.00	5.00	5.00	5.00
Std. deviation	.8819	.7243	.8729	.8803	.7153	.8897	.8768	.8776
Variance	.7778	.5246	.7620	.7750	.5117	.7915	.7688	.7701
Skewness	-.044	.078	-.063	-.031	.149	-.051	-.042	-.038
Std. error of skewness	.096	.096	.096	.096	.096	.096	.096	.096
Kurtosis	-.538	.254	-.501	-.536	.105	-.562	-.526	-.590
Std. error of Kurtosis	.191	.191	.191	.191	.191	.191	.191	.191

OCJV1, Innovation; OCJV2, Entrepreneurship; OCJV3, Decisiveness; OCJV4, Security; OCJV5, Supportiveness; OCJV6, Emphasis on Performance; OCJV7, Team Spirit; OCJV8, Preciseness

Table 4.3 Basic statistics for perceived organizational culture, Japan

	ICJV1	ICJV2	ICJV3	ICJV4	ICJV5	ICJV6	ICJV7	ICJV8
Mean	6.3400	6.3385	6.3400	6.3400	6.3400	6.3462	6.3400	6.3385
Std. error of mean	1.859E-02	1.857E-02	1.859E-02	1.859E-02	1.859E-02	1.867E-02	1.859E-02	1.857E-02
Median	6.0000	6.0000	6.0000	6.0000	6.0000	6.0000	6.0000	6.0000
Mode	6.00	6.00	6.00	6.00	6.00	6.00	6.00	6.00
Std. deviation	.4741	.4736	.4741	.4741	.4741	.4761	.4741	.4736
Variance	.2247	.2243	.2247	.2247	.2247	.2267	.2247	.2243
Skewness	.677	.684	.677	.677	.677	.648	.677	.684
Std. error of skewness	.096	.096	.096	.096	.096	.096	.096	.096
Kurtosis	-1.546	-1.536	-1.546	-1.546	-1.546	-1.585	-1.546	-1.536
Std. error of Kurtosis	.191	.191	.191	.191	.191	.191	.191	.191

ICJV1, Innovation; ICJV2, Entrepreneurship; ICJV3, Decisiveness; ICJV4, Security; ICJV5, Supportiveness; ICJV6, Emphasis on Performance; ICJV7, Team Spirit; ICJV8, Preciseness

Table 4.4 Covariance matrix of the observed organizational culture

	OCJV1	OCJV2	OCJV3	OCJV4	OCJV5	OCJV6	OCJV7	OCJV8
OCJV1	.7778							
OCJV2	.1328	.5246						
OCJV3	.7492	.1201	.762					
OCJV4	.7617	.1394	.7502	.775				
OCJV5	.1322	.5089	.1148	.1327	.5117			
OCJV6	.7746	.1458	.757	.7678	.1376	.7915		
OCJV7	.7588	.1195	.7531	.7581	.1234	.7604	.7688	
OCJV8	.7609	.1351	.7461	.7526	.1314	.7732	.7494	.7701

Table 4.5 Correlation matrix of the observed organizational culture

	OCJV1	OCJV2	OCJV3	OCJV4	OCJV5	OCJV6	OCJV7	OCJV8
OCJV1	1.0000							
OCJV2	.2079	1.0000						
OCJV3	.9732	.1900	1.0000					
OCJV4	.9811	.2186	.9762	1.0000				
OCJV5	.2095	.9823	.1839	.2107	1.0000			
OCJV6	.9873	.2263	.9748	.9804	.2162	1.0000		
OCJV7	.9812	.1881	.9839	.9822	.1968	.9747	1.0000	
OCJV8	.9831	.2126	.9739	.9741	.2094	.9904	.9740	1.0000

their personal relationship. This is reflected in the correlation matrix (Table 4.5) of the observed organizational culture.

From the analysis of the covariance and correlation matrices (Tables 4.4 and 4.5), we can say that the eight values that affect organizational culture are interdependent.

From the matrices in Tables 4.4 and 4.5, we can see that OCJV1 (Innovation) has close links with Decisiveness (OCJV3), Security of Employment (OCJV4), Emphasis of Performance (OCJV6), Team Spirit (OCJV7) and Preciseness (OCJV8), but it has relatively little relationship with Entrepreneurship (OCJV2) and Supportiveness (OCJV5). However, Entrepreneurship has close links with Supportiveness but not with the other values. Decisiveness has close link with Security of Employment, Emphasis on Performance, Team Spirit, and Preciseness. Security of Employment has close links with Emphasis on Performance, Team Spirit, and Preciseness. Emphasis on Performance has close links with both Team Spirit and Preciseness. Team Spirit is closely related to Preciseness. Thus, most of these values that compose organizational culture are closely linked except for two, Entrepreneurship and Supportiveness. Entrepreneurship comes from the top managers, and Supportiveness is a societal value attached to the organizational culture but unrelated to the operational behavior of the organization. That may be the possible explanation of their relative independent characteristics.

Factor Analysis for the observed organizational culture

Factor analysis (in Tables 4.6, 4.7, and 4.8) is used here to uncover the latent structure or dimensions of a set of variables estimated from the scores obtained from the survey of opinions of the employees in Japan. Here the analysis of the perceived ideas of the employees regarding the organizational culture they experience in Japan is presented. The exploratory factor analysis is carried on to find out which factors are relatively more important to influence organizational culture in Japanese multinational company.

The Eigen values are called characteristic roots. The Eigen value is a measure of amount of variance in relation to total. The Eigen value of a factor can be computed as the sum of its squared factor loadings for all the variables. Here two indicators have significant Eigen values (obtained from the communalities matrix). Thus, these indicators, *Entrepreneurship* and *Supportiveness*, are very important to influence the variable organizational culture.

Entrepreneurship is defined here in terms of independent managerial activity and knowledge management. Japanese system of management has its *Kaizen* or continuous improvement as its main element. Without the support of the *Kaizen* activities, Japanese product-development system cannot operate efficiently to outwit the rival companies both in Japan and in the rest of the world. Thus, managers are empowered to take decisions in the local operations if that is needed to enhance competitive advantages for the company. Supportiveness is a cultural trait that the Japanese learn in their primary schools and subsequently in every walk of life, where team effort and not individual achievements are the norm.

Comparison between "perceived" organizational culture and the "observed" organizational culture

Organizational culture is a very important factor in determining how well an individual fits into an organizational context. The concept of a person–organization fit has a psychological perspective in which both the individual and the culture combine to affect an individual's response to the organization (O'Reilly et al., 1991). In quantifying the "person–organization fit," researchers have taken two different roads (O'Reilly et al., 1991). The first is the explorations of interrelationship between individual characteristics and occupational attributes. The second is to relate the skills of the individuals and job requirements. These have relationships with the congruence between individual's personality and the organizational culture. Caldwell and O'Reilly (1990) developed a profile-matching process to evaluate the person–organization fit. This is based on the idea that organizations have cultures that are more or less attractive to certain types of individuals. This begins with a set of values, which typically act as the definitions

Table 4.6 Factor analysis: total variance explained

Total variance explained

Component	Initial eigen values			Extraction sums of squared			Rotation sums of squared loadings		
	Total	% of variance	Cumulative	Total	% of variance	Cumulative	Total	% of variance	Cumulative
1	6.023	75.284	75.284	6.023	75.284	75.284	5.854	73.171	73.171
2	1.857	23.217	98.501	1.857	23.217	98.501	2.026	25.33	98.501
3	4.09E-02	0.511	99.012						
4	2.74E-02	0.343	99.354						
5	2.48E-02	0.31	99.664						
6	1.29E-02	0.161	99.825						
7	8.00E-03	1.00E-01	99.925						
8	5.98E-03	7.48E-02	100						

Extraction Method: Principal Component Analysis

Table 4.7 Factor analysis in the parent unit in Japan: observed organizational culture

	Supportiveness	Entrepreneurship	Communality
(Factor loadings)			
Innovation	.987	.107	.986
Entrepreneurship	.106	.99	.991
Decisiveness	.985	.008	.978
Emphasis on stability	.984	.113	.982
Supportiveness	.103	.99	.991
Performance orientation	.986	.12	.987
Team spirit	.987	.009	.983
Preciseness	.985	.11	.982
Eigen value	6.023	1.857	
Percent variance explained	75.284	23.217	

Table 4.8 Results of factor analysis on observed organizational culture

Most important factors	Related to
Supportiveness	Entrepreneurship
Entrepreneurship	Innovations, decisiveness,
	Performance emphasis, team spirit, preciseness

around which norms, symbols, rituals, and other cultural activities revolve. It is based on the notion of a psychological process of identity formation in which individuals appear to seek a social identity that provides meaning and connectedness (Harrison and Caroll, 1991). Values thus, provide the instruments to create a person–organization fit. Thus, it is essential whether there is a congruence between individual's values (we call it ideal organizational culture) and those of the organization (we call it actual organizational culture) as a measure of the relationship between the organizational culture and commitment.

High-perceived-fit individuals apparently respond as if they are congruent with the top management value system, and thus may in fact stimulate other individuals in the organization to respond to them as if they are congruent (i.e., more positively than they otherwise would). This process may enable these individuals to socially construct their own interpretation of the values of the organization (Kristof, 1996) and to maintain that construction over time. Thus, perceptions of a high degree of fit between oneself and the job environment may have the added effects of motivating employees to act on their own values (because they believe they are consistent with those of the organization), producing expectations that such action will be rewarded and stimulating others in the environment to share these perceptions.

In addition to asking employees to identify the current culture that prevailed within their organization, the survey instrument used in this research also asked respondents to allocate points to their "preferred" or "ideal" type of culture. It is therefore possible to compare the current or existing culture within organization with the preferred or ideal culture type using discriminant analysis (Table 4.2 and 4.3). For the discriminant analysis, the items on the samples scores for the employees in Japan for ideal or perceived and observed organizational culture, as described in Tables 4.2 and 4.3, were combined together.

Type 1 is perceived, and Type 2 is observed organizational culture, as given in the samples for the employees in Japan. The standardized discriminant function coefficients in the table above serve the same purpose as beta weights in multiple regression: they indicate the relative importance of the independent variables in predicting the dependent. In this case, in the Type 1 as we can see from the Classification Function Coefficients table given below Decisiveness has the maximum impacts on ideal culture as perceived by the employees in Japan, followed by Supportiveness, Entrepreneurship, Preciseness, and Team Spirit. In the actual organizational culture, the relative importances of the values are similar. Thus, there is no significant difference in the perceptions of the employees on perceived and observed organizational culture. They put their emphasis on the same values. Type 1 indicates the perceived values and Type 2 indicates the observed values of the organization culture in Table 4.9

As we can see the Table 4.9, the canonical correlation .663 is satisfactory. Wilk's lambda is not high at all, and chi-square is still high. Thus, the two samples in terms of value are somehow similar. So, we can fairly conclude that that there is no significant difference between perceived and observed organizational culture as given by these value scores in the sample for the employees in their home operation in Japan.

Sekiguchi (2006) supported this idea in the context of Japan. Foong and Richardson (2008) in their study of cultural factors in ethnocentric multinational corporation and employee morale also support this idea. However, recent adaptations of Western practices in Japanese companies have created a gap between the ideal and actual organizational culture. During the old days, the gap was non-existent, but has been widened recently. Although that may be true about some Japanese companies with Western executives (Olympus is an example), major Japanese multinational companies, particularly the one which is under our investigation in this research are very proud of their organizational culture and want to maintain it in order not to disturb the harmony in the workplace. As the enhancement of harmony in the workplace is one of the most important long-term corporate objectives of this Japanese company, we can safely assume that it will not accept any alien concepts to maximize its short-term profit.

Implications for theory

Implication of this analysis is very clear. The dimensions of individual preferences and those of organizational cultures should be comparable. The evidence of

Table 4.9 Classification function coefficients, Eigen values, and Wilk's lambda

Classification function coefficients

	Type	
	1.0	*2.0*
ICJV1	0.84	0.549
ICJV2	5.951	4.856
ICJV3	10.756	10.353
ICJV4	–3.886	–3.372
ICJV5	7.885	6.402
ICJV6	–9.272	–9.403
ICJV7	4.123	3.787
ICJV8	5.713	5.755
Constant	–70.744	–52.125

Eigen values

Function	Eigen values	% of variance	Cumulative %	Canonical correlation
1	.784	100.0	100.0	.663

1 Canonical discriminant functions were used in the analysis

Wilk's lambda

Test of function	Wilks' lambda	Chi-Square	DF	Sig
1	.560	749.252	8	.000

such comparability would indicate that "the types of cultures individuals indicate they want are generally equivalent to the cultures organizations offer" (O'Reilly et al., 1991; Kilmann, 1981; Ouchi, 1981). That creates commitments. "Lack of comparability would reduce the meaningfulness of person–organization fit" or in other words commitments of the individuals. This high degree of a person–organization fit provides a committed employees, thus magnifying the returns from investments in employee development activities (Ouchi, 1981).

Interpersonal interactions are to a large extent determined by real and relevant differences or similarities between interaction partners in belief structures and desired outcomes. Value congruence theory implies that actual beliefs and the resultant interactions will dominate attitudes about the interaction environment. Thus, if actual value congruence is high, attitudes should be positive regardless of perceived fit, based on experienced interactions that demonstrate common cognitive structures, enhanced communication, and agreement about value-relevant goals, value fulfillment, and clear role expectations. If actual congruence is low, high perceived fit may mitigate negative effects of the lack of actual value congruence such that attitudes may be moderately positive because of personality effects, leadership interactions, and other processes not directly related to actual value congruence. When both the perceived and actual fit are low, attitudes should be negative overall.

Social information-processing or social construction approaches to understanding reactions to the work environment imply that beliefs about, rather than actual, organizational fit should dominate (Kristof-Brown, 2000). That is, if employees believe, for whatever reasons, that they fit well with their organization, positive attitudes result, whereas if they believe they are a poor fit with the organizational environment, their attitudes will tend to be poor unless perceptions are overridden by actual positive interactions with fellow employees (high actual congruence). This social construction approach suggests that under conditions of high perceived fit, employees will express positive perceptions and attitudes regardless of the level of actual fit (Enz, 1986). Under conditions of low perceived fit, high actual fit may to some extent enhance attitudes via the mechanisms of improved communication, reduced uncertainty, and other value congruence processes. When both perceived and actual fit are low, attitudes should be poor (Kristof, 1996).

An individual's perception of whether or not he or she fits well with the organization most likely produces expectations regarding the quality of interaction to be encountered on the job. Whether or not this expectation is fulfilled depends on the actual level of fit the individual has with the organization. Research in this area primarily has examined the notion that met expectations tend to produce positive attitudes, whereas unmet expectations lead to negative attitudes (Ployhart, 2012). This approach suggests that those individuals who are correct in their perception of their degree of fit with the organization (perceived and actual fit are consistent) should express the most positive job attitudes because their interactions with others bear out their predictions, as compared to those individuals who are wrong about their degree of fit. This argument, however, is not very compelling in that it ignores actual interaction events and their positive or negative nature and that it places all emphasis on the uncertainty reduction effects of the ability to predict.

Implications for practice

There are complex interactions between societal and ethnic cultures. If there were similarities of values of the organization and the employees in the subsidiary operations, it would imply that employee's values are becoming more homogeneous and converging toward the organizational culture of the parent operation. This research has verified the value-based composition of organizational culture in the parent operation of this Japanese multinational company as the benchmark. Formations of values are important issues to be analyzed. Research has shown that human beings develop a sense of self, which is a combination of beliefs, feelings, and knowledge used to evaluate, organize, and regulate one's intellectual, emotional, and behavioral reactions to the physical and social environment (Meyer, Irving, and Allen, 1998; Basu and Miroshnik, 1999; Lok, Westwood, and Crawford, 2005). The "self" is constructed via experience as the primary source for humans to interpret and respond to external events.

This measure of cultural fit is referred to as *enculturation* (Selmer and De Leon, 1996). The acculturation process in the Japanese company has created sets of values in the management system, which the members have embraced irrespectively of their personal cultural preferences (Hayashi, 1989, 2002).

O'Reilly et al. (1991) emphasized the notion of person–organization fit, and they put forward the concept that some organizations have cultures that are attractive to some individuals. O'Reilly et al.'s examination of this linkage was important to examine the relationship between the person–organization fit and commitment, satisfaction, and performance of the individual employees. In evaluating the person–organization fit, we need to examine, first, preferences that individuals have for organizational cultures, and second, the relationship between preferences of the employee and the existing organizational culture. It assumes that organizations with strong organization cultures mold individuals within the organization to have similar perceptions regarding organizational culture (Lok et al., 2005). If it is correct, then enculturation (Kranias, 2000; Selmer and De Leon, 1996; Harrison and Caroll, 1991) is possible.

Using this logic, it seems difficult to accept that organizations with such strong organizational culture would select individuals whose perceptions are not similar to those of the organization itself (Del Campo, 2006). If the person–organization fit is low, it may result in high levels of employee turnover. This type of misalignment between an individual and the organization could increase conflict, alienation, and dissatisfaction. Thus, a relative difference in individual preferences and that of the organization is a better evaluator of workplace relationships and eventual outcomes than the absolute magnitude of individual preferences. As an individual cannot see the preference of the organization, he or she can try to compare his or her individual preferences with the existing situation within the given organizational culture of the workplace.

Appendix
Questionnaire for organizational culture

		7	6	5	4	3	2	1
1	Being innovative							
2	Being quick to take advantage of opportunities							
3	Being willing to experiment							
4	Taking risks							
5	Being careful							
6	Being rule oriented							
7	Having stability							
8	Having predictability							
9	Having security of employment							
10	Not being constrained by many rules							
11	Being fair							
12	Having respect for individual's rights							
13	Being tolerant							
14	Being achievement oriented							
15	Having high expectations for performance							
16	Being results oriented							
17	Being action oriented							
18	Being analytical							
19	Paying attention to detail							
20	Being precise							
21	Being team oriented							
22	Working in collaboration with others							
23	Being people oriented							
24	Being competitive							
25	Being socially responsible							

5 Transmission of organizational culture to Thailand

Introduction

The transmission of organizational culture from the headquarters (HQ) to the overseas subsidiaries can form an international strategy to create unique organizational resources and the mechanism of managing overseas subsidiaries of the multinational companies. During the cultural transmission, a parent unit of a company can successfully transfer the set of the core values that is composing its parent organizational culture to the overseas subsidiaries, to enhance firm's overall performance by utilizing its unique resources and dynamic capabilities (Newbert, 2008; Peteraf and Bergen, 2003). This process can be called strategic cultural control of the subsidiaries to enhance their competitiveness (Jaeger, 1983; Selmer and De Leon, 1996; Kranias, 2000; Brannen and Salk, 2000; Sekiguchi, 2006)

The control of subsidiaries through organizational culture means transmission of the parent organizational culture as a part of the strategic planning process of the multinational company so as to mold the foreign employees psychologically to carry forward the original organizational purpose of the parent company (Brannen and Salk, 2000). This transmission of organizational culture would reduce transaction cost by reducing uncertainly regarding the motive and behavior of the foreign employees. Transplantations of organizational culture of the parent operation to its overseas subsidiaries create certainty regarding the behavior of the employees of host national origins.

Successful multinational firms transcended national cultural differences to develop a common pattern of business performance by creating company citizenships. These included a primary focus on such values as organizational innovation and goal orientation. Corporate purpose of the company, its espoused values, and vision of the leaders create values of its corporate management and operations management systems and for the organizational culture of the company as a whole. These values ultimately create commitment of the employees. Creation of commitment is an important index of a firm's successful corporate performance. Organizational cultures that encouraged trust, participations of the employees, and entrepreneurial behavior were effective across the globe, both in the home country and in the host countries all over the world with the implementation of appropriate human resource management system (Brannen and Salk, 2000; Basu, Miroshnik, and Uchida, 2001). This is a strategy to create unique competitive resources (Miroshnik, 2012; Hatch and Dyer, 2004; Lant, Milliken, and Batra, 1992).

Proposition and hypothesis

There are some specific espoused values in every important multinational company, which form their organizational cultures and create values, which in turn can form commitment of its employees worldwide. These commitments are the indicator of successful performance of a company because creation of commitment leads to success of the company both in the parent operation and in the subsidiaries. We can call the interrelationship between organizational culture of the parent and subsidiaries company citizenship. This company citizenship can be transmitted from one part of the globe to another by a multinational company through the transmission of its organizational culture as reflected by its corporate management and operations management system. This is a part of the company's strategic management process.

Formation of this company citizenship based on firm's organizational culture creates unique competitive advantage of a multinational company as the part of its international strategy. This concept of company citizenship is directly opposed to two very important theories put forward in recent years. Freedman (Freedman, 2006) has coined the term "flat world" to describe a world where people have the "jet-set culture" (Triandis, 2006) of the high Anglo-American executive class, with a similar language, education, tastes, and preference but with varied citizenships and nationalities. Emergence of this global culture is the result of the globalization process that started in 1990. This has created a new breed of managerial class whose culture is global, not national. If that is the case, organizational systems that were developed using national characteristics are undergoing changes to include global characteristics (Schneider, 1988; Weber, Shanker, and Raveh, 1996).

There is also the powerful argument of Hofstede (2002) who thinks organizational culture is related to the national culture of the country where the company is located and, as a multinational company, cannot avoid the strong influences of the national culture of the host country.

This chapter, drawing upon the experiences of a major Japanese multinational automobile company, has examined the core values of corporate management and operations management systems in Japan, the home country for Toyota, and in Thailand, the host country, to demonstrate that the theories of Freedman (2006) and Hofstede (2002) are not exactly valid. A company citizenship can be formed even in a country with a very different national culture because the strong organizational culture of a multinational company, which gave rise to the values of corporate management and operations management, can override difference in national culture between the home and the host countries of a multinational company. As there are different multinational companies with different organizational culture, there would be different company citizenships for different multinational companies rather than just one Anglo-American jet-set global culture.

Hypothesis

The hypothesis of this research is that a company citizenship can be formed by a multinational company by linking the original values of its organizational culture to the individual values of the employees of the subsidiary companies in a host country anywhere in the world. That follows the fundamental idea of the Roman philosopher Cicero that human values are universal (Bayertz, 1996).

Organizational culture, which exists globally in a multinational company, is formed by the major values introduced by of the founder/top management of that corporation, and it may or may not necessarily be influenced by the values of the country where that multinational corporation is operating. Values interact with aspects of culture to influence individual's attitude and response that we can call commitments (Eisenberger, Fasolo, and Davis-LaMastro, 1990). The concept of a person–organization fit, a psychological perspective in which both individual and the culture combine to affect an individual's response to the organization (O'Reilly, 1989; O'Reilly, Chatman, and Caldwell, 1991; Cable and Judge, 1997b), is defined as the compatibility between individuals and organizations (Cable and Edwards, 2004; Aselage and Eisenberger, 2003; Schneider, 2001; Vandenberghe, 1999; Kristof, 1996). The person–organization fit can be related to job satisfaction, organizational commitment, and turnover (Finegan, 2000). People are happier in settings that satisfy their individual needs or are suitable with their dispositions (Cable, Aiman-Smith, Mulvey, and Edwards, 2000). Organizational culture is a very important factor in determining how well an individual fits an organizational context and thus, the analysis of the person–organization fit is related to the analysis of the relationship between organizational culture and commitment (Barney, 1986, 2005; Van Vianen, 2000). If the employees are attached to these central values of the organization, performance of the organization increases because of the increased commitment of the members of the employees (Aselage and Eisenberger, 2003). It is essential to explore whether the employees have similar values as espoused by the organization, which create commitment of the employees.

Commitment and motivation help the firm to pursue strategic goals by discovering opportunities and utilizing existing opportunities. Entrepreneurship requires innovative activity, and strategic management requires stability (Hitt, Ireland, Sirmon, and Trahms, 2011). To achieve the balance between exploration and exploitation, specifications of organizational structure capable of supporting these twin needs are required. An effective organizational structure can combine existing resources and innovate future resources to create value for the organization and its stakeholders. The question is how formal and informal structures of the organization can create such a super structure for enhanced performance and entrepreneurial activities (Alvarez and Barney, 2010). The analysis presented in this chapter is an attempt to answer that question by elaborating the interrelationship between different components of the levels of cultures and the structures they support.

In quantifying the person–organization fit, researchers have taken two different roads (O'Reilly et al., 1991; Schneider, 2001; Cable and DeRue, 2002; Cable and Edwards, 2004; Carless, 2005; Kristof-Brown, Zimmerman, and Johnson, 2005; Ostroff, Shin, and Kinicki, 2005). The first is the exploration of interrelationship between individual characteristics and occupational attributes. The second is to relate the skills of the individuals and job requirements. These have relationships with the congruence between individual's personality and the organizational culture, which has close relationship with commitments of the individual.

Recent works in interactional psychology try to identify the characteristics of effective techniques to address the issue of person-organization-fit effects. O'Reilly et al. (1991) developed a profile-matching process to evaluate the person–organization fit. This is based on the idea that organizations have cultures that are more or less attractive to certain types of individuals. This begins with a set of values, which typically act as the definitions around which norms, symbols, rituals, and other cultural activities revolve (Kanter, 1968). It is based on the notion of a psychological process of identity formation in which individuals appear to seek a social identity that provides meaning and connectedness (Kilmann, 1981).

Values thus, provide the instruments to create a person–organization fit. Thus, it is essential whether there is a congruence between individuals' values (we call it ideal organizational culture) and those of the organization (we call it actual organizational culture) as a measure of the relationship between the organizational culture and commitment of the employees to stay in the organization. An employee may not leave the organization because he or she cannot get an alternative job, which pays just as much as he or she receives or in the same locality or of the same type. In those cases, he or she has limited psychological commitment for the organization. That may have effects on his or her ability to work in the most efficient way. A psychological attachment would be formed if the person is satisfied that he or she has obtained in his or her organization a similar organizational culture as he or she had imagined as the ideal organizational culture.

O'Reilly et al. (1991) focused more on the concept that certain types of organizations have cultures that are more or less attractive to certain types of individuals. In assessing a person–organization fit, two components should be examined: first, preferences that individuals have for organizational cultures must be demonstrated; and second, the relationship between individual preferences and existing organizational culture should be evaluated (Park, Mitsuhashi, Fey, and Bjrkman, 2003; Del Campo, 2006).

In this chapter, we have tried to combine these two concepts by comparing the ideal organizational culture as perceived by the employees and the organizational culture they in reality observe in the organization in both the parent operation of a Japanese multinational company and in its subsidiary operation in Thailand. If the ideal and the observed organizational culture are similar, then a person–organizational fit exists in that organization. As a result of this harmony, the committed employees are expected to give their best to maximize the potentiality of the organization. For a multinational company it is not enough, as foreign subsidiaries provide important intermediate products along with the market for final products, manufactured either in the parent company or in the subsidiaries. Thus, a person–organization fit ideally should be achieved both in the parent operation and in the subsidiaries.

Company citizenship in Japanese multinational companies

The analysis of Japanese culture and organizations by outsiders so far suffers from a number of defects. They do not try to understand the effects of the Japanese value system on their organizations. So far, a success of Japanese companies was analyzed only in terms of their unique production and operations management system (Lincoln and Kalleberg, 1990). However, the interrelationship between the production and operations management system, which is a part of the organizational culture, and the specific human resources management system it requires for its proper implementation, was not given sufficient attention (Lincoln, Kerbo, and Wittenhagen, 1995).

In a Japanese company, the leadership styles and the organizational culture are designed by the human resources management system; these are not coming from outside as the leaders are recruited from inside the organization. Effective corporate performance is the result of these underlying determinants of organizational culture and leadership style. Thus, in a Japanese organization, leadership style is rooted in the human resources management system, which emerges from the values of the organizational culture (Sekiguchi, 2006).

The similarity of organizational culture creates a similar attachment for the employees in the subsidiaries as in the home operations of the Japanese multinational companies. Whether this attachment of the employees can have impacts on the performance of the company is the fundamental issue. The companies with organizational commitment among its employees have strong organizational cultures, which are rooted in their values, beliefs, and assumptions. Continuous progress and respect that can be gained to be associated with a company with continuous growth is the end objective of the employees. These feelings lead them to develop a family feeling within the workplace and responsibility toward the fellow employees and the community at large. They believe they have a responsibility toward the organization and the local and global societies (Okabe, 2005).

Whether efficient corporate performances can be repeated in foreign locations depends on the transmission mechanism of the Japanese organizational culture, which in turn depends on the adaptations of Japanese style human resources management system. That can face obstacles due to different values in a foreign society, and as a result, organizational culture in a foreign location may be different from the organizational culture of the company in Japan. Adaptation of operations management system alone will not create effective performance of a Japanese company in a foreign location. Creation of an appropriate human resources management system and as a result, appropriate organizational culture is essential for effective performance (Sekiguchi, 2006; Ouchi, 1981).

An organization with informal cultural control relies on an implicit organization-wide culture within the organization for the control of the members of that organization. In a classical bureaucratic model of organization, control relies on the use of explicit formal rules and regulations. Japanese organizations follow the first type of control through culture (Baliga and Jaeger, 1984). Japanese corporations have strived to fulfill that goal to create a harmonious organizational climate through the corporate management system and operations management system not only for their main operation in Japan but also in their overseas subsidiaries (Basu et al., 2001; Miroshnik, 2012). Japanese management system utilizing its layers of value system effectively tries to utilize strategic entrepreneurship inherent within its value system. This can be done by combining environmental, organizational, and personal attributes into a dynamic process of creation of opportunities to enhance competitiveness (Ouchi, 1981; Jaeger, 1983).

Japanese multinational companies with their proven competitive advantages in operational management practices normally give priorities to the team spirit and involvement of the employees in quality enhancements. They have long and continuous training program to infuse the values of the parent units on the employees of the subsidiaries (Basu et al., 2001; Jaeger, 1983). They try to replicate these features in their overseas operations. This research demonstrated, in precise quantitative way, that the management system can create competitive resources for a multinational company in its subsidiaries by implementing a common value system.

Methodology and its implementation

This method adopted in this study is different from the methods adopted in existing literature, because the purpose is different here. The purpose is to examine whether employees, after experiencing the organizational culture of the company for years, are still unhappy because their expected an ideal organizational culture are different. In this research, the question of the person–organization fit is evaluated in the Japanese main operation of a major Japanese multinational automobile company by comparing the values of the observed organizational culture and the ideal organizational culture as perceived by the employees.

To evaluate organizational culture in Japanese operations of this multinational automobile company, this research follows the same method as that in the previous chapter. Thereafter, in each of the operations in Japan and Thailand, surveys of opinions of the 150 managers, who have spent a considerable number of years to understand the organizational culture of the organization, were executed. The purpose is to analyze the values that may be important to the workers self-concept or identity, as well as relevant to the organization's central value system.

The instrument contains a set of value statements that can be used to assess both the extent to which certain values characterize a target organization and an

Table 5.1 Characteristics of the sample for Thailand

Items	Employees in Thailand
Number of respondents	150
Tenure	
Length of service (mean)	9.35 years
Age	
Under 35	39.60%
35–45	56.70%
Above 45	3.70%
Educational level	
Senior High School	1.10%
University Graduate	91.50%
Post-graduate	7.40%
Nationality	
Japanese	0.10%
Thai	98.50%
Other Asian	1.40%
Formal cultural training	
Posted abroad	1.70%
Received cultural training	73.10%
Received language training	42.50%

Table 5.2 Eigen values, Thailand

Function	Eigen values	% of variance	Cumulative %	Canonical correlation
1	14.863	100.000	100.000	0.968

individual's preference for that particular configuration of values as in the previous chapter.

In addition to asking employees to identify the current culture that prevailed within their organization, the survey instrument used in this research also asked respondents to allocate points to their "preferred" or "ideal" type of culture. It is therefore possible to compare the current or existing culture within organization with the preferred or ideal culture type using discriminant analysis. Type 1 is perceived and Type 2 is observed organizational culture as given in the samples for the employees in Japan.

The standardized discriminant function coefficients in the table above serve the same purpose as beta weights in multiple regressions. They indicate the relative importance of the independent variables in predicting the dependent. In

Table 5.3 Wilk's lambda, Thailand

Wilks' Lambda				
Test of function	Wilks' Lambda	Chi-Square	DF	Sig
1	.063	3576.631	8	.000

this case in the Type 1, as we can see from the classification function coefficients in Table 5.3, Decisiveness has the maximum impacts on ideal culture as perceived by the employees in Japan, followed by Supportiveness, Entrepreneurship, Preciseness, and Team Spirit. In the actual organizational culture, the relative importance of the values are similar. Thus, there is no significant difference in the perceptions of the employees on perceived and observed organizational culture. They put their emphasis on the same values.

As we can see from the tables, the canonical correlation is satisfactory. Wilk's lambda is not high at all, and chi-square is still high; thus the two samples in terms of value are somehow similar. Thus, we can fairly conclude that that there is no significant difference between perceived and observed organizational culture as given by these value scores in the sample for the employees in their home operation in Japan.

Implication of this analysis is very clear. A person–organization fit is related to the normative value-based commitment. The dimensions of individual preferences and organizational cultures should be comparable (Kirkman and Shapiro, 2001). Evidence of such comparability would indicate that "the types of cultures individuals indicate they want are generally equivalent to the cultures organizations offer" (O'Reilly et al., 1991, Kilmann, 1981, Ouchi, 1981). That creates commitments. "Lack of comparability would reduce the meaningfulness of the person–organization fit" or, in other words commitments, of the individuals.

The high degree of a person–organization fit in Japan for this organization under our study indicates that it has a competitive advantage over its rivals internationally (Barney, 1986, 2005). This high degree of a person–organization fit provides committed employees, thus magnifying the returns from investments in employee development activities (Ouchi, 1981; Park et al., 2003).

Value-based organizational character in the Thai subsidiary

The purpose of the survey used in this study in the subsidiary operation in Thailand is to identify the current organizational culture and the "espoused" or perceived organizational culture in this Japanese multinational company. It is therefore possible to compare the realized or observed organizational culture with the espoused or perceived organizational culture of this Japanese multinational organization type using discriminant analysis.

Both perceived and actual organizational fit have been examined primarily from the perspective of core work values (Sekiguchi, 2006). The theoretical orientation underlying both perceived and actual values-based research is that the sharing of work values, or beliefs concerning what one should or ought to do at work, relates to the sharing of methods of cognitive classification and interpretation, thus reducing uncertainty regarding interpersonal interactions (Schein, 1984; Miroshnik, 2002). Kluckhohn (1951) noted that if individuals possess similar values, their role expectations become clearer and more predictable. The needs–supplies perspective suggests that individuals with high organization fit will find their values fulfilled by the organization. Therefore, value congruence has been hypothesized to increase satisfaction, commitment, and other positive work attitudes.

If we compare the means of various items, we can see from the Table 5.4 that the differences are not significant for the Values 2 and 5 (Entrepreneurship and Supportiveness), as their Wilk's lambdas are quite small. For others, it is not very large either, always less than .6. The smaller the Wilk's lambda, the more important is the independent variable to the discriminant function, that is, the differences between the two samples, perceived (ideal) and observed (actual), will be smaller and insignificant. This is also supported by the Eigen value and canonical correlation. The Eigen value is small, and the canonical correlation is very high. Thus, we may say that there is no significant difference between the perceived and observed organizational culture in the Japanese subsidiary operation in Thailand as perceived by the employees in Thailand.

Onishi (2006) and Swierczek and Onishi (2003) in their study of Japanese managers and Thai subordinates in Japanese subsidiaries in Thailand have observed

Table 5.4 Classification function coefficients, Thailand

	Type	
	1.0	*2.0*
ICTHV1	12.193	14.914
ICTHV2	14.807	30.811
ICTHV3	−3.228	−4.264
ICTHV4	16.249	19.998
ICTHV5	−.177	−13.79
ICTHV6	8.575	1.005
ICTHV7	−20.167	−21.225
ICTHV8	22.86	34.637

Fisher's Linear Discriminant Functions

[Type 1 = Ideal; Type 2 = Observed].

ICTHV1, Innovation; ICTHV2, Entrepreneurship; ICTHV3, Decisiveness; ICTHV4, Security; ICTHV5, Supportiveness; ICTHV6, Emphasis on Performance; ICTHV7, Team Spirit; ICTHV8, Preciseness similar features. Andrews (2001) has noticed similar characteristics in Thai subsidiaries of Japanese multinational companies; however, for other multinational companies, that may not be the case (Lawler and Atmiyanandana, 2003; Lawler, Atmiyanada, and Zaidi, 1992; Niffenegger, Kulviwat, and Engchanil, 2006).

The perception of congruence is the important construct in part because unrecognized or unnoticed congruence should not necessarily have positive relationships to job attitudes (Enz, 1986). Research employing perceptions of congruence has also found that value congruence between employees and their organization is related to satisfaction, commitment, and intentions to quit (Cable and Judge, 1997a; Morley, 2007).

Enz (1986) discusses the role that perceived value congruence may play in the social construction of organizational reality (Weiss, 1978). At the subunit level, Enz (1986) observed that perceptions of value congruence were more predictive of perceptions of subunit power than actual congruence. She interpreted this finding as indicating that perceptions of value congruence may shape other perceptions – in this case, perceptions of the power structure of the organization – and thus the social reality in which employees exist.

Currently, the predominant approach to examining both actual and perceived fit, and their relationship to each other, has focused on the possibility that actual fit leads to perceived fit (Judge and Cable, 1997). These studies observe a mediating effect; that is, actual fit (typically based on values) is mediated by perceptions of fit in its effects on such outcomes as organizational attraction. This approach relies on employees accurately perceiving their environment as a good or poor fit, and responding accordingly. Judge and Cable (1997) found that perceived fit accounted for any variance explained by actual fit (full mediation).

As we can see similar characteristics in their subsidiary operation in Thailand, can we fairly conclude that the organization may have successfully transmitted its Japanese organizational culture to its subsidiary operation in Thailand as well, as given by the opinion of their Thai employees? One of two basic purposes of Japanese corporations is to achieve employees satisfaction, and the other is to achieve customers satisfaction (Hayashi, 1989, 2002; Basu and Miroshnik, 1999). Just like in Japan, in Thai subsidiary operations as well employees are reasonably satisfied as their personal idea about a preferred or ideal organizational culture more or less matches their experience regarding the prevailing organizational culture. Similar experiences are realized in the case of Japanese subsidiary operations in the United States and Germany (Lincoln and Kalleberg, 1990; Lincoln et al., 1995; Park et al., 2003). We can infer that due to the successful transmission of organizational culture from the parent to the Thai subsidiary, this similarity of the ideal values of the employees with the prevailing values in their workplaces can be observed. However, for a decisive proof, we can examine the similarity between the observed organizational culture in the parent and in the Thai subsidiary, which is given in Table 5.5 and Figure 5.1. The structural equation model is fitted to find out a very high degree of relationship between these two organizational cultures. Thus, cultural transmission is successful where the values of the organizational culture of the subsidiary in Thailand are similar to that of the parent operation.

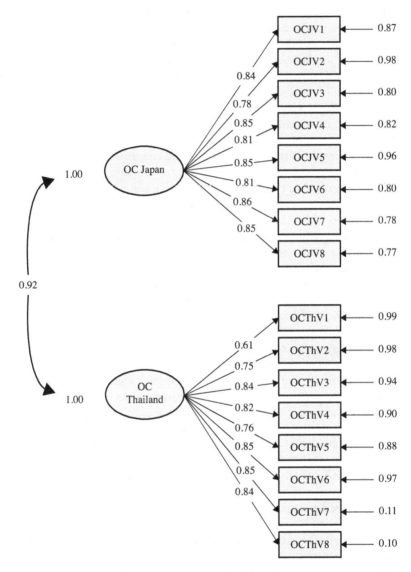

Figure 5.1 Path diagram of the relationship between organizational culture of the parent unit in Japan and the subsidiary in Thailand

Chi-square = 2953.34; Normed chi-square = 2518.60; RMSEA = 0.16; Standardized RMR = 0.14; CFI = 0.87;

(The meaning of the statistical terms indicating goodness of fit are in the Appendix)

Table 5.5 Structural equation model: factor scores regression

	Organizational culture – Japan	Organizational culture – Thailand
Innovation	.84	.61
Entrepreneurship	.78	.75
Decisiveness	.85	.84
Stability	.81	.82
Supportiveness	.85	.76
Performance	.81	.85
Team spirit	.86	.85
Preciseness	.85	.84

If the person–organization fit would be low, high levels of employee turnover may result. This type of misalignment between individual and the organization could increase conflict, alienation, and dissatisfaction. Thus, relative difference between individual preferences and that of the organization is a better evaluator of workplace relationships and eventual outcome than the absolute magnitude of individual preferences. As an individual cannot see the preference of the organization, he can try to compare his individual preferences with the existing situation within the given organizational culture of the workplace.

Comments

Successful multinational firms transcended national cultural differences to develop a common pattern of business performance by creating company citizenships (Miroshnik, 2012; Basu et al., 2001; Husted, 2003; Organ and Konovsky, 1989). These included a primary focus on such values as organizational innovation and a goal orientation (Bird and Stevens, 2003). These values ultimately create commitment of the employees and create a perfect person–organization fit. Creation of commitment, an important index of a firm's successful corporate performance, in turn forms a company citizenship. Organizational cultures that "encouraged trust, *participativeness*, and entrepreneurial behavior were effective across" the globe, both in the home country and in the host countries all over the world.

In the context of a multinational company, the role of culture should not be ignored, as culture implies resources of high economic significance. A multinational company with strong organizational culture can provide a global company citizenship compared to a company with weak organizational culture.

This research provides the evidence from a major multinational automobile company that instead of the proposed co-called jet-set or monolith-type of global culture as described by Triandis (2006) or Freedman (2006) or fusion-type global culture as proposed by Sheth (2006), many different company citizenships of various multinational companies may be emerging as a new organizational form in the era of globalizatin.

Appendix
Meaning of the statistical criteria regarding goodness of fit

- RMSEA represents how well a model fits a population, not just the sample used for estimation. Lower RMSEA values indicate better fit.
- The root mean square residual (RMR) is the square root of the mean of the standardized residuals. Lower RMR values represent better fit, and higher values represent worse fit.
- The goodness-of-fit index (GFI) is analogous to a squared multiple correlation. Thus, GFI = 1.0 indicates a perfect model fit, GFI > .90 may indicate good fit, and values close to zero indicate very poor fit.
- Adjusted goodness-of-fit index (AGFI) differs from the GFI only in that it adjusts for the number of degrees of freedom in the specified model.
- The Normed fit index (NFI) is the difference in the value for the fitted model and the null model divided by the value for the null model. It ranges between zero to one. A Normed fit index of one indicates perfect fit.
- The relative fit index (RFI) represents a derivative of the NFI; as with both the NFI and CFI, the RFI coefficient values range from zero to one with values close to one indicating superior fit
- The comparative fit index (CFI) is an incremental fit index that is an improved version of the NFI. The CFI is normed so that values range between zero to one, with higher values indicating better fit.
- The Tucker–Lewis Index (TLI) is conceptually similar to the NFI, Models with good fit have values that approach one.
- NPAR stands for the number of parameters, and CMIN is the minimum discrepancy and represents the discrepancy between the unrestricted sample covariance matrix S and the restricted covariance matrix. Df stands for degrees of freedom, and P is the probability value.

6 Corporate management in India

Corporate governance is a process, relation, and mechanism setup for the corporations and firms based on certain guidelines and principles by which a company is controlled and directed. The principles provided in the system ensure that the company is governed in a way that it is able to set and achieve its goals and objectives in the context of the social, regulatory, and market environment, and is able to maximize profits and also benefit those whose interest is involved in it, in the long run. The division and distribution of rights and responsibilities among different participants in the corporation (such as the board of directors, managers, shareholders, creditors, auditors, regulators, and other stakeholders) and inclusion of the rules and procedures for making decisions in corporate affairs are identified with the help of the corporate governance mechanism and guidelines.

The Organization for Economic Cooperation and Development (1999) published its Principles of corporate governance giving a very comprehensive definition of corporate governance a set of relationships between a company's management, its board, its shareholders and other stakeholders. Corporate governance also provides the structure through which the objectives of the company are set, and the means of attaining those objectives and monitoring performance are determined. Good corporate governance should provide proper incentives for the board and management to pursue objectives that are in the interests of the company and shareholders, and should facilitate effective monitoring; thereby encouraging firms to use recourses more efficiently. Corporate governance has the explicit purpose to create a healthy culture to stimulate harmony and corporate effectiveness.

As far as structural and regulatory changes are concerned, India has witnessed several enactments – the Companies Act of 2013 and SEBI (Security and Exchange Board of India) listing obligations and disclosure requirements regulations, which have contributed significantly in strengthening governance norms and increasing accountability by way of disclosures. Interestingly, these changes have been inspired by the Anglo-Saxon model of corporate governance, which is probably one of the key reasons behind current practices of corporate governance not achieving the desired level of fruition.

In the last decade, the frequencies of corporate frauds and governance failures that have dotted the global corporate map have witnessed comparably vigorous efforts of improving corporate governance practices. India has liberalized the regulatory fabric of the country to align its corporate governance norms with those of developed countries and has invited the flood of corruption, nepotism, or outright theft.

One-third of Indian companies are controlled by one or more family members who have founded the company. As a result, Indian corporate scene is a minefield of corruption, tax evasions, violence, and outright theft. The intensity of family ownership in India is comparable to that found throughout Asia, the Middle East, Italy, and Spain. There are certain advantages of a family-owned enterprise, including committed owners, long-term strategies, industry knowledge accumulated over generations, and such values as trust, stewardship, and longevity. The concentration of power may lead to quick decisions; information and transaction costs may be lower; and access to capital may be easier, when few external alternatives are available

These situations all run counter to corporate governance's foundations of transparency, accountability, and boards' effective stewardship – foundations that go a long way in building trust of the shareholders. The value destruction from imploded family-owned companies is another powerful driver for reform. The Birlas split after three generations, the Ambanis in the second generation, and the Bajajs in the third generation.

Family bonding is important, and the concept of the extended family is still very much prevalent. Often the entire business is considered to be a part of the extended family; the distinction between what belongs to the family legally and what belongs to the company is lost. Traditionally, Indian businesses have always run on personal relationship and trust. The owner–manager often bestows his trust on a set of people, irrespective of their place in the organizational hierarchy. Independent directors are often chosen on the basis of whether the person would fit into the organization's culture and be agreeable to the family.

In Indian business environment a related-party transaction can present a potential or actual conflict of interest by advancing the self-interests of families holding a majority stake to the detriment of minority shareholders. The practice can lead to situations in which funds are tunneled out of the company into another entity, a "related party," or can result in a lost business opportunity. India's body of laws, regulations, and codes directly or indirectly lays down the "dos and don'ts" of related-party transactions.

In an economy where family-owned businesses dominate, the desire and opportunity to use a known party is great, particularly when trust is involved. Secrecy may also be a consideration to prevent competitors from learning about a business strategy. Cultural factors have raised the threshold for tolerance. The lack of timely disclosures prevents shareholders from questioning the deals.

Indian companies need only obtain board approval for related-party transactions, even large ones, not broader shareholder approval. Stock exchange listing rules merely mandate audit committees to review related-party transactions and disclose them in the quarterly compliance reports and corporate governance sections of annual reports of listed companies.

A "promoter" generally means the entrepreneur – whether an individual, a corporate entity, or a government institution – that establishes and continues to exert control of the business. The status of "promoter" gets effectively transferred through sale of the business to a new owner. The Satyam case illustrates the perils of promoters. In December 2008, Satyam Chief Executive Officer B. Ramalinga Raju announced that the company would acquire a 100 percent stake in Maytas properties for $1.3 billion and a 51 percent stake in Maytas infrastructure for $300 million. The Raju family owned roughly one-third of each takeover target. The maneuver was seen as a way of diverting cash from Satyam's shareholders to the Raju family through these acquisitions at highly overvalued prices. Because the Raju family's ownership of Satyam was a minority share (8.75 percent), the deal required shareholder approval and was eventually rejected. In January 2009, Raju confessed that this scramble for acquisitions was an effort to cover up fraud amounting to $1 billion, or 94 percent of the company's cash. The "independent" directors were not truly independent, and the auditors often acted in collusion to perpetrate the corruption. Companies now need to provide details of shares pledged by promoters.

The family's "groupthink" may prevail. Familial ties may create a division between "insiders" and "outsiders" regarding influence and perceptions of what constitutes the best interests of the company and shareholders. Opinions and decisions during board meetings may reflect "family convocations" held outside the boardroom. Objectivity may be skewed by family priorities, disputes, interpersonal relationships, and shared understandings.

In Indian society, respect for elders is paramount; it is customary to demonstrate deference to their views. This cultural trait often influences the selection of directors and boardroom dynamics. If controlling shareholders cease to be pleased with the efforts of an independent director, such a director can be certain that his or her term will not be renewed, even if such director is spared the more disastrous consequence of being removed from the board.

In January 2017, SEBI, India's capital markets regulator, released a "Guidance Note on Board Evaluation." This note elaborated on different aspects of performance evaluation by laying down the means to identify objectives, different criteria and method of evaluation. The role of independent directors in performance evaluation is key.

For the last 25 years down the line, independent directors have hardly been able to make the desired impact. The regulator on its part has, time and again, made the norms tighter – introduced comprehensive definition of independent directors, defined a role of the audit committee, etc. Despite all the governance reforms, the regulator is still found wanting.

While independent directors have been generally criticized for playing a passive role on the board, instances of independent directors not siding with promoter decisions have not been taken well – they were removed from their position by promoters. Under law, an independent director can be easily removed by promoters or majority shareholders. This inherent conflict has a direct impact on independence. Empowerment of independent directors has to be supplemented with greater duties for, and accountability of directors. In this regard, Indian company law, revamped in 2013, mandates that directors owe duties not only toward the company and shareholders, but also toward the employees, community, and for the protection of environment. Although these general duties have been imposed on all directors, directors including independent directors have been complacent due to lack of enforcement action.

In India, founders' ability to control the affairs of the company has the potential of derailing the entire corporate governance system. Unlike developed economies, in India, identity of the founder and the company is often merged. The founders, irrespective of their legal position, continue to exercise significant influence over the key business decisions of companies and fail to acknowledge the need for succession planning. Family-owned Indian companies suffer an inherent inhibition to let go of control.

The need to make corporate governance in India transparent was felt after the high profile corporate governance failure scams like the stock market scam, the UTI scam, Ketan Parikh scam, and Satyam scam, which were severely criticized by the shareholders. Thus, corporate governance is not just company administration but more than that, and it includes monitoring the actions, policies, practices, and decisions of corporations, their agents, and affected stakeholders thereby ensuring fair, efficient, and transparent functioning of the corporate management system.

The framework of corporate governance consists of (a) express or implied contracts between the stakeholders and the company for the distribution of rights, duties, rewards, and liabilities, etc. among different participants in the corporation; (b) procedure for proper control and supervision of information flow in the company, that is, a proper mechanism of checks-and-balances; and (c) procedures for resolving and reconciling the conflicting interests and decisions of different participants in the corporation. This mechanism ensures accountability of the Board of Directors to all stakeholders of the corporation, that is, managers, shareholders, suppliers, creditors, auditors, regulators, employees, customers, and society in general, for giving the company a fair, clear, and efficient administration. So, it is not just mere company administration, but a corporate management system.

A company that has good corporate governance has a much higher-level of confidence amongst the shareholders associated with that company. Active and independent directors contribute toward a positive outlook of the company in the financial market, positively influencing share prices. Corporate governance is one of the important criteria for foreign institutional investors to decide on which company to invest in. The corporate practices in India emphasize the functions of audit and finances that have legal, moral, and ethical implications for the business and its impact on the shareholders. The Indian Companies Act of 2013 introduced innovative measures to appropriately balance legislative and regulatory reforms for the growth of the enterprise and to increase foreign investment, keeping in mind international practices. The rules and regulations are measures that increase the involvement of the shareholders in decision making and introduce transparency in corporate governance, which ultimately safeguards the interest of the society and shareholders. Corporate governance safeguards not only the management, but the interests of the stakeholders as well, and it fosters the economic progress of India.

7   Failure of Dunlop in India

Dunlop–India, incorporated in 1926, manufactures tires, tubes, flaps, fan and belts, brake hoses, textile and steel-cord belting, transmission belting, PVC belting, repair material, hoses, etc. It used to be the only manufacturer of air tires in India. The company established technical collaboration with Sumitomo Rubber Japan, Dunlop Ltd, UK, BTR Belting, UK, and Mitsubishi Belting, Japan.

In 1980s, Dunlop was the undisputed leader with about one-third of market share. By the 2000s, the brand had all but vanished from tire dealers' showrooms, and a winding-up petition is under review in the Supreme Court.

Dunlop's journey from dominance to dereliction is a reflection of total corruption and theft on the part of the of the owners. Manu Chabria, who purchased Dunlop from Goenka, ran away to Dubai after borrowing Rupee 1 billion from the United Bank of India, and then died or was killed. Later Dunlop was purchased by a loan defaulter Pawan Ruia, who is in prison after he has tried to set fire to Jessop, a railway equipment company, which he also purchased.

When Dunlop's near-monopoly was shielded by high tariff walls, it was able to cater to everything, from the humble bicycle to heavy vehicles and airplanes, at one point, manufacturing 300 kinds of tires. In 1984, Manu Chhabria, the Dubai-based takeover tycoon, and R P Goenka acquired Dunlop. Initially, it was a success. A tumultuous working relationship between Chhabria and Goenka finally culminated in the latter's exit from the company. In 1996, the Dunlop and Shaw Wallace unions made a joint representation to the finance minister and the Prime Minister's Office, seeking Chhabria's removal. By 2000, the factory was closed. In 2005, Ruia bought Dunlop from the Chhabria family. Dunlop's operations have never really been revived.

Management style in Dunlop–India

There are significant differences in the management styles in Dunlop–India and those in a typical Japanese company. These possibly explain the outcome of the Dunlop–India and why it has failed.

In response to the question, "How does your superior dress at work, compared to others in the group?" the reply from a Japanese plant of Toyota was "Same as others," but in Dunlop–India, the response was "He dresses up differently to demonstrate his status." In Toyota and in other major companies in Japan and in subsidiary plants in foreign countries, everyone dresses the same way irrespective of his or her status, with their names written on top of their uniform. Thus, in Japanese plants, there is no difference between people; they are all same. They park their cars in the same space; there is no special place for the executives. They eat in the same canteen together.

In response to the question, "How often does your superior eat lunch with other members of the group?" the reply in Toyota was "Regularly, but there are lunch time meetings sometimes for the team leaders only." In Dunlop–India, the reply is "Never." Thus, in Japanese plants, the communication between the leader and the members are intimate, but in Dunlop–India, they maintain a clear separation because of differences in status. In a Japanese plant, the Plant Manager and Directors of the company stand in the same queue to buy lunch and sit at the same table with workers to create a family atmosphere and harmony. In Dunlop–India, with executives aware of their status; they kept themselves separate from the workers. In response to the question, "Where does your superior usually eat lunch?" the answer in Dunlop–India is "In a separate room."

As a result, there is a serious communication gap between the supervisor and the ordinary workers in Dunlop–India. In response to the question, "When members experience personal difficulties, do they tell their superior about them?" the reply in Dunlop–India was negative, in the Japanese plant, the answer was "Yes, of course."

In response to the question, "When your superior learns that a member is experiencing personal difficulties, does your superior discuss the matter sympathetically with the person concerned?" the response in the Dunlop–India was "never," and the response in the Japanese plant was "yes, of course." Given this close relationship between the supervisor and the ordinary worker, it is not a surprise that Japanese system creates "human-ware," as Shingo (1985) described.

This is reflected in close participation of the workers in Japanese plants in the production process. In response to the questions, "About how many suggestions for work improvements would your superior hope that you would make each month?" and "When group members make suggestions for improvements, what does your superior usually do?" the response in Dunlop–India was very negative, whereas in the Japanese plants it was highly positive.

Rather than separating workers from the strategy and progress in the plants in Japanese companies, workers are consulted regularly on the matters of work, future plans, and strategy. In response to the question, "How much of the information available to your superior concerning the organization's plans and performance is shared with the group?" the reply in Dunlop–India was very negative, but in Japanese plants the response was that the workers discuss these issues in their group meetings and in the trade union meetings. In the Appendix to this chapter, we provide detailed information regarding the result of the survey on the management style in Dunlop–India. Our estimates satisfy the goodness-of-fit criteria; however, the relationship between the latent variables is very weak. In Figure 7.1, we can see that the organizational culture in Japan (OCJP) is

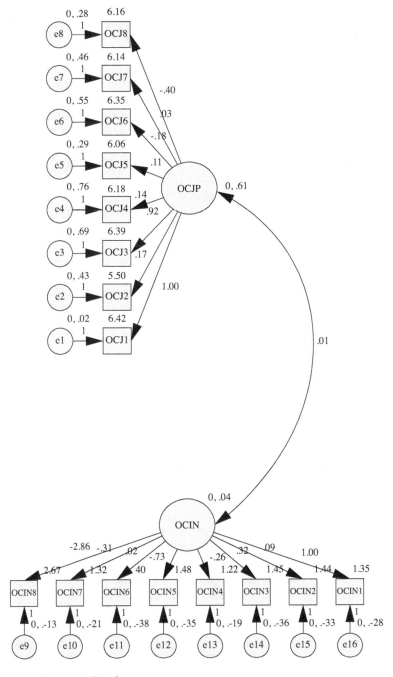

Figure 7.1 Toyota vs Dunlop

Minimum was achieved, chi-square = 222.022, degrees of freedom = 103

unrelated to organizational culture in India (OCIN). Thus, the management system of Toyota has no relationship with the management system of Dunlop. These are separate systems, and that can possibly explain why Toyota is successful and why Dunlop disappeared.

Explanations of the statistical criteria

If the probability value of the chi-square test is smaller than.05, we would reject the null hypothesis that the model fits the data.

Tucker-Lewis Index (TLI) and the Comparative Fit Index (CFI) compare the absolute fit of our specified model to the absolute fit of the independence model. The greater the discrepancy between the overall fit of the two models, the larger the values of these descriptive statistics.

These fit statistics are similar to the adjusted R2 in a multiple regression analysis: the parsimony fit statistics penalize large models with many estimated parameters and few leftover degrees of freedom.

If the estimates are assumed to be population values, they maximize the likelihood (probability) that the data (the observed covariances) were drawn from the population (the expected covariances). Maximum likelihood estimation methods are appropriate for nonnormally distributed data and small sample size.

Hu and Bentler (1999) recommend the Root Mean Square Error of Approximation (RMSEA) values below .06 and Tucker–Lewis Index values of .95 or higher. the comparative fit index (CFI) is equal to the discrepancy function adjusted to the sample size. The CFI ranges from 0 to 1 with a larger value indicating a better model fit. An acceptable model fit is indicated by a CFI value of 0.90 or greater (Hu and Bentler, 1999).

The RMSEA indicates the amount of unexplained variance or residual. The RMSEA value is larger than the 0.06 or less can satisfy the goodness of fit criteria. The CFI and NFI (Normed Fit Index) values should meet the criteria (0.90 or larger) for an acceptable model fit.

The RMSEA is related to residual in the model. The RMSEA values range from 0 to 1 with a smaller RMSEA value indicating a better model fit. If the model fit is acceptable, the parameter estimates are examined. The ratio of each parameter estimate to its standard error is distributed as a z statistic and is significant at the 0.05 level if its value exceeds 1.96, and at the 0.01 level if its value exceeds 2.56.

The AMOS output (i.e., the output from the Software package AMOS) also displays the unstandardized and standardized regression coefficients. Each unstandardized regression coefficient represents the amount of change in the dependent or mediating variable for each one unit change in the variable predicting it.

Standardized estimates allow one to evaluate the relative contributions of each predictor variable to each outcome variable.

There is not much difference between the standardized and unstandardized coefficients in this example, probably because the units are derived from survey measurement items. By contrast, variables with very different measurement scales entered into the same model can result in sharp discrepancies between the standardized and unstandardized regression coefficient output.

The goodness-of-fit index (GFI) was the very first standardized fit index (Joreskog and Sorbom, 1999). It is analogous to a squared multiple correlation, except that the GFI is a kind of matrix proportion of explained variance. Thus, GFI = 1.0 indicates a perfect model fit, GFI > .90 may indicate good fit, and values close to zero indicate very poor fit. However, the GFI values can fall outside the range 0–1.0. Values greater than 1.0 can be found with just identified models or with overidentified models with an almost perfect fit; negative values are most likely to happen when the sample size is small or when the model fit is extremely poor.

Another index originally associated with AMOS is the adjusted goodness-of-fit index (AGFI; Joreskog and Sorbom, 1999). It corrects downward the value of the GFI based on model complexity. The AGFI differs from the GFI only in that it adjusts for the number of degrees of freedom in the specified model. The GFI and AGFI can be classified as absolute indices. The parsimony goodness-of-fit index (PGFI) corrects the value of the GFI by a factor that reflects a model complexity, but it is sensitive to the model size.

The normed fit index (NFI) is one of the original incremental fit indices. It is a ratio of the difference in the value for the fitted model and the null model divided by the value for the null model. It ranges between zero to one. A Normed fit index of one indicates perfect fit.

The relative fit index (RFI) represents a derivative of the NFI; as with both the NFI and CFI, the RFI coefficient values range from zero to one with values close to one indicating superior fit (Hu and Bentler, 1999).

The comparative fit index (CFI) is an incremental fit index that is an improved version of the NFI. The CFI is normed so that values range between zero to one, with higher values indicating better fit. Because the CFI has many desirable properties, including its relative, but not complete, insensitivity to model complexity, it is among the widely used indices. The CFI values above 0.90 are usually associated with a model that fits well, and a revised cut off value close to 0.95 was suggested by Hu and Bentler (1999)

The Tucker–Lewis Index (TLI) is conceptually similar to the NFI, but it varies in that it is actually a comparison of the normed chi-square values for the null and specified model, which to some degree takes into account model complexity. Models with good fit have values that approach one (Hu and Bentler, 1999), and a model with a higher value suggests a better fit than a model with a lower value.

RMSEA represents how well a model fits a population, not just the sample used for estimation. Lower RMSEA values indicate better fit. The root mean square residual (RMR) represents the average residual value derived from the filling of the variance–covariance matrix for the hypothesized model to the variance–covariance matrix of the sample data. Therefore, the RMR is the square root of the mean of the standardized residuals. Lower RMR values represent better fit, and higher values represent worse fit. A recommended RMR value is < 0.02.

NPAR stands for the number of parameters, and CMIN is the minimum discrepancy and represents the discrepancy between the unrestricted sample covariance matrix S and the restricted covariance matrix. Df stands for degrees of freedom, and P is the probability value.

The RMSEA should be below the recommended limit of 0.05, and the RMR should be below the recommended limit of 0.02. This can be interpreted as meaning that the model explains the correlation to within an average error (Hu and Bentler, 1999). Hence the model shows an overall acceptable fit. The confirmatory factor analysis showed an acceptable overall model fit, and hence, the theorized model fits well with the observed data. It can be concluded that the hypothesized model fits the sample data very well.

Appendix
Management style in Dunlop: questionnaire

Would your superior show disapproval of a member who regularly arrived late for work by a certain amount of time?

Answer: Of course.
Mean = 4.79; S. D = .18

How does your superior dress at work, compared to others in the group?

Answer: He had to reflect his superior position;
Mean = 4.69; S. D = .15

Where does your superior usually eat lunch?

Answer: In a separate room.
Mean = 4.51; S. D = .27

How often does your superior eat lunch with other members of the group?

Answer: Never
Mean = 4.67; S. D = .27

When members experience personal difficulties, do they tell their superior about them?

Answer: No
Mean = 4.21; S. D = .78

When your superior learns that a member is experiencing personal difficulties, does your superior discuss the matter sympathetically with the person concerned?

Answer: No
Mean = 4.85; S. D = .56

On average, how often does your superior check with members concerning the quality of their work?

Answer: Regularly
Mean = 4.57; S. D = .13

On average, how often does your superior talk about progress in relation to a work schedule?

Answer: When he needs to.
Mean = 4.37; S. D = .32

On average, how often does your superior demonstrate or us any of the equipment used by the group?

Answer: Whenever it is required.
Mean = 3.76; S. D = .24

On average, how often does your superior send you written notes or memos instead of speaking to you in person?

Answer: Whenever he wants, quite often,
Mean = 4.92; S. D = .16

About how many suggestions for work improvements would your superior hope that you would make each month?

Answer: None. We are not supposed to suggest anything.
Mean = 3.85; S. D = .27

When group members make suggestions for improvements, what does your superior usually do?

Answer: He ignores it or asks us to mind our business.
Mean = 4.71; S. D = .31

For what proportion of the day are you within sight of your superior?

Answer: Most of the time.
Mean = 4.67; S. D = .32

How often do you spend time with your superior socially?

Answer: Never
Mean =-
Mean = 4.75; S. D = .31

How often do you spend time with your superior discussing your career plans?

Answer: Never;
Mean = 4.06; S. D = .38

How often do you spend time with your superior talking about immediate work problems?

Answer: Whenever needed; Mean = 4.82; S. D = .35

Does your superior's evaluation depend more on your own work or on that of the group as a whole?

Answer: On our own work. We do not work as a group
Mean = 4.5; S. D = .37

On average, how often does your superior meet the group for social or recreational purpose outside working hours?

Answer: Very rare
Mean = 4.2; S. D = .35

How do you address your superior?

Answer: By surname, with obligatory "Sir."
Mean = 4.56; S. D = .34

How much of the information available to your superior concerning the organizations plans and performance is shared with the group?

Answer: We do not share anything. We are never consulted.
Mean = 4.89; S. D = .26

How often does this group as a whole have meetings with your superior?

Answer: Only when we have a dispute.
Mean = 4.86; S. D = .14

How many hours do you usually spend discussing work problems with three or more People from your own workgroup at the same time?

Answer: It varies from group to group, at the time of any dispute or industrial action.
Mean = 4.56; S. D = .32

How frequently do you communicate with members of other workgroup in the organization on the same level as yourself?

Answer: At the time of any dispute or industrial action
Mean = 4.21; S. D = .39

How does your superior react when you communicate with members of other workgroups?

Answer: With fear as he would suspect that we are planning an industrial action.
Mean = 4.52; S. D = .38

How does your superior react when you help coworkers with their work problems?

Answer: He does not like that.
Mean = 4.06; S. D = .38

Means and S. D are calculated using a Likert scale (Likert, 1932) from 1 (disagree) to 5 (strongly agree)

Statistical analysis of the management style

Maximum likelihood estimates

Regression weights

			Estimate	S.E.	C.R.	P	Label
OCJ8	←	Ocjp	1.000				
OCJ7	←	Ocjp	.123	.091	1.356	.175	par_1
OCJ6	←	Ocjp	−.082	.111	−.736	.461	par_2
OCJ5	←	Ocjp	.086	.076	1.122	.262	par_3
OCJ4	←	Ocjp	−.041	.123	−.332	.740	par_4
OCJ3	←	Ocjp	−.558	.103	−5.412	***	par_5
OCJ2	←	Ocjp	−.753	.074	−10.190	***	par_6
OCJ1	←	Ocjp	−.681	.100	−6.817	***	par_7
OCIN8	←	Ocin	1.000				
OCIN7	←	Ocin	2.290	6.315	.363	.717	par_8
OCIN6	←	Ocin	−5.339	14.253	−.375	.708	par_9
OCIN5	←	Ocin	−3.099	8.118	−.382	.703	par_10
OCIN4	←	Ocin	14.068	35.653	.395	.693	par_11
OCIN3	←	Ocin	−28.637	72.531	−.395	.693	par_12
OCIN2	←	Ocin	11.859	30.116	.394	.694	par_13
OCIN1	←	Ocin	−6.375	16.458	−.387	.698	par_14

Covariances:

			Estimate	S.E.	C.R.	P	Label
ocin	↔	ocjp	.011	.028	.394	.693	par_15

Correlations: (Group number 1 – Default model)

			Estimate
OCIN	↔	OCJP	.315

Total effects (Group number 1 – Default model)

	ocjp	*ocin*
OCIN1	.000	−6.375
OCIN2	.000	11.859
OCIN3	.000	−28.637
OCIN4	*.000*	14.068
OCIN5	.000	−3.099
OCIN6	.000	−5.339
OCIN7	.000	2.290
OCIN8	.000	1.000
OCJ1	−.681	.000
OCJ2	−.753	.000
OCJ3	−.558	.000
OCJ4	−.041	.000
OCJ5	.086	.000
OCJ6	−.082	.000
OCJ7	.123	.000
OCJ8	1.000	.000

Model fit summary

CMIN

Model	NPAR	CMIN	DF	P	CMIN/DF
Default model	49	513.050	103	.000	4.981
Saturated model	152	.000	0		
Independence model	16	861.636	136	.000	6.336

Baseline Comparisons

Model	NFI Delta1	RFI rho1	IFI Delta2	TLI rho2	CFI
Default model	.405	.214	.459	.254	.435
Saturated model	1.000		1.000		1.000
Independence model	.000	.000	.000	.000	.000

Parsimony-Adjusted measures

Model	PRATIO	PNFI	PCFI
Default model	.757	.306	.329
Saturated model	.000	.000	.000
Independence model	1.000	.000	.000

NCP

Model	NCP	LO 90	HI 90
Default model	410.050	343.095	484.528
Saturated model	.000	.000	.000
Independence model	725.636	636.663	822.092

FMIN

Model	FMIN	F0	LO 90	HI 90
Default model	4.311	3.446	2.883	4.072
Saturated model	.000	.000	.000	.000
Independence model	7.241	6.098	5.350	6.908

RMSEA

Model	RMSEA	LO 90	HI 90	PCLOSE
Default model	.183	.167	.199	.000
Independence model	.212	.198	.225	.000

AIC

Model	AIC	BCC	BIC	CAIC
Default model	611.050	627.383		
Saturated model	304.000	354.667		
Independence model	893.636	898.969		

ECVI

Model	ECVI	LO 90	HI 90	MECVI
Default model	5.135	4.572	5.761	5.272
Saturated model	2.555	2.555	2.555	2.980
Independence model	7.510	6.762	8.320	7.554

HOELTER

Model	HOELTER .05	HOELTER .01
Default model	30	33
Independence model	23	25

8 Failure of Hindustan Motors in India

Hindustan Motors is an Indian automotive manufacturer based in India. It is owned by the Birla family. The company was the largest car manufacturer in India before 1990. Hindustan Motors was the producer of the Ambassador motorcar, based on 1956 Morris Oxford, which was once a mainstream car in India. It was in production from 1957 until 2014. Production of the Ambassador was closed in 2014.

It was founded in 1942 by Mr. B. M. Birla. The company was tuned into a monopoly producer because of the support of the government patronage. In 2017, Hindustan Motors sold its brand name to the French company Peugeot. Post-Independence in 1948, vehicle production was shifted to West Bengal. Hindustan and General Motors have had several collaborations to produce Bedford Trucks, Vauxhall Motors, and Opel Astra. In early 1999, General Motors India purchased the plant from Hindustan Motors. Hindustan motors used to make earthmovers, initially in collaboration with Terex–USA, and beginning in 1984, with Caterpillar Inc. The operation was sold to Caterpillar in 2000. The company began manufacturing tractors in 1963, in collaboration Motokov–Praha (Zetor) of Czechoslovakia. In 1999, Mahindra Tractors purchased 60 percent of the company, and in 2001, it completed purchasing the rest of the company, renaming it Mahindra Gujarat Tractors Ltd.

In 1982, Hindustan formed collaboration with Isuzu to assemble and sell the Isuzu trucks in India. They were discontinued mainly due to falling sales and poor service facilities.

Hindustan began a joint venture with Mitsubishi in 1998. It was not successful.

Management style in Hindustan Motors

There are significant differences in management style in Hindustan Motors with their Japanese counterpart in Japan. Just like in Dunlop–India, management in Hindustan Times is oppressive. There is no psychological contact between the supervisor and the ordinary workers. They are very far from each other. The relationship is one of hostility not harmony. In the Appendix to this chapter, we provide the detail regarding the result of the survey on the management style in Hindustan Motors.

In response to the question, "Would your superior show disapproval of a member who regularly arrived late for work by a certain amount of time?" the answer was "He gets very angry." In response to the question, "How often does your superior eat lunch with other members of the group?" the answer in the Hindustan Motors was "very rarely if at all." In response to the question, "when members experience Personal difficulties, do they tell their superior about them?" the answer was no.

There was no link between the executive and the ordinary worker in the Hindustan Times. When we have asked, "When your superior learns that a member is experiencing personal difficulties, does your superior discuss the matter sympathetically with the person concerned?" the answer we got in the Hindustan Motors was no. Again, when we asked the question, "When your superior learns that a member is experiencing personal difficulties, does your superior discuss the matter in the person's absence with other members?" the answer was no.

In response to the question, "When your superior learn that a member is experiencing personal difficulties, does your superior arrange for other members to help with the person's workloads?" the answer was no.

In response to the question, "How does your superior dress at work, compared to others in the group?" the reply from Hindustan Motors was "He dressed up differently to demonstrate his status."

As a result, there is a serious psychological gap between the supervisor and the ordinary workers in Hindustan Motors. This is reflected in the absence of any participation of the workers in Hindustan Motors plants in the production process. In response to the question, "About how many suggestions for work improvements would your superior hope that you would make each month?" and "When group members make suggestions for improvements, what does your superior usually do?" the responses in Hindustan Motors were negative.

In Hindustan Motors, workers had nothing to do with the strategy and progress in the plants. Workers were not consulted regularly on matters of work, future plans, and strategy. In response to the question, "How much of the information available to your superior concerning the organization's plans and performance is shared with the group?" the reply in Hindustan Motors was totally negative.

From Figure 8.1, we can see that Toyota's management system is unrelated to the Hindustan Motors' management system. Full explanations of the statistical criteria are presented in the Appendix to this chapter. Both the covariance and the regression coefficients are very small. Toyota's management system is designed to enhance both customer's satisfaction and worker's satisfaction. In Hindustan Motors, there was no concern for the worker's satisfaction or for the customer's satisfaction. The management was complacent

From Figure 8.1, we can see that Toyota's management system is unrelated to the Hindustan Motor's management system. Full explanations of the statistical criteria are presented in the Appendix to this chapter. Both the covariance and the regression coefficient are very small. Toyota's management system is designed to enhance both customer's satisfaction and worker's satisfaction. In Hindustan

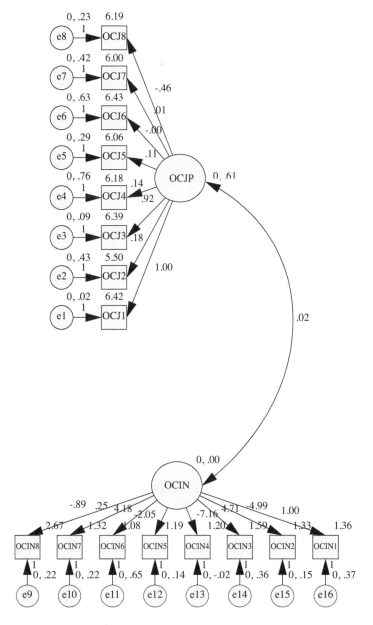

Figure 8.1 Toyota vs Hindustan Motors

Motors, there was no concern for the worker's satisfaction or for the customer's satisfaction. The management was complacent.

From Figure 8.1, we can see that Toyota's management system is unrelated to the Hindustan Motors' management system. Full explanations of the statistical criteria are presented in the Appendix to this chapter. Our estimation satisfies all goodness-of-fit criteria, but the relationship between the latent variables is very weak. Both the covariance and the regression coefficient are very small. Toyota's management system is designed to enhance both customer's satisfaction and worker's satisfaction. In Hindustan Motors, there was no concern for the worker's satisfaction or for the customer's satisfaction. The management was complacent and often corrupt.

One of the central purposes of management is to facilitate communication across all of the organization's boundaries, so that the entire company works together to address given business challenges. With efficient dissemination of management system, the company's ability to make impacting decisions increases dramatically, because individuals throughout the firm gain access to important strategic ideas. This improves the organization's ability to make rapid decisions and execute them. To create a management system appropriate for transforming tacit knowledge into communal, explicit knowledge, fear-based approaches to management must be abandoned in preference for a harmonious relationship-oriented management. The key is to create an environment of understanding, shared control, compassion, and learning. In Hindustan Motors, there was none of these. Because of the monopoly rights given to Birla Brothers by the Nehru–Gandhi family, the company survived, but then, when it had to face competition, it collapsed.

Human beings are creatures *ruled by reasons.* It must be admitted that workers in present-day firms are given few reasons to want to be cooperative and creative. In these, human beings are viewed much the same as organisms ("termites," according to Herzberg, 1980) ruled by quasi-instinctive impulses or external stimuli. Therefore, the present-day behavioral sciences of organisms must be replaced by a theory that advocates that people must find by themselves and for themselves *reasons for working with* more *creativity than what is presently being asked of them.*

Appendix
Management style in Hindustan Motors

Questionnaire

Would your superior show disapproval of a member who regularly arrived late for work by a certain amount of time?

Answer: He gets very angry
Mean = 4.93, S. D = .26

How many hours per week is your superior usually at work compared to official work hours?

Answer: For all the official hours; Mean = 4.96; S. D = 1.16

How does your superior dress at work, compared to others in the group?

Answer: He dress up differently to demonstrate his status.
Mean = 4.82; S. D = 1.34

Where does your superior usually eat lunch?

Answer: Separately in their canteen
Mean = 4.51; S. D = 1.27

How often does your superior eat lunch with other members of the group?

Answer: very rarely if at all
Mean = 4.58; S. D = 1.45

When members experience personal difficulties, do they tell their superior about them?

Answer: No,
Mean = 4.21; S. D = 1 .78

When your superior learns that a member is experiencing personal difficulties, does your superior discuss the matter sympathetically with the person concerned?

Answer: No
Mean = 4.85; S. D = 1.56

When your superior learns that a member is experiencing personal difficulties, does your superior discuss the matter in the person's absence with other members?

Answer: No
Mean = 4.97; S. D = 1.85

When your superior learns that a member is experiencing personal difficulties, does your superior arrange for other members to help with the person's workloads?

Answer: No
Mean = 4.51; S. D = 1.32

On average, how often does your superior check with members concerning the quality of their work?

Answer: Continuously;
Mean = 4.17; S. D = 2.13

On average, how often does your superior talk about progress in relation to a work schedule?

Answer: Regularly, Sometime more often than that.
Mean = 4.37; S. D = 2.32

On average, how often does your superior demonstrate or us any of the equipment used by the group?

Answer: Rarely, if there is a need.
Mean = 4.76; S. D = 1.24

On average, how often does your superior instruct you on how to increase your job skills?

Answer: Whenever needed
Mean = 4.86; S. D = 2 .32

On average, how often does your superior send you written notes or memos instead of speaking to you in person?

Answer: Some time, whenever he needs.
Mean = 4.92; S. D = 2.35

On average, how often does your superior explain to you how to carry out a new task?

Answer: If there is a need.
Mean = 4.78; S. D = 1.81

About how many suggestions for work improvements would your superior hope that you would make each month?

Answer: Never.
Mean = 3.85; S. D = 2.27

When group members make suggestions for improvements, what does your superior usually do?

Answer: He ignores
Mean = 4.71; S. D = 2. 51

For what proportion of the day are you within sight of your superior?

Answer: Most of the time or sometime less, it depends on the type of work;
Mean = 4.67; S. D = 1.52

How often do you spend time with your superior socially?

Answer: Rarely
Mean = 4.75; S. D = 2.31

How often do you spend time with your superior discussing your career plans?

Answer: Rarely;
Mean = 4.66; S. D = 1.38

How often do you spend time with your superior talking about immediate work problems?

Answer: Whenever needed
Mean = 4.32; S. D = 2.35

Does your superior's evaluation depend more on your own work or on that of the group as a whole?

Answer: On my own work
Mean = 4.87; S. D = 2.34

On average, how often does your superior meet the group for social or recreational purpose outside working hours?

Answer: Not normally.
Mean = 4.6; S. D = 2.55

What does your superior do when he or she believes that there is a substantial problem in the group's work procedures?

Answer: Discuss in the group meeting and in the trade union meeting.
Mean = 4.61; S. D = 1.89

Who is consulted when substantially new work procedures are being discussed?

Answer: Trade Union and most workers
Mean = 4.96; S. D = 2.17

How much of the information available to your superior concerning the organization's plans and performance is shared with the group?

Answer: We do not share any details;
Mean = 4.65; S. D = 2.26

How often does this group as a whole have meetings with your superior?

Answer: Very rarely
Mean = 4.86; S. D = 2.34

How frequently do you communicate with members of other workgroup in the organization on the same level as yourself?

Answer: Quite often; Mean = 4.41; S. D = 1.39

How does your superior react when you communicate with members of other workgroups?

Answer: He does not like it.
Mean = 4.52; S. D = 1.88

How does your superior react when you help coworkers with their work problems?

Answer: With discouragement
Mean = 4.66; S. D = 2.38

How does your superior react when you undertake work additional to the hours for which you are paid?

Answer: That is not the practice; Mean = 4.76; S. D = 1.81
Notes: Means and S. D are calculated using a Likert scale (Likert, 1932) from 1 (disagree) to 5 (strongly agree).

Statistical analysis of the management system

Maximum likelihood estimates

Regression weights

			Estimate	S.E.	C.R.	P	Label
OCJ1	←	OCJP	1.000				
OCJ2	←	OCJP	.183	.086	2.129	.033	par_1
OCJ3	←	OCJP	.924	.057	16.256	***	par_2
OCJ4	←	OCJP	.142	.114	1.252	.210	par_3
OCJ5	←	OCJP	.113	.070	1.616	.106	par_4
OCJ6	←	OCJP	-.003	.103	-.033	.974	par_5
OCJ7	←	OCJP	.012	.085	.145	.885	par_6
OCJ8	←	OCJP	-.457	.065	-7.002	***	par_7
OCIN1	←	OCIN	1.000				
OCIN2	←	OCIN	-4.988	4.803	-1.038	.299	par_8
OCIN3	←	OCIN	4.708	4.595	1.025	.306	par_9
OCIN4	←	OCIN	-7.164	6.896	-1.039	.299	par_10
OCIN5	←	OCIN	-2.047	2.041	-1.003	.316	par_11
OCIN6	←	OCIN	4.179	4.188	.998	.318	par_12
OCIN7	←	OCIN	.254	.774	.328	.743	par_13
OCIN8	←	OCIN	-.891	1.125	-.792	.428	par_14

Standardized regression weights

			Estimate
OCJ1	←	OCJP	.982
OCJ2	←	OCJP	.213
OCJ3	←	OCJP	.927
OCJ4	←	OCJP	.127
OCJ5	←	OCJP	.163
OCJ6	←	OCJP	-.003
OCJ7	←	OCJP	.015
OCJ8	←	OCJP	-.596
OCIN1	←	OCIN	.097
OCIN2	←	OCIN	-.602
OCIN3	←	OCIN	.420
OCIN4	←	OCIN	-1.063
OCIN5	←	OCIN	-.309
OCIN6	←	OCIN	.293
OCIN7	←	OCIN	.032
OCIN8	←	OCIN	-.112

Covariances

			Estimate	S.E.	C.R.	P	Label
OCIN	↔	OCJP	.025	.024	1.013	.311	par_15

Correlations

			Estimate
OCIN	↔	OCJP	.534

Squared multiple correlations

	Estimate
OCIN8	.013
OCIN7	.001
OCIN6	.086
OCIN5	.095
OCIN4	1.130
OCIN3	.176
OCIN2	.362
OCIN1	.009
OCJ8	.355
OCJ7	.000
OCJ6	.000
OCJ5	.026
OCJ4	.016
OCJ3	.859
OCJ2	.045
OCJ1	.965

Standardized total effects

	OCJP	OCIN
OCIN8	.000	−.112
OCIN7	*.000*	.032
OCIN6	.000	.293
OCIN5	.000	−.309
OCIN4	.000	−1.063
OCIN3	.000	.420
OCIN2	.000	−.602
OCIN1	.000	.097

	OCJP	OCIN
OCJ8	−.596	.000
OCJ7	.015	.000
OCJ6	−.003	.000
OCJ5	.163	.000
OCJ4	.127	.000
OCJ3	.927	.000
OCJ2	.213	.000
OCJ1	.982	.000

Model fit summary

CMIN

Model	NPAR	CMIN	DF	P	CMIN/DF
Default model	49	497.283	103	.000	4.828
Saturated model	152	.000	0		
Independence model	16	861.636	136	.000	6.336

Baseline comparisons

Model	NFI Delta1	RFI rho1	IFI Delta2	TLI rho2	CFI
Default model	.423	.238	.480	.283	.457
Saturated model	1.000		1.000		1.000
Independence model	.000	.000	.000	.000	.000

Parsimony-adjusted measures

Model	PRATIO	PNFI	PCFI
Default model	.757	.320	.346
Saturated model	.000	.000	.000
Independence model	1.000	.000	.000

NCP

Model	NCP	LO 90	HI 90
Default model	394.283	328.549	467.547
Saturated model	.000	.000	.000
Independence model	725.636	636.663	822.092

FMIN

Model	FMIN	F0	LO 90	HI 90
Default model	4.179	3.313	2.761	3.929
Saturated model	.000	.000	.000	.000
Independence model	7.241	6.098	5.350	6.908

RMSEA

Model	RMSEA	LO 90	HI 90	PCLOSE
Default model	.179	.164	.195	.000
Independence model	.212	.198	.225	.000

AIC

Model	AIC	BCC	BIC	CAIC
Default model	595.283	611.616		
Saturated model	304.000	354.667		
Independence model	893.636	898.969		

ECVI

Model	ECVI	LO 90	HI 90	MECVI
Default model	5.002	4.450	5.618	5.140
Saturated model	2.555	2.555	2.555	2.980
Independence model	7.510	6.762	8.320	7.554

HOELTER

Model	HOELTER .05	HOELTER .01
Default model	31	34
Independence model	23	25

Result

Minimum was achieved
Chi-square = 497.283
Degrees of freedom = 103

9 Conclusion

Modern sociology sees "powerlessness alienation" as a consequence of (a) the separation from ownership of the means of production, (b) the inability to influence general managerial policies, (c) the lack of control over the conditions of employment, and (d) the lack of control over the immediate work process.

In the full development of capitalism, however, still stronger fetters were forged; the worker became a commodity, a piece of industrial raw material, a mere adjunct to the machine, a pure function of capital, and the capitalist mode of production. The owners of private property commanded the non-owners into the narrow slots that the capitalist factory division of labor dictated. The command seemed personal; the worker appeared powerless to disobey although strictly in terms of Marx's economics, wages were determined by the forces of the cold and impersonal market, which held both worker and employer in its sway.

Inventions were invariably labor-saving inventions. These in turn gave rise to a chronic excess supply of labor: "the industrial reserve army." "Only in association with others has each individual the means of cultivating his talents in all directions. Only in a community, therefore, is personal freedom possible." Each separate individual potentially represented humanity as a whole, his real or natural development led to that of the universality of man; unfettered self-realization through genuine (un-alienated) labor led to the fulfillment of what Marx called man's species life.

Just as alienated labor transforms free and self-directed activity into a means, so it transforms the species life of man into a means of physical existence. In becoming an alienated being, man became isolated from real humanity, from himself, from his fellows, and from nature.

The capitalist economy gives rise to a false kind of production and to an industrial system that does not satisfy human needs but only those "imaginary appetites" that the system itself has created. The true destiny of man is one of "self-realization." This takes the form of a continual "dialogue" or reciprocal relationship between himself, his fellow beings, and the objects of surrounding nature.

Barney (1991) defines resources as valuable "when they enable a firm to conceive of or implement strategies that improve its efficiency and effectiveness" and "when they exploit opportunities or neutralize threats in a firm's environment."

The view of organizations as "repositories of productive knowledge" is expanded upon by Nelson and Winter (1982), who maintain that an organization's productive knowledge is to be found in its operational routines. Organizational routines are the basis of a firm's distinctiveness and are, therefore, the source of its competitiveness. Thus, the resource-based view considers the firm as a repository of knowledge (Fransman, 1998; Simon, Hitt, and Ireland, 2007). Japanese major companies have used this concept effectively, but it was ignored by the Indian private sector companies who spend almost nothing on research and knowledge development.

Corporate purpose of the company, its espoused values, and vision of the leaders create values of its corporate management and operations management systems and for the organizational culture of the company as a whole. These values ultimately create commitment of the employees. Creation of commitment, an important index of a firm's successful corporate performance, in turn forms a company citizenship. Organizational cultures that "encouraged trust, participative-ness, and entrepreneurial behavior were effective across" the globe, both in the home country and in the host countries all over the world (Basu, Miroshnik, and Uchida, 2001). This is a strategy to create unique competitive resources (Miroshnik, 2012; Hatch and Dyer, 2004). Japanese major companies create these competitive resources, but Indian private sector companies cannot, and as a result, they fail.

In both Dunlop and Hindustan Motors, we have seen unsympathetic management who did not care about the customers or the workers and who led these companies into total disaster. In both companies, corruption and monopoly rights of the promoters have protected these companies for some time, but this could not be sustainable. The Japanese companies on the other hand have taken care of both the customers and the workers.

Bibliography

Ackoff, R.L. 1970. *A concept of corporate: Planning*. New York, NY: Wiley.

Adegbesan, J.A. 2009. On the origins of competitive advantage: Strategic factor markets and heterogeneous resource complementarity. *Academy of Management Review*, 34, 463–475.

Adler, N. 1982. Cross-cultural management: Conceptual analyses. *International Studies of Management and Organization*, 12, 4, 7–45.

Adler, N., and Jelinek, M. 1986. Is "organization culture" culture bound? *Human Resources Management*, 25, 1, 73–90.

Adler, N.J., and Gundersen, A. 2007. *International dimensions of organizational behavior*. Mason, Ohio: Thompson South Western.

Åhlström, P. 1998. Sequences in the implementation of lean production. *European Management Journal*, 16, 3, 327–334.

Aitken, H.G. 1960. Taylorism at Watertown Arsenal: scientific management in action, 1908–1915. Cambridge, Mass: Harvard University Press.

Aitken, H.G. 1985. *Scientific management in action: Taylorism at Watertown Arsenal, 1908–1915*. Princeton, NJ, USA: Princeton University Press.

Aktouf, O. 1992. Management and theories of organizations in the 1990s: Toward a critical radical humanism? *The Academy of Management Review*, 17, 3.

Aktouf, O. 1986. Une approche ethnographique et une perspective interculturelle Canada/Algérie. *Le travail humain*, Jan 1, .237–248.

Allaire, Y., and Firsirotu, M.1984. Theories of organizational culture. *Organizational Studies*, 5, 193–226.

Alvarez, S.A., and Barney, J.B. 2010. Entrepreneurship and epistemology: The philosophical underpinnings of the study of entrepreneurial opportunities. *Academy of Management Annals*, 4, 1, 557–583.

Amit, R., and Schoemaker, P.J.H. 1993. Strategic assets and organizational rent. *Strategic Management Journal*, 14, 1, 33–46.

Andersson, U., Björkman, I., and Forsgren, M. 2005. Managing subsidiary knowledge creation: The effect of control mechanisms on subsidiary local embeddedness. *International Business Review*, 14, 5, 521–538.

Andrews, T.G. 2001. Downsizing the Thai subsidiary corporation: A case analysis. *Asia Pacific Business Review*, 8, 2, 149–170.

Aoki, K. 2008. Transferring Japanese Kaizen activities to overseas plants in China. *International Journal of Operations & Production Management*, 28, 6, 518–539.

Aoki, M. 1990. Towards an economic model of the Japanese firm. *Journal of Economic Literature*, 28, 1–27.

Appleyard, D.R., Field, A.J., Jr., and Cobb, S.L. 2006. *International economics.* Boston: McGraw-Hill.

Arab Times. 2010. Indian family firms businesses decline. www.ifc.org/wps/wcm/connect/1fe292804a4785e6824d9faa52ef3b86/

Argyris, C. 1957. The individual and organization: Some problems of mutual adjustment. *Administrative science quarterly,* 1–24.

Aselage, J., and Eisenberger, R. 2003. Perceived organizational support and psychological contracts: A theoretical integration. *Journal of Organizational Behavior,* 24, 5, 491–509.

Axel, M. 1995. Culture-bound aspects of Japanese management. *Management International Review,* 35, 2, 57–73.

Balasubramanian, B., Black, B., and Khanna, V. 2009. *Firm-level corporate governance in emerging markets: A case study of India.* Law Working Paper, 119/2009. European Corporate Governance Institute. http://papers.ssrn.com/sol3/papers.cfm?abstract_id=992529&rec=1&srcabs=914440

Baliga, B.R., and Jaeger, A.M. 1984. Multinational corporations: Control systems and delegation issues. *Journal of International Business Studies,* 15, 2, 25–40.

Baliga, B.R., and Jaeger, A.M.1985. Control systems and strategic adaptation: Lessons from the Japanese experience. *Strategic Management Journal,* 6, 115–134.

Bartlett, C.A., and Yoshihara, H. 1988. New challenges for Japanese multinationals: Is organization adaptation their Achilles Heel. *Human Resources Management,* 27, 1, 19–43.

Bartlett, C.A., and Ghoshal, S. 1989. *Managing across the borders: The transnational solution.* Boston: Harvard Business School Press.

Bartlett, C.A., and Ghoshal, S. 1992. *What is a global manager?* Cambridge: Harvard Business School Press.

Barney, J.B. 1983. Semiotics and the study of occupational and organizational cultures. *Administrative Science Quarterly,* 28, 393–413.

Barney, J.B. 1986. Organizational culture: Can it be a source of sustained competitive advantage. *Academy of Management Review,* 11, 3, 656–665.

Barney, J.B. 1991. Firm resources and sustained competitive advantages. *Journal of Management,* 17, 1, 99–120.

Barney, J.B. 2001. Is the resource-based view a useful perspective for strategic management research? *Academy of Management Review,* 26, 1, 41–57.

Barney, J.B. 2005. Where does inequality come from? The personal and intellectual roots of resource-based theory. In K.G. Smith and M.A. Hitt, eds., *Great minds in management: The process of theory development,* 280–303. Oxford, UK: Oxford University Press.

Barney, J.B., and Clark, D.N. 2007. *Resource-based theory: Creating and sustaining competitive advantage.* Oxford, UK: Oxford University Press.

Basu, D., and Miroshnik, V. 1999. Strategic human resources management of Japanese multinational companies in UK. *Journal of Management Development,* 18, 9, 714–732.

Basu, D., Miroshnik, V., and Uchida, S. 2001. Leadership in management of Japanese multinational companies in home and host countries. *Keiei to Keizai,* 81, 2, 109–144.

Basu, D., Miroshnik, V., and Uchida, S. 2011. Transmission of management system from Japan to Britain. *Keiki to Keizai,* 90, 4, 27–48.

Basu, S. 1999. *Corporate purpose.* New York, NY: Garland Publishers.

Bayertz, K. 1996. Human dignity: Philosophical origin and scientific erosion of an idea. In K. Bayertz, ed., *Sanctity of life and human dignity*, 73–90. Boston: Kluwer Academic.

Beechler, S., and Yang, J.Z. 1994. The transfer of Japanese-style management to American subsidiaries: Contingencies, constraints, and competencies. *Journal of International Business Studies*, 467–491.

Beissinger, M.R. 1988. *Scientific management, socialist discipline, and Soviet power*. London: I.B. Tauris.

Bellak, C.A., and Weiss, A. 1993. A note on the Austrian "diamond." *Management International Review*, 33, 2, 109–118.

Bereznoy, A. 2015. Changing competitive landscape through business model innovation: The new imperative for corporate market strategy. *Journal of the Knowledge Economy*, October 27, 1–22.

Besser, T.L. 1993. The commitment of the Japanese and U.S. workers: Reassessment of the literature. *American Sociological Review*, 58, 873–881.

Bhattacharyya, A. 2016. *Corporate governance in India: Change and continuity*. Oxford, UK: Oxford University Press.

Bird, A., and Stevens, M.J. 2003. Toward an emergent global culture and the effects of globalization on obsolescing national cultures. *Journal of International Management*, 9, 4, 395–407.

Biswas, S., and Puri, M. 2011. India inc. vouches for senior executives at board levels: Next can wait. *Economic Times*, April 27. http://articles.economictimes.indiatimes.com/2011-04-27/news/29479221_1

Bloom, N., and Van Reenen, J. 2010. Why do management practices differ across firms and countries? *The Journal of Economic Perspectives*, 24, 1, 203–224.

Bloom, N., Christos, G., Raffaella, S., and Van Reenen, J. 2012. Management practices across firms and countries. *The Academy of Management Perspectives*, 26, 1, 12–33.

Bloskie, C. 1995. Leadership and integrity. *Optimum*, 26, 2, 37–56.

Bodwell, W., and Chermack, T. 2010. Organizational ambidexterity: Integrating deliberate and emergent strategy with scenario planning. *Technological Forecasting & Social Change*, 77, 1, 193–202.

Bogaert, S., Boone, D., and Declerck, C. 2008. Social value orientation and cooperation in social dilemmas: A review and conceptual model. *British Journal of Social Psychology*, 47, 453–480.

Bolt, J., and Tailor, F. 1985. Executive development to strategy. *Harvard Business Review*, November–December, 168–176.

Bonaglia, F., Goldstein, A., and Mathews, J. 2007. Accelerated internationalization by emerging markets's multinationals: The case of the white goods sector. *Journal of World Business*, 42, 369–383.

Bolwijn, P.T., and Kumpe, T. 1990. Manufacturing in the 1990s–productivity, flexibility and innovation. *Long Range Planning*, 23, 4, 44–57.

Brannen, M.Y., and Salk, J.E. 2000. Partnering across borders: Negotiating organizational culture in a German-Japanese joint venture. *Human Relations*, 53, 4, 451–487.

Bridoux, F., Coeurderoy, R., and Durand, R. 2011. Heterogeneous motives and the collective creation of value. *Academy of Management Review*, 36, 4, 711–730.

Brown, J.L., and Schneck, R. 1979. A structural comparison between Canadian and American industrial organizations. *Administrative Science Quarterly*, 24, 1, 24–47.

Business Standard. 2011. Poor corporate governance leads to higher risk and lower returns. May 27. www.businessstandard.com/India

Cable, D.M., and Judge, T.A. 1997a. Applicant personality, organizational culture, and organization attraction. *Personnel Psychology*, 50, 2, 359–394.

Cable, D.M., and Judge, T.A. 1997b. Interviewers' perceptions of person-organization fit and organizational selection decisions. *Journal of Applied Psychology*, 82, 546–581.

Cable, D.M., Aiman-Smith, L., Mulvey, P.W., and Edwards, J.R. 2000. The sources and accuracy of job applicants' beliefs about organizational culture. *Academy of Management Journal*, 43, 6, 1076–1086.

Cable, D.M., and DeRue, D.S. 2002. The convergent and discriminant validity of subjective fit perceptions. *Journal of Applied Psychology*, 87, 5, 875–884.

Cable, D.M., and Edwards, J.R. 2004. Complementary and supplementary fit: A theoretical and empirical integration. *Journal of Applied Psychology*, 89, 5, 822–834.

Caldwell, D.F., and O'Reilly, C.A. 1990. Measuring person-job fit with a profile-comparison process. *Journal of Applied Psychology*, 75, 6, 648–657.

Caldwell, S.D., Herold, D.M., and Fedor, D.B. 2004. Toward an understanding of the relationships among organizational change, individual difference, and changes in person-environment fit: A cross level study. *Journal of Applied Psychology*, 89, 868–882.

Calori, R., and Sarnin, P. 1991. Corporate culture and economic performance: A French study. *Organization Studies*, 12, 1, 49–74.

Cameron, K.S., and Quinn, R.E. 1999. *Diagnosing and changing organizational culture: Based on the competing values framework*. Reading, MA: Addison-Wesley.

Cameron, K.S., and Quinn, R.E. 2011. *Diagnosing and changing organizational culture: Based on the competing values framework*. Hoboken, NJ: John Wiley & Sons.

Carless, S.A. 2005. Person-job fit versus person-organization fit as predictors of organizational attraction and job acceptance intentions: A longitudinal study. *Journal of Occupational and Organizational Psychology*, 78, 3, 411–429.

Carlock, R. 2010. *When family businesses are best*. INSEAD Faculty and Research WorkingPaper2010/42/EFE. Fontainebleau: INSEAD.

Carr, C., and Collis, D. 2011. Should you have a global strategy? *Sloan Management Review*, September 21.

Carroll, A.B. 1979. A three-dimensional conceptual model of corporate performance. *Academy of Management Review*, 4, 4, 497–505.

Carroll, D.T. 1983. A disappointing search for excellence. *Harvard Business Review*, November–December, 78–88.

Chakrabarti, R. 2005. Corporate governance in India: Evolution and challenges. *ICFAI Journal of Corporate Governance*, October. https://pdfs.semanticscholar.org/ce61/23a86eaf591ed71a3253a0cca4cac

Chakrabarti, R., Megginson, W., and Yadav, P. 2008. Corporate governance in India. *Journal of Applied Corporate Finance*, 20, 1, 59–72.

Chatterjee, B., Mir, M.Z., and Farooque, O. 2009. The current status of related party disclosure in India: A longitudinal analysis. In M. Tsamenyi and S. Uddin, eds., *Accounting in emerging economies (Research in accounting in emerging economies)*, Vol. 9, 287–319. Bingley, Yorkshire: Emerald.

Chen, M.J., and Miller, D. 2010. West meets East: Toward an ambicultural approach to management. *Academy of Management Perspective*, 24, 17–24.

Chen, M.J., and Miller, D. 2011. The relational perspective as a business mindset. *Academy of Management Perspectives*, 25, 3, 6–18.

Chew, I.K.H., and Putti, J. 1995. Relationship on work-related values of Singaporean and Japanese managers in Singapore. *Human Relations*, 48, 10, 1149–1170.

Chhokar, J.S., Brodbeck, F.C., and House, R.J., eds. 2008. *Culture and leadership across the world: The GLOBE book of in-depth studies of 25 societies*. New York, NY: Taylor & Francis.

Child, J. 1972. Organizational structure, environment and performance: The role of strategic choice. *Sociology*, 6, 1, 1–22.

Child, J., and Rodrigues, S. 2005. The internationalization of Chinese firms: A case for theoretical extension. *Management and Organization Review*, 1, 3, 381–410.

Clark, T. 1991. Review of the competitive advantage of nations, by M. E. Porter. *Journal of Marketing*, October, 118–120.

Clugston, M., Howell, J.P., and Dorfman, P.W. 2000. Does cultural socialization predict multiple bases and foci of commitment? *Journal of Management*, 26, 1, 5–30.

Coase, R.H. 1937. The nature of the firm. *Economica*, 4, 16, 386–405.

Colbert, B.A. 2004. The complex resource-based view: Implications for theory and practice in strategic human resource management. *Academy of Management Review*, 29, 3, 341–358.

Collis, D.J. 1991. A resource-based analysis of global competition: the case of the bearings industry. *Strategic Management Journal*, 12, S1, 49–68.

Cutcher-Gershenfeld, J. 1991. The impact on economic performance of a transformation in industrial relations. *Industrial and Labor Relations Review*, 44, 241–260.

Daniels, J.D. 1987. Bridging national and global marketing strategies through regional operations. *International Marketing Review*, 4, 3, 29–44.

Das, S.C. 2016. *Corporate governance in India: An evaluation*. New Delhi: Taxmann, ICCA.

Davies, H., and Ellis, P.D. 2000. Porter's "competitive advantage of nations": Time for a final judgment? *Journal of Management Studies*, 37, 8, 1189–1213.

Deal, T.E., and Kennedy, A.A.1982. *Corporate cultures: The rites and rituals of corporate life*. Reading, MA: Addison-Wesley.

Del Campo, R.G. 2006. The influence of culture strength on person-organization fit and turnover. *International Journal of Management*, 9, 71–88.

Denison, D.R., and Mishra, A.K. 1995. Toward a theory of organizational culture and effectiveness. *Organizational Science*, 6, 2, 204–223.

Dibrell, C., Craig, J.B., and Neubaum, D.O. 2013. Linking the formal strategic planning process, planning flexibility, and innovativeness to firm performance. *Journal of Business Research*, 67, 9, 2000–2007.

Drucker, P. 1959. Long-range planning: Challenge to management science. *Management Science*, 5, 235–249.

Drucker, P. 1971. What we can learn from Japanese management. *Harvard Business Review*, March, 1–26.

Drucker, P. 1995. L'inforination dont un dirigeant a vraiment besoin. *L'Expansion Management Review*, 77, 6–14.

Durand, R., and Calori, R. 2006. Sameness, otherness? Enriching . . . considerations on the same and the other. *Academy of Management Review*, 31, 1, 93–114.

Dyer, J.H., and Ouchi, W.G. 1993. Japanese-style partnerships: giving companies a competitive edge. *Sloan Management Review*, 35, 1, 51–63

Easterby-Smith, M., Lyles, M.A., and Peteraf, M.A. 2009. Dynamic capabilities: Current debates and future directions. *British Journal of Management*, 20, 1, S1–S8.

Economic Times. 2011. No voting rights for interested groups: Sebi. http://articles.economictimes.indiatimes.com/February,2011-2-08/news/

Edström, A., and Lorange, P. 1984. Matching strategy and human resources in multinational corporations. *Journal of International Business Studies*, 15, 2, 125–137.

Edwards, J.R., Cable, D., Williamson, I.O., Schurer, L., Lambert, J., and Shipp, A. 2006. The phenomenology of fit: Linking the person and environment to the subjective experience of person-environment fit. *Journal of Applied Psychology*, 91, 4, 802–839.

Eisenberger, R., Fasolo, P., and Davis-LaMastro, V. 1990. Perceived organizational support and employee diligence, commitment, and innovation. *Journal of Applied Psychology*, 75, 1, 51–59.

Eisenberger, R., Fasolo, P., and Davis-LaMastro, V. 1990. Perceived organizational support and employee diligence, commitment, and innovation. *Journal of Applied Psychology*, 75, 1, 51–59.

Eisenhardt, K.M., and Martin, J.A. 2000. Dynamic capabilities: What are they? *Strategic Management Journal*, 21, 10, 1105–1121.

Engels, F., and Marx, K. 1987. *Anti-DUhring: Dialectics of nature*. Moscow: Progress Publisher.

Enz, C.A. 1986. *Power and shared values in corporate culture*. Ann Arbor, MI: UMI Research.

Etchegoyen, A. 1990. *Les entreprises ont-elles une âme?* Paris: F. Bourin.

Farh, J.L., Hackett, R.D., and Liang, J. 2007. Individual level cultural values as moderators of perceived organizational support-employee outcome relationship in China. *Academy of Management Journal*, 50, 715–729.

Fedor, D.B., Caldwell, S.D., and Herold, D.M. 2006. The effects of organizational changes on employee commitment: A multilevel investigation. *Personal Psychology*, 59, 1–29.

Fehr, E., and Gintis, H. 2007. Human motivation and social cooperation: Experimental and analytical foundations. *Annual Review of Sociology*, 33, 43–64.

Felin, T., and Hesterly, W.S. 2007. The knowledge based view, heterogeneity, and the individual: Philosophical considerations on the locus of knowledge. *Academy of Management Review*, 32, 195–218.

Fey, C.F., and Furu, P. 2008. Top management incentive compensation and knowledge sharing in multinational corporations. *Strategic Management Journal*, 29, 12, 1301–1323.

Finegan, J.E. 2000. The impact of person and organizational values on organizational commitment. *Journal of Occupational and Organizational Psychology*, 73, 2, 149–169.

Florida, R., and Kenney, M. 1991. Transplanted organizations: The transfer of Japanese industrial organization to the U.S. *American Sociological Review*, 6, 1–98.

Flynn, B.B., Schroeder, R.G., Flynn, E.J., Sakakibara, S., and Bates, K.A. 1997. World-class manufacturing project: Overview and selected results. *International Journal of Operations & Production Management*, 17, 7, 671–685.

Foong, Y.P., and Richardson, S. 2008. The perceptions of Malaysians in a Japanese company. *Cross Cultural Management: An International Journal*, 15, 3, 221–243.

Fransman, M. 1998. Information, knowledge, vision, and theories of the firm. In G. Dosi, D.J. Teece, and J. Chytry, eds., *Technology, organisation, and competitiveness:*

Perspectives on industrial and corporate change, 147–192. New York, NY: Oxford University Press.

Fredrickson, B.L., Cohen, M.A., Coffey, K.A., Pek, J., and Finkel, S.M. 2008. Open hearts build lives Positive emotions, induced through loving kindness meditation build consequential personal resources. *Journal of Personality and Social Psychology*, 95, 1045–1062.

Freedman, T. 2006. *The world is flat: The globalized world in the twenty-first century.* New York, NY: Picador.

Fujie, H., and Shimada, H. 2017.*Results of JETRO's 2016 survey on business conditions of Japanese companies in Asia and Oceania.* Tokyo: JETRO.

Fujino, T. 1998. How Japanese companies have globalized. *Management Japan*, 31, 2, 1–28.

Fukuda, K.J. 2011. *Japanese-style management transferred.* New York, NY: Routledge.

Ghoshal, S. 2005. Bad management theories are destroying good management practices. *Academy of Management Learning and Education*, 4, 1, 75–91.

Girin, J. 1990. Problèmes du langage dans les organisations. *Dans L'individu dans l'organisation: les dimensions oubliées*, 37–78.

Glick, W.H. 1985. Conceptualizing and measuring organizational and psychological climate: Pitfalls in multilevel research. *Academy of Management Review*, 10, 3, 601–616.

Golden, K.A., and Ramanujam, V. 1985. Between a dream and a nightmare: On the integration of the human resource management and strategic business planning processes. *Human Resource Management*, 24, 4, 429–452.

Grant, R.M. 1996. Toward a knowledge-based theory of the firm. *Strategic Management Journal*, 17, 109–122.

Grant, R.M. 2003. Strategic planning in a turbulent environment: Evidence from the oil majors. *Strategic Management Journal*, 24, 6, 491–518.

Grey, C., and Antonacopoulou, E., eds. 2003. *Essential readings in management learning.* London: Sage Publications.

Grey, C. 2004. Reinventing business schools: The contribution of critical management education. *Academy of Management Learning and Education*, 3, 2, 178–186.

Grey, C., and Willmott, H.C. 2005.*Critical management studies: A reader.* Oxford, UK: Oxford University Press.

Guillen, M., and Garcia-Canal, E. 2009. The American model of the multinational firm and the "new" multinationals from emerging economies. *Academy of Management Perspectives*, 23, 2, 23–35.

Gunnell, M. 2016. A comparison of the GLOBE and Geert Hostede findings and their Implications for Global Business Leaders. www.linkedin.com/pulse/comparison-findings-globe-geert-hostede-implications-global-gunnell

Gupta, A., and Govindarajan, V. 2000. Knowledge flows within multinational corporations. *Strategic Management Journal*, 21, 4, 473–496.

Gupta, A. 2011. The relational perspective and East meets West. *Academy of Management Perspectives*, 25, 3, 19–27.

Gupta, V., Hanges, P.J., and Dorfman, P.W. 2002a. Clustering of societal cultures. In R.M. House, P.J. Hanges, M. Javidan, P.W. Dorfman, V. Gupta, and GLOBE Associates, eds., *Cultures, leadership, and organizations.* Bingley, Yorkshire: Emerald. www.emeraldinsight.com/doi/full/10.1108/EJTD-03-2016-0016

Gupta, V., Hanges, P.J., and Dorfman, P.W. 2002b. Cultural clustering: Methodologies and findings. *Journal of World Business*, 37, 1, 11–15.

Hainbrick, D.C. 1984. The top management team: Key to strategic success. *California Management Review*, Fall, 88–109.

Haire, M., Ghiselli, E.E., and Porter, L.W. 1966.*Managerial thinking*. Berkeley: Wiley.

Hall, J.W. 1972. A comparison of Halpin and Croft's organizational climates and Likert and Likert's organizational systems. *Administrative Science Quarterly*, 17, 4, 586–590.

Hall, P.A., and Soskice, D. 2001. *Varieties of capitalism: The institutional foundations of comparative advantage*. Oxford, UK and New York, NY: Oxford University Press.

Hamel, G., and Prahalad, C.K. 1990. Strategic intent. *Harvard Business Review*, 67, 3, 63–76.

Harrison, J.R., and Caroll, G.R. 1991. Keeping the faith, a model of cultural transmission in formal organization. *Administrative Science Quarterly*, 36, 552–582.

Harrison, J.R., and Caroll, G.R. 1998. Organizational demography and culture, insights from a formal model. *Administrative Science Quarterly*, 43, 637–667.

Harrison, J.R., and Caroll, G.R. 2000. *The dynamics of cultural influence networks*. Berkeley: U.C. Berkeley.

Harrison, J.R., and Caroll, G.R. 2001. Modelling organizational culture, demography and influence networks. In J. Chatman, T. Cummings, P.C. Early, N. Holden, P. Sparrow, and W. Starbuck, eds., *Handbook of organizational culture and culture*. New York, NY: Wiley.

Harzing, A. 2000. An empirical analysis and extension of the Bartlett and Ghoshal typology of multinational companies. *Journal of International Business Studies*, 31, 1, 101–120.

Hassard, J. 1988. Overcoming hermeticism in organization theory: An alternative to paradigm incommensurability. *Human Relations*, 41, 3, 247–259.

Hatch, N.W., and Dyer, J.H. 2004. Human capital and learning as a source of sustainable competitive advantage. *Strategic Management Journal*, 25, 12, 1155–1178.

Hayashi, M. 2002. A historical review of Japanese management theories: The search for a general theory of Japanese management. *Asian Business & Management*, 1, 2, 189–207.

Hayashi, S. 1989. *Culture and management in Japan*. Tokyo: University of Tokyo Press.

Heckscher, E.F. 2006. *International trade, and economic history*. Cambridge: MIT Press.

Hedlund, G. 1994. A model of knowledge management and the N-form corporation. *Strategic Management Journal*, 15, special Issue: Strategy: Search for New Paradigms, 73–90.

Helfat, C., and Peteraf, M. 2009. Understanding dynamic capabilities: Progress along a developmental path. *Strategic Organization*, 7, 1, 91–118.

Henson, R.M. 2012. Industrial-organizational and strategy are integrated in practice! *Industrial and Organizational Psychology*, 5, 1, 82–86.

Herold, D.M., Fedor, D.B., and Caldwell, S.D. 2007. Beyond change management: A multilevel investigation of contextual and personal influences on employees' commitment to change. *Journal of Applied Psychology*, 92, 942–951.

Herzberg, F. 1980. Humanities, practical management education. *Industry Week*, 206, 7, 69–72.

Hill, C. 2007. *International business competing in the global marketplace*. McGraw-Hill.

Hiller, N.J., DeChurch, L.A., Murase, T., and Doty, D. 2011. Searching for outcomes of leadership: A 25-year review. *Journal of Management*, 37, 1137–1177.

Hitt, M.A., Ireland, R.D., Sirmon, D.G., and Trahms, C.A. 2011. Strategic entrepreneurship: Creating value for individuals, organizations, and society. *The Academy of Management Perspectives*, 25, 2, 57–75.

Hofstede, G. 1980. *Culture's consequences: International differences in work-related values*. Beverly Hills, CA: Sage Publications.

Hofstede, G. 1985. The interaction between national and organisational value system. *Journal of Management Studies*, 22, 3, 347–357.

Hofstede, G. 1990. Measuring organizational cultures: A qualitative and quantitative study across twenty cases. *Administrative Science Quarterly*, 35, 286–316.

Hofstede, G.1993.Cultural constraints in management theories. *Academy of Management Executive*, 7, 1, 81–94.

Hofstede, G. 2002. *Culture's consequences: Comparing values, behaviors, institutions, and organizations across nations*. Thousand Oaks, CA: Sage Publications.

Hofstede, G., and Bond, M.H. 1988. The Confucius connection: From cultural roots to economic growth. *Organizational dynamics*, 16, 4, 5–21.

Hofstede, G., Hofstede, G.J., and Minkov, M. 2010. *Cultures and organizations: Software of the mind: Intercultural cooperation and its importance for survival*. New York, NY: McGraw-Hill.

Hong, J., Easterby-Smith, M., and Snell, R. 2006. Transferring organizational learning systems to Japanese subsidiaries in China. *Journal of Management Studies*, 43, 5, 1027–1058.

Hoskisson, R., Hitt, M., and Wan, W. 1999. Theory and research in strategic management: Swings of a pendulum. *Journal of Management*, 25, 3, 417–456.

House, R.J. 1999. Cultural influences on leadership: Project GLOBE. In W. Moblet, J. Gessner, and V. Arnold, eds., *Advances in global leadership*, Vol. 1, 171–234. Greenwick, CT: JAI Press.

House, R.J., Hanges, P.J., Javidan, M., Dorfman, P.W., and Gupta, V. 2004. *Culture, leadership, and organizations: The GLOBE study of 62 societies*. Thousand Oaks, CA: Sage Publications.

Hout, T., and Carter, J. 1996. Les habits neufs des cadres dirigeants. *L'expansion Management Review*, 81, 51–61.

Hu, L.T., and Bentler, P.M. 1999. Cutoff criteria for fit indexes in covariance structure analysis: Conventional criteria versus new alternatives. *Structural Equation Modeling: A Multidisciplinary Journal*, 6, 1, 1–55.

Hunt, S.D., Wood, V.R., and Chonko, L.B. 1989. Corporate ethical values and organizational commitment in marketing. *Journal of Marketing*, 53, 3, 79–90.

Husted, B.W. 2003. Globalization and cultural change in international business research. *Journal of International Management*, 9, 4, 427–433.

Ichniowski, C., Shaw, K., and Prennushi, G. 1995. *The effects of human resource management practices on productivity*. NBER Working Paper 5333. Washington, DC: NBER.

Ikeda, K. 1987. Nihon oyobi nihonjin ni tsuiteno imeji (Image of Japan and Japanese). In A. Tsujimura, K. Furuhata, and H. Akuto, eds., *Sekai wa Nihon wo Dou Miteiruka (How does the world see Japan)*, 12–31. Tokyo: Nihon Hyoronsa.

Imai, M. 1986. *Kaizen: The key to Japan's competitive success*. New York, NY: McGraw-Hill.

Jackling, B., and Johl, C. 2009. Board structure and firm performance: Evidence from India's top companies. *Corporate Governance: An International Review*, 17, 4, 492–509.

Jaeger, A.M. 1983. The transfer of organizational culture overseas: An approach to control in the multinational corporation. *Journal of International Business Studies*, 14, 2, 91–114.

Jaeger, A.M., and Baliga, B.R. 1985. Control systems and strategic adaptation: Lessons from the Japanese experience. *Strategic Management Journal*, 6, 2, 115–134.

Javidan, M., Dorfman, P.W., Sully de Luque, M., and House, R.J. 2006. In the eye of the beholder: Cross cultural lessons in leadership from Project GLOBE. *Academy of Management Perspectives*, 20, 1, 67–90.

Javidan, M., House, R., Dorfman, P., Hanges, P., and De Luque, M. 2006. Conceptualizing and measuring cultures and their consequences: A comparative review of GLOBE's and Hofstede's approaches. *Journal of International Business Studies*, 37, 6, 897–914.

Javidan, M., and Dastmalchian, A. 2009. Managerial implications of the GLOBE project: A study of 62 societies. *Asia Pacific Journal of Human Resources*, 47, 1, 41–58.

Jelinek, M. 1992. The competitive advantage of nations by Porter, Michael E. *Administrative Science Quarterly*, 37, 507–510.

Jirjahn, U., Mohrenweiser, J., and Backes-Gellner, U. 2011. Works councils and learning: On the dynamic dimension of codetermination. *Kyklos*, 64, 3, 427–447.

Joreskog, K.G., and Sorbom, D. 1999. *LISREL 8.30: User's reference guide*. Chicago: Scientific Software.

Judge, T.A., and Cable, D.M. 1997. Applicant personality, organizational culture, and organization attraction. *Personnel Psychology*, 50, 2, 359–394.

Kahle, L.R., Best, R.J., and Kennedy, R.J. 1988. An alternative method for measuring value-based segmentation and advertisement positioning. *Current Issues in Research in Advertising*, 11, 139–155.

Kahle, L.R., and Kennedy, P. 1988. Using the List of Values (LOV) to understand consumers. *The Journal of Services Marketing*, 2, 4, 49–56.

Kanter, R. 1968. Commitment and social organization: A Study of commitment mechanisms in utopian communities. *American Sociological Review*, 33, 4, 499–517.

Kaplan, R.S., and Norton, D.P.1996. *Translating strategy into action: The balanced scorecard*. Boston: Harvard Business School Press.

Kaplan, S., and Beinhocker, E.D. 2003. The real value of strategic planning. *MIT Sloan Management Review*, Winter. http://sloanreview.mit.edu/article/the-real-value-of-strategic-planning/

Kaplan, S. 2012. *The business model innovation factory: How to stay relevant when the world is changing*. Hoboken, NJ: Wiley.

Kar, P. 2010. *Fighting abusive related party transactions in Asia: Workshop on implementation*. OECD Asian Roundtable on Corporate Governance. www.gcgf.org/ifcext/cgf.nsf/Content/RTP_Publication

Kato, T. 2003. The recent transformation of participatory employment practices in Japan. In S. Ogura, T. Tachibanaki, and D. Wise, eds., *Labor markets and firm benefit policies in Japan and the United States*. Washington, DC: NBER.

Katz, H.C., Kochan, T.A., and Gobeille, K.R. 1983. Industrial relations performance, economic performance and QWL programs. *Industrial and Labor Relations Review*, 37, 3–17.

Khanna, V., and Black, B. 2007. Can corporate governance reforms increase firms' market values: Evidence from India. *Journal of Empirical Legal Studies*, 4. http://papers.ssrn.com/sol3/papers.cfm?abstract_id=914440&rec=1&srcabs=1012222

Kilmann, R.H. 1981. Toward a unique/useful concept of values for interpersonal behavior: A critical review of literature on value. *Psychological Reports*, 48, 3, 939–959.

Kilman, R.H., Saxton, M.J., and Serpa, R. 1985. Introduction: Five key issues in understanding and changing culture. In R. Kilman, M. Gaxton, and R. Serpa, eds., *Gaining control of the organizational culture*, 1–16. San Francisco: Jossey-Bass Publishers.

Kim, H., Kim, H.S., Lee, J.H., Jung, J.M., Lee, J.Y., and Do, N.C.2006. A framework for sharing product information across enterprises. *International Journal of Advanced Manufacturing Technology*, 27, 610–618.

Kiritsis, D., Bufardi, A., and Xirouchakis, P. 2003. Research issues on product lifecycle management and information tracking using smart embedded systems. *Advanced Engineering Informatics*, 17, 3–4, 189–202.

Kirkman, B.L., and Shapiro, D.L. 2001. The impact of team members' cultural values on productivity, cooperation, and empowerment in self-managing work teams. *Journal of Cross-Cultural Psychology*, 32, 5, 597–617.

Kluckhohn, C. 1951. Value and value orientations in the theory of action. In T. Parsons and E. Shils, eds., *Toward a general theory of action*. Cambridge, MA: Harvard University Press.

Kobayashi, N. 1980. *Nihon no Takokuseki Kigyo (Japanese multinational corporations)*. Tokyo: Chuo Keizaisha.

Kor, Y.Y., and Leblebici, H. 2005. How do interdependencies among human-capital deployment, development, and diversification strategies affect firms' financial performance? *Strategic Management Journal*, 26, 10, 967–985.

Kotter, J., and Heskett, L.1992.*Corporate culture and performance*. New York, NY: Free Press.

Kranias, D.S. 2000. Cultural control: The case of Japanese multinational companies and their subsidiaries in the UK. *Management Decision*, 38, 9, 638–648.

Kristof, A. 1996. Person-organization fit: An integrative review of its conceptualizations, measurement, and implications. *Personnel Psychology*, 49, 1–49.

Kristof-Brown, A.L. 2000. Perceived applicant fit: Distinguishing between recruiters' perceptions of person-job and person-organization fit. *Personnel Psychology*, 53, 3, 643–671.

Kristof-Brown, A.L., Zimmerman, R.D., and Johnson, E.C. 2005. Consequences of individual's fit at work: A meta-analysis of person-job, person-organization, person-group, and person-supervisor fit. *Personnel Psychology*, 58, 2, 281–342.

Krugman, P. 1994. Competitiveness: A dangerous obsession. *Foreign Affairs*, 73, 2, 28–44.

Kujawa, D. 1979. The labour relations of US multinationals abroad: Comparative and prospective views. *Labour and Society*, 4, 3–25.

Kumagai, F. 1996. *Nihon Teki Seisan Sisutemu in USA (Japanese production system in USA)*. Tokyo: JETRO.

Kumazawa, M., and Yamada, J. 1989. Jobs and skills under the lifelong Nenko employment practice. In S. Wood, ed., *The transformation of work*, 56–79. London: Unwin Hyman.

Kahneman, D., and Tversky, A. (1979). On the interpretation of intuitive probability: A reply to Jonathan Cohen. *Cognition*, 7, 4, 409–411.

Lant, T.K., Milliken, F.J., and Batra, B. 1992. The role of managerial learning and interpretation in strategic persistence and reorientation: An empirical exploration. *Strategic Management Journal*, 13, 8, 585–608.

Lawler, J., Atmiyanada, V., and Zaidi, M. 1992. Human resource management practices in multinational and local firms in Thailand. *Journal of Southeast Asian Business*, 8, 1, 16–33.

Lawler, J., and Atmiyanandana, V. 2003. HRM in Thailand: A post-1997 update. *Asia Pacific Business Review*, 9, 4, 165–185.

Lee, H.J., Yoshikawa, K., Reade, C., and Arai, R. 2013. The Confucian Asian Cluster? Cultural, economic and institutional explanations of leadership challenges of Japanese managers in China, Association of Japanese Business Studies 2013 Conference Proceedings. www.recruit-ms.co.jp/research/thesis/pdf/2013AJBS_Proceedings.pdf

Laibson, D., and Zeckhauser, R. 1998. *Journal of Risk and Uncertainty*, 16, 1, 7–47.

Likert, R. (1932). A technique for the measurement of attitudes. *Archives of Psychology*. 140: 1–55.

Liden, R. 2012. Leadership research in Asia: A brief assessment and suggestions for the future. *Asia Pacific Journal of Management*, 29, 205–212.

Liker, J.K., and Morgan, J.M. 2006. The Toyota Way in services: The case of lean product development. *Academy of Management Perspectives*, 20, 2, 5–20.

Lillrank, P., and Kano, N. 1989. *Continuous improvement*. Ann Arbor, MI: University of Michigan.

Lincoln, J.R., and Kalleberg, A.L. 1985. Work organization and workforce commitment: A study of plants and employees in the U.S. and Japan. *American Sociological Review*, 50, 6, 738–760.

Lincoln, J.R., Hanada, M., and McBride, K. 1986. Organizational structures in Japanese and U.S. manufacturing. *Administrative Science Quarterly*, 31, 338–364.

Lincoln, J.R., and Kalleberg, A.L. 1990. *Culture, control and commitment: A study of work organization and work attitudes in the U.S and Japan*. Cambridge: Cambridge University Press.

Lincoln, J.R., Kerbo, H.R., and Wittenhagen, E. 1995. Japanese companies in Germany: A case study in cross cultural management. *Industrial Relations*, 34, 417–441.

Lindblom, C.E. 1979. Still muddling, not yet through. *Public Administration Review*, 39, 6, 517–526.

Lok, P., Westwood, R., and Crawford, J. 2005. Perceptions of organizational subculture and their significance for organizational commitment. *Applied Psychology: An International Review*, 54, 4, 490–514.

Locke, E.A. 1997. The motivation to work: What we know. *Advances in motivation and achievement* (10, 375–412). Bingley, Yorkshire: Emerald.

Locke, E.A., and Latham, G.P. 1990. *A theory of goal setting & task performance.* Englewood Cliffs, NJ: Prentice-Hall, Inc.

Locke, E.A., and Latham, G.P. 2002. Building a practically useful theory of goal setting and task motivation: A 35-year odyssey. *American psychologist*, 57(9), 705–717.

Marcoulides, G.A., and Heck, R.H. 1993. Organization culture and performance: Proposing and testing a model. *Organization Science*, 14, 2, 209–225.

Maslow, A.H. 1954. The instinctoid nature of basic needs 1. *Journal of Personality*, 22, 3, 326–347.

Maslow, A.H. 1969. The farther reaches of human nature. *The Journal of Transpersonal Psychology*, 1, 1, 1–9.

Mathews, J. 2006. Dragon multinationals: New players in 21st century globalization. *Asia-Pacific Journal of Management*, 23, 1, 5–27.

McGregor, D. 1960. *The human side of enterprise*. New York, NY: McGraw-Hill.

Meyer, J. P., and Allen, N. J. 1984. Testing the "side-bet theory" of organizational commitment: Some methodological considerations. *Journal of Applied Psychology*, 69, 3, 372–378.

Meyer, J.P., and Allen, N.J. 1991. A three-component conceptualization of organizational commitment. *Human Resource Management Review*, 1, 61–89.

Meyer, J.P., Irving, P.G., and Allen, N.J. 1998. Examination of the combined effects of work values and early work experiences on organizational commitment. *Journal of Organizational Behavior*, 19, 1, 29–52.

Miles, I., Saritas, O., and Sokolov, A. 2016. *Foresight for science, technology and innovation*. Heidelberg, New York, Dordrecht, and London: Springer.

Mintzberg, H. 1989. *Inside our strange world of organizations*. New York: Simon and Schuster.

Mintzberg, H. 1994. *The rise and fall of strategic planning: Reconceiving the roles for planning, plans, planners*. Free Press and Prentice-Hall International.

Mintzberg, H. 1995. Un tour d'horizon des vraies fonctions du dirigeant. *L'expansion Management Review*, 76, 29–40.

Mintzberg, H. 1988. *Opening up the definition of strategy: The strategy process*. Englewood Cliffs: Prentis Hall.

Mintzburg, H., Simon, R., and Basu, K. 2002. Beyond selfishness. *Sloan Management Review*, 44, 1, 67–74.

Miroshnik, V. 2002. Culture and international management: A review *Journal of Management Development*, 21, 7.

Miroshnik, V. 2009. Organizational culture and corporate performance of Japanese companies: Atheoretical model. In D. Basu, ed., *Economic models: Methods, theory & applications*. London: Imperial College Press and World Scientific Publishing.

Miroshnik, V. 2012. Company citizenship creation in the developing countries in the era of globalization: Evidence from the Toyota Motor company in India. *Journal of Management Development*, 31, 6.

Mischel, W. 1977. The interaction of person and situation. In D. Magnusson and N.S. Endler, eds., *Personality at the crossroads: Current issues in interactional psychology*. Hillsdale, NJ: Lawrence Erlbaum Associates.

Miyajima, H.1996. *The evolution and change of contingent governance structure in the J-firm system: An approach to presidential turnover and firm Performance*. Working Paper No. 9606, Institute for Research in Contemporary Political and Economic Affairs. Tokyo: Waseda University.

Mootee, I. 2016. The end of strategic planning and the rise of strategic foresight. http://idr.is/the-endof-strategic-planning-and-the-rise-of-strategic-foresight/

Morgan, P.V. 1986. International human resource management: Fact or fiction. *Personnel Administrator*, 31, 9, 43–47.

Morishima, M. 1996. Renegotiating psychological controls, Japanese style. In C.L. Cooper, ed., *Trends in organizational behavior* (Vol. 3, 149–165). New York, NY: John Wiley & Sons.

Morita, A. 1992. A moment for Japanese management. *Japan-Echo*, 19, 2, 1–12.

Morley, M.J. 2007. Person-organization fit. *Journal of Managerial Psychology*, 22, 2, 109–117.

Morris, J., and Wilkinson, B. 1995. The transfer of Japanese management techniques to Alien institutional environments. *Journal of Management Studies*, 32, 6, 719–730.

Morris, J., Wilkinson, B., and Munday, M. 2000. Farewell to HRM? Personal practices in Japanese manufacturing plants in the UK. *International Journal of Human Resource Management*, 11, 6, 1047–1060.

Mowday, R.T., Steers, R.M., and Porter, L.W. 1979. The measurement of organizational commitment. *Journal of Vocational Behavior*, 14, 224–247.

Mowday, R.T., Porter, L.W., and Steers, R.M. 1982. *Organizational linkages: The psychology of commitment, absenteeism, and turnover*. San Diego, CA: Academic Press.

Nag, R., and Gioia, D.A. 2012. From common to uncommon knowledge: Foundations of firm-specific use of knowledge as a resource. *Academy of Management Journal*, 55, 2, 421–457.

Nakane, G. 1970. *Japanese society*. Harmondsworth: Penguin.

Narula, R. 2006. Globalization, new ecologies, new zoologies, and the purported death of the eclectic paradigm. *Asia Pacific Journal of Management*, 23, 2, 143–151.

Nash, D. 2013. *Case studies: Identifying foresight methods and practices in American corporate planning*. Prescott Valey, AZ: Northcentral University.

Nelson, R.R., and Winter, S.G. 1982. *An evolutionary theory of economic change*. Cambridge, MA: Harvard University Press.

Newbert, S.L. 2007. Empirical research on the resource-based view of the firm: An assessment and suggestions for future research. *Strategic Management Journal*, 28, 2, 121–146.

Newbert, S.L. 2008. Value, rareness, competitive advantage, and performance: A conceptual-level empirical investigation of the resource-based view of the firm. *Strategic Management Journal*, 29, 7, 745–768.

Nickerson, J., and Zenger, T. 2008. Envy, comparison costs and the economic theory of the firm. *Strategic Management Journal*, 29, 1429–1449.

Niffenegger, P., Kulviwat, S., and Engchanil, N. 2006. Conflicting cultural imperatives in modern Thailand: Global perspectives. *Asia Pacific Business Review*, 12, 4, 403–420.

Nohara, H. 1985. Technologies Electroniques et Gestion de la main-d'œuvre dans l'industrie Japonaise. *Revue d'économie industrielle*, 34, 1, 15–32.

Nord, W.R. 1974. The failure of current applied behavioral science-A Marxian perspective. *The Journal of Applied Behavioral Science*, 10, 4, 557–578.

O.E.C.D. 1999. *OECD principles of corporate governance, OECD: Paris in contemporary political and economic affairs*. Tokyo: Waseda University.

Ogasavara, M.H., and Hoshino, Y. 2007. The impact of ownership, internalization, and entry mode on Japanese subsidiaries' performance in Brazil. *Japan and the World Economy*, 19, 1, 1–25.

Ohlin, B. 1938. Economic progress in Sweden. *The Annals of the American Academy of Political and Social Science*, 197, 1, 1–6.

Okabe, Y. 2005. Organizational commitment in the restructuring age: A comparison of British and Japanese managers in manufacturing industries. *Asian Business & Management*, 4, 3, 251–270.

Oliver, N., and Wilkinson, B. 1992. *The Japanization of British industry*. Cambridge, MA: Blackwell.

Onishi, J. 2006. The transferability of Japanese HRM practices to Thailand. *Asia Pacific Journal of Human Resources*, 44, 3, 260–275.

O'Reilly, C.A., and Chatman, J. 1986. Organizational commitment and psychological attachment: The effects of compliance, identification, and internalization on pro-social behavior. *Journal of Applied Psychology*, 71, 3, 492–499.

O'Reilly, C.A. 1989. *Corporations, culture, and commitment: Motivation and social control in organizations.* Berkeley: University of California Press.

O'Reilly, C.A., Chatman, J.A., and Caldwell, D. 1991. People and organizational culture: A Q-sort approach to assessing person-organization fit. *Academy of Management Journal,* 34, 487–516.

Organ, D.W., and Konovsky, M. 1989. Cognitive versus affective determinants of organizational citizenship behavior. *Journal of Applied Psychology,* 74, 1, 157–186.

Ostroff, C., Shin, Y., and Kinicki, A.J. 2005. Multiple perspectives of congruence: Relationship between value congruence and employee attitudes. *Journal of Organizational Behaviour,* 26, 6, 591–623.

Ouchi, W.1981. *Theory Z: How American business can meet the Japanese challenge.* Reading, MA: Addison-Wesley.

Pagès, M. 1984. *L'emprise de l'organisation.* Paris: Presses universitaires de France.

Palich, L.E., Horn, P.W., and Griffeth, R.W. 1995. Managing in the international context: Testing cultural generality of sources of commitment to ultinational enterprises. *Journal of Management,* 21, 4, 671–690.

Parboteeah, K.P., Bronson, J.W., and Cullen, J.B. 2005. Does national culture affect willingness to justify ethically suspect behaviors? A focus on the GLOBE national culture scheme. *International Journal of Cross Cultural Management,* 5, 2, 123–137.

Park, H.J., Mitsuhashi, H., Fey, C.F., and Bjrkman, I. 2003. The effect of human resource management practices on Japanese MNC subsidiary performance: A partial mediating model. *The International Journal of Human Resource Management,* 14, 8, 1391–1406.

Pascale, R., and Athos, A. 1982. *The art of Japanese management: Applications for American executives.* New York, NY: Simon & Schuster.

Pavett, C., and Morris, T. 1995. Management styles within a multinational. *Human Relations,* 48, 10, 1171–1191.

Peabody, D. 1985. *National characteristics.* Cambridge: Cambridge University Press.

Perrow, C. 1979. *Organizational theory in a society of organizations.* Paris: Ecole Nationale d'Administration Publique.

Perlmutter, H.V. 1969. Some management problems in spaceship earth: The megafirm and the global industrial estate. In *Academy of management proceedings* (1969, 1, 59–87). Briarcliff Manor, NY 10510: Academy of Management.

Peteraf, M.A. 1993. The cornerstones of competitive advantage: A resource-based view. *Strategic Management Journal,* 14, 3, 179–191.

Peteraf, M.A., and Bergen, M.E. 2003. Scanning dynamic competitive landscape: A market based and resource based framework. *Strategic Management Journal,* 24, 1027–1041.

Peters, T., and Watermann, R. 1982. *In search of excellence.* New York, NY: Harper and Row.

Peters, T.J. 1987. *Thriving on chaos: Handbook for a management revolution.* New York, NY: Harper and Row.

Piramal, G. 2009. Satyam and the Indian family business. *Harvard Business Review Blog,* January 26. http://blogs.hbr.org/cs/2009/01/satyam_and_indian_family_busin.html

Pinder, C. C. 1998. *Work motivation in organizational behavior.* Upper Saddle River, NJ: Prentice Hall.

Ployhart, R.E. 2012. From possible to probable: The psychology of competitive advantage. *Industrial and Organizational Psychology,* 5, 1, 120–126.

Porter, M.E. 1990. The competitive advantage of nations. *Competitive Intelligence Review*, 1, 1, 14–14.

Porter, M.E. 1996. Competitive advantage, agglomeration economies, and regional policy. *International regional science review*, 19, 1–2, 85–90.

Prahalad, C.K., and Doz, Y. 1987. *The multinational mission: Balancing local demands and global vision*. New York: The Free Press.

Priem, R.L., and Butler, J.E. 2001. Is the resource-based "view" a useful perspective for strategic management research. *Academy of Management Review*, 26, 1, 22–40.

Puranam, P., Raveendran, M., and Knusden, T. 2012. Organization design: The epistemic interdependence perspective. *Academy of Management Review*, 37, 3, 419–440.

Ralston, D.A., Holt, D.H., Terpstra, R.H., and Kai-Cheng, Y.2008. The impact of national culture and economic ideology on managerial work values: A study of the United States, Russia, Japan, and China. *Journal of International Business Studies*, 39, 8–26.

Ravlin, E.C., and Ritchie, C.M. 2006. Perceived and actual organizational fit: Multiple influences on attitudes. *Journal of Managerial Issues*, 175–192.

Raykov, T., and Marcoulides, G.A. 2000. *A first course in structural equation modeling*. London: Lawrence Erlbaum Associates.

Reich, R. 1991. *The work of nations: Preparing ourselves for twenty-first century capitalism*. New York: Knopf.

Ricardo, D. 1821. *The principles of taxation and political economy*. London: JM Dent.

Rohrbeck, R., and Schwarz, J.O. 2013. The value contribution of strategic foresight: Insights from an empirical study of large European companies. *Technological Forecasting & Social Change*, 80, 5, 1593–1606.

Rohrbeck, R., Battistella, C., and Huizingh, E.2015. Corporate foresight: An emerging field with a rich tradition. *Technological Forecasting & Social Change*, 101, 1, 1–9.

Rokeach, M. 1973. *The nature of human values*. New York, NY: Free Press.

Ronen, S., and Shenkar, O. 1988. Using employee attitudes to establish MNC regional divisions. *Personnel*, 65, 8, 32–39.

Roth, M.S. 1995. The effects of culture and socioeconomics on the performance of global brand image strategies. *Journal of Marketing Research*, 32, 2, 163–175.

Ruff, F. 2006. Corporate foresight: Integrating the future of business environment into innovation and strategy. *International Journal of Technology Management*, 34, 3–4, 278–295.

Ruff, F. 2015. The advanced role of corporate foresight in innovation and strategic management: Reflections on practical experiences from automotive industry. *Technological Forecasting & Social Change*, 101, 1, 37–48.

Rugman, A.M. 1987. Strategies for national competitiveness. *Long Range Planning*, 20, 3, 92–97.

Rugman, A.M. 1992. Porter takes the wrong turn. *Business Quarterly*, 56, 3, 59–64.

Rugman, A.M., and Verbeke, A. 1993. Foreign subsidiaries and multinational strategic management: An extension and correction of Porter's single diamond framework. *Management International Review*, 2, 71–84.

Rugman, A.M., and Verbeke, A. 2003. Extending the theory of the multinational enterprise: Internalization and strategic management perspectives. *Journal of International Business Studies*, 34, 2, 125–137.

Rugman, A.M. 2005. *The regional multinationals*. Cambridge: Cambridge University Press.

Rugman, A.M., and Verbeke, A. 2008. Internalization theory and its impact on the field of international business. In J.J. Boddewyn, ed., *International business scholarship: AIB fellows on the first 50 years*, 155–174. Bingley, Yorkshire: Emerald.

Sagiv, L., and Schwartz, S.H. 2000. Value priorities and subjective well-being: Direct relations and congruity effects. *European Journal of Social Psychology*, 30, 177–198.

Sainsaulieu, R. 1983. La régulation culturelle des ensembles organisés. *L'Année sociologique*, 33, 195–217.

Sandberg, Å. 1995. Enriching production: Perspectives on Volvo's Uddevalla plant as an alternative to lean production. https://mpra.ub.uni-muenchen.de/10785/

Schein, E.H. 1968. Organizational socialization and the profession of management. *Industrial Management Review*, 9, 1–15.

Schein, E.H. 1984. Coming to a new awareness of corporate culture. *Sloan Management Review*, 25, 2, S 3, 3–16.

Schein, E.H.1990. Organizational culture. *American Psychologist*, 45, 2, 109–119.

Schein, E.H. 1997. *Organizational culture and leadership*. San-Francisco: Jossey-Bass Publishers.

Schein, E.H. 1998. Organizational socialization and the profession of management. *Industrial Management Review*, 1–15.

Schneider, B. 2001. Fits about fit. *Applied Psychology: An International Review*, 50, 141–152.

Schneider, S.C. 1988. National vs. corporate culture: Implications for human resource management. *Human Resource Management*, 27, 2, 231–246.

Schwartz, S.H. 1992. Universals in the content and structure of values: Theoretical advances and empirical tests in 20 countries. In M. Zanna, ed., *Advances in experimental social psychology*. San Diego, CA: Academic Press.

Schwartz, S.H. 1994. Beyond individualism/collectivism: New cultural dimensions of value. In U. Kim, H.C. Triandis, C. Kagitcibasi, S.C. Choi, and G. Yoon, eds., *Individualism and collectivism: Theory, method and applications*, 85–122. Thousand Oaks, CA: Sage Publications.

Schwartz, S.H.1996. Value priorities and behavior: Applying a theory of integrated value systems. In C. Seligman, J.M. Olson, and M.P. Zanna, eds., *The psychology of values: The Ontario symposium*, Vol. 8, 1–24. Hillsdale, NJ: Erlbaum.

Schwartz, S.H. 1999. A theory of cultural values and some implications for work. *Applied Psychology: An International Review*, 48, 1, 23–47.

Scroggins, R. 2015. Strategic management theories. *Global Journal of Computer Science and Technology*, 15, 1240–1248.

Sekiguchi, T. 2006. How organizations promote person-environment fit: Using the case of Japanese firms to illustrate institutional and cultural influences. *Asia Pacific Journal of Management*, 23, 1, 47–69.

Selmer, J., and De Leon, C. 1993. Organizational acculturation in foreign subsidiaries. *The International Executive*, 35, 4, 321–338.

Selmer, J., and De Leon, C. 1996. Parent cultural control through organizational acculturation. *Journal of Organizational Behaviour*, 17, 557–572.

Selmer, J. 2007. Which is easier, adjusting to a similar or to a dissimilar culture? American business expatriates in Canada and Germany. *International Journal of Cross Cultural Management*, 7, 2, 185–201.

Shenkar, O. 2012. Beyond cultural distance: Switching to a friction lens in the study of cultural differences. *Journal of International Business Studies*, 43, 1, 12–17.

Sheth, J.N. 2006. Clash of cultures or fusion of cultures: Implications for international business. *Journal of International Management*, 12, 218–221.

Shibata, H. 2008. The transfer of Japanese work practice to plants in Thailand. *International Journal of Human Resource Management*, 19, 2, 330–345.

Shim, W.S., and Steers, R.M. 2012. Symmetric and asymmetric leadership cultures: A comparative study of leadership and organizational culture at Hyundai and Toyota. *Journal of World Business*, 47, 581–591.

Shimada, H. 1993. Japanese management of auto-production in the United States: An overview of human technology in international labour organization. In *Lean production and beyond*, 23–47. Geneva: ILO.

Shingo, S. 1985. *A revolution in manufacturing: The SMED System*. Tokyo: Productivity Press.

Siehl, C., and Martin, J. 1988. Measuring organizational culture: Mixing qualitative and quantitative methods. In M.O. Jones, M.D. Moore and R.C Snyder, eds., *Inside organizations: Understanding the human dimension*, 79–103. Newbury Park, CA: Sage Publications.

Simon, D.G., Hitt, M.A., and Ireland, R.D. 2007. Managing firm resources in dynamic environments to create value: Looking inside the black box. *Academy of Management Review*, 32, 1, 273–292.

Simonin, B.L. 1999. Ambiguity and the process of knowledge transfer in strategic alliances. *Strategic Management Journal*, 20, 7, 595–623.

Smith, A. 1776. *An inquiry into the nature and causes of the wealth of nations: Volume One*. London: W. Strahan and T. Cadell.

Smith, C.A., Organ, D.W., and Near, J.P. 1983. Organizational citizenship behavior: Its nature and antecedents. *Journal of Applied Psychology*, 68, 653–663.

Smith, C.A., and Elger, T. 2000. The societal effects school and transnational transfer: The case of Japanese investment in Britain. In M. Maurice and A. Sorge, eds., *Embedding organizations: Societal analysis of actors, organizations and socio economic context*. Amsterdam: John Benjamins.

Steers, R.M., Sanchez-Runde, C., and Nardon, L. 2012. Leadership in a global context: New directions in research and theory development. *Journal of World Business*, 47, 479–482.

Sun, J., and Wang, X. 2010. Value differences between generations in China: A study in Shanghai. *Journal of Youth Studies*, 13, 1, 65–81.

Suzuki, Y. 1994. The competitive advantage of Japanese industries: Developments, dimensions and directions. *Journal of Far Eastern Business*, 1, 1, 37–51.

Swierczek, F.W., and Onishi, J. 2003. Culture and conflict: Japanese managers and Thai subordinates. *Personnel Review*, 32, 2, 187–210.

Szulanski, G. 1996. Exploring internal stickiness: Impediments to the transfer of best practice within the firm. *Strategic Management Journal*, 17, 27–43.

Takahashi, K., Ishikawa, J., and Kanai, T. 2012. Qualitative and quantitative studies of leadership in multinational settings: Meta-analytic and cross-cultural reviews. *Journal of World Business*, 47, 530–538.

Taylor, B. 1999. Patterns of control within Japanese manufacturing plants in China: Doubts about Japanization in Asia. *Journal of Management Studies*, 36, 6, 853–873.

Taylor, S., Levy, O., Boyacigiller, N.A., and Beechler, S. 2008. Employee commitment in MNCs: Impacts of organizational culture, HRM and top management orientations. *International Journal of Human Resource Management*, 19, 4, 501–527.

Thaper, M., and Sharma, A. 2017. Corporate governance in India: An analysis. *Journal of Economic and Social Development*, 4, 1, 81–96.

Thurow, L. 1990. Review of the competitive advantage of nations, by Porter, Michael E. *Sloan Management Review*, 32, 1, 95–97.

Torrens, R. 1816. *A letter to the right honorable the earl of liverpool, on the state of the agriculture of the United Kingdom: And on the means of relieving the present distress of the farmer, and of securing him against the recurrence of similar embarrassment.* London: J. Hatchard.

Triandis, H.C., and Gelfand, M. 1998. Converging measurements of horizontal and vertical individualism and collectivism. *Journal of Personality and Social Psychology*, 74, 1, 118–128.

Triandis, H.C. 2006. Cultural aspects of globalization. *Journal of International Management*, 12, 208–217.

Tung, R. 1981. Selection and training of personnel for overseas assignments. *Columbia Journal of World Business*, 16, 1, 68–78.

Tung, R. 1982. Selection and training procedures of U.S., European, and Japanese multinationals. *Columbia Management Review*, 25, 1, 57–71.

Tung, R. 1988. *Managing human resource abroad.* New York, NY: Ballinger.

Quinn, R.E. 1988. *Beyond rational management: Mastering the paradoxes and competing demands of high performance.* San Francisco, CA: Jossey-Bass.

Vandenberghe, C. 1999. Organizational culture, person-culture fit, and turnover: A replication in the health care industry. *Journal of Organizational Behavior*, 20, 2, 175–184.

Vandenberghe, C., Stinglhamber, F., Bentein, K., and Delhaise, T. 2001. An examination of the cross-cultural validity of a multidimensional model of commitment in Europe. *Journal of Cross-Cultural Psychology*, 32, 3, 322–344.

Van Vianen, A.E.M. 2000. Person-organization fit: The match between newcomers' and recruiters' preferences for organization cultures. *Personnel Psychology*, 53, 1, 113–149.

Varottil, U. 2010. Evolution and effectiveness of independent directors in Indian corporate governance. *Hastings Business Law Journal*, 7, 1, 281–287.

Vecchiato, R., and Roveda, C.2010. Strategic foresight in corporate organizations: Handling the effect and response uncertainty of technology and social drivers of change. *Technological Forecasting & Social Change*, 77, 9, 1527–1539.

Vecchiato, R. 2012. Environmental uncertainty, foresight and strategic decision making. *Technological Forecasting & Social Change*, 79, 3, 436–447.

Vecchiato, R. 2015. Strategic planning and organizational flexibility in turbulent environments. *Foresight*, 17, 3, 257–273.

Vera, D., and Crossan, M. 2004. Strategic leadership and organizational learning. *Academy of Management Review*, 29, 222–240.

Verbeke, A. 2009. *International business strategy.* Cambridge: Cambridge University Press.

Wang, H.C., He, J., and Mahoney, J.T. 2009. Firm-specific knowledge resources and competitive advantage: The roles of economic-and relationship-based employee governance mechanisms. *Strategic Management Journal*, 30, 12, 1265–1285.

Watanabe, S. 1998. Manager-subordinate relationship in cross-cultural organizations: The case of Japanese subsidiaries in the United States. *International Journal of Japanese Sociology*, 7, 23–43.

Waverman, L. 1995. A critical analysis of Porter's framework on the competitive advantage of nations. In A.M. Rugman, J. van den Broek, and A. Verbeke, eds.,

Research in global strategic management (Vol.5): Beyond the diamond. Greenwich, CT: JAI Press.

Weber, Y., Shanker, O., and Raveh, A. 1996. National and corporate cultural fit in mergers/acquisitions: An exploratory study. *Management Science*, 42, 8, 1215–1227.

Weick, K.E. 1979. *The social psychology of organizing.* Columbus, OH: McGraw-Hill.

Weiss, H.M. 1978. Social learning of work values in organizations. *Journal of Applied Psychology*, 63, 1, 711–718.

West, E.G. 1969. The political economy of alienation: Karl Marx and Adam Smith. *Oxford Economic Papers*, 21, 1, 1–23.

Wickens, P., and Lopez, A.R. 1987. *The road to Nissan: Flexibility, quality, teamwork.* Basingstoke: Macmillan.

Williamson, O. 2000. The new institutional economics: Taking stock, looking ahead. *Journal of Economic Literature*, 38, 595–613.

Wiltbank, R., Dew, N., Read, S., and Sarasvathy, S.D. 2006. What to do next? The case for non-predictive strategy. *Strategic Management Journal*, 27, 10, 981–998.

Winter, S. 2003. Understanding dynamic capabilities. *Strategic Management Journal*, 24, 10, 991–995.

Witt, M.A. 2011. *China: What varieties of capitalism?* INSEAD Working Paper No. 2010/88/EPS. http://papers.ssrn.com/sol3/papers.cfm?abstract_id=1695940 #%23

Weitzman, M. 1984. *The share economy: Conquering stagflation.* Cambridge: Harvard University Press.

Yamashiro, A., ed. 1967. *Ringiteki Keiei to Ringi Seido (Ringi management and the ringi system).* Tokyo: Toyo Keizai, 117–119, 181–182.

Yeh, R.S. 1986. *Values and intraorganisational influence: A comparative study of Taiwanese, Japanese and American firms in Taiwan.* Ph.D. dissertation, Temple University, Philadelphia, USA.

Yeh, R.S. 1988. On Hofstede's treatment of Chinese and Japanese values. *Asia Pacific Journal of Management*, 6, 1, 149–160.

Yoda, T. 2013. Corporate foresight in Japan. https://dspace.jaist.ac.jp/dspace/bit-stream/10119/11745/1/kouen28_407.pdf

Yonaha, J. 2011. *Chinalizing Japan-1000 years of cultural crush between Japan and China. (in Japanese).* Tokyo, Japan: Bungei-Shunju

Yoshikawa, T. 2018. *Asian corporate governance: Trends and challenges.* Cambridge: Cambridge University Press.

Youssef, C.M., and Luthans, F. 2007. Positive organization behavior in the workplace. *Journal of Management*, 33, 774–800.

Yu, J., and Meyer-Ohle, H. 2008. Working for Japanese corporations in China: A qualitative study. *Asian Business and Management*, 7, 33–51.

Zaheer, S., Schomaker, M.S., and Nachum, L. 2012. Distance without direction: Restoring credibility to a much-loved construct. *Journal of International Business Studies*, 43, 1, 18–27.

Index

Note: Page numbers in *italic* indicate a figure and page numbers in bold indicate a table on the corresponding page.